THEORY AND REALITY
IN FINANCIAL
ECONOMICS

Essays Toward A New Political Finance

THEORY AND REALITY
IN FINANCIAL
ECONOMICS

Essays Toward A New Political Finance

George M. Frankfurter

Professor Emeritus, Louisiana State University, USA

NEW JERSEY · LONDON · SINGAPORE · BEIJING · SHANGHAI · HONG KONG · TAIPEI · CHENNAI

Published by

World Scientific Publishing Co. Pte. Ltd.

5 Toh Tuck Link, Singapore 596224

USA office: 27 Warren Street, Suite 401-402, Hackensack, NJ 07601

UK office: 57 Shelton Street, Covent Garden, London WC2H 9HE

Library of Congress Cataloging-in-Publication Data
Frankfurter, George M.
    Theory and reality in financial economics : essays toward a new political
finance / by George M Frankfurter.
      p. cm.
    Includes bibliographical references and index.
    ISBN-13: 978-981-270-791-8
    ISBN-10: 981-270-791-3
    1. Finance. 2. Economics. I. Title.

    HG173.F688 2007
    332.01--dc22

                  2007033434

British Library Cataloguing-in-Publication Data
A catalogue record for this book is available from the British Library.

Typeset by Stallion Press
Email: enquiries@stallionpress.com

Printed in Singapore by World Scientific Printers (S) Pte Ltd

Foreword

It is quite unusual to see the words "theory" and "reality" together in the title of a book on financial economics. It is even more unusual to see the word "political" in its subtitle. For most finance professors, reality is something you use to test your theories, but the theories themselves are deliberately unrealistic. And if the theories are not consistent with reality, the blame falls on reality and not on the theories. Politics is something that impedes the efficient functioning of markets, which, if left to their own devices, will deliver the greatest good to the greatest number of people.

George Frankfurter is uniquely qualified to challenge these conventional views. His distinguished academic career has given him a thorough background in the theories that form the foundation of financial economics. Unlike most of his professional colleagues, however, he has not hesitated to expose the cracks that would topple large parts of the structure were it not for a quasi-religious faith in the feats that rational economic men are capable of accomplishing when they are given free rein in free markets. He has not been afraid to confront the academic publication and promotion system that ensures no one is allowed to question the real issues too closely.

George is one of the few financial economists who has a sufficiently broad perspective beyond the campus to see how this faith not only props up academic theories, but also sustains a form of elite capitalism that serves its masters and their political allies better than it serves the rest of us. Any number of astonishing deceptions and disturbing inequities are excused as the inevitable consequences of a competitive market.

Since Microsoft has acquired an overwhelming dominance in the market for personal computer operating systems, it must be as a result of superior innovation and performance. Since for-profit universities are successfully making money selling degrees, they must be the best means to create an educated and engaged citizenry. Since Enron's stock price was soaring, it must have represented the future of the nation's energy management. And if we couldn't believe their auditors — the venerable Arthur Andersen — that all was well, then who could we believe?

It seems so obvious, then, that if we want to ensure adequate medical care for everyone, insurance and healthcare companies will take care of it. If we want to enhance the nation's security through energy independence, oil companies will create the alternatives to imported petroleum. If we want to eliminate poverty, there are small businesses desperate to hire the poor at the right wage. Through the magic of free markets, everyone can make money and build a just and equitable society at the same time.

Not content to just expose what has gone wrong, George is able to suggest reforms to both the academic and the political-economic systems that might make markets truly efficient. Fair, not just free, markets are capable of giving us greater wealth and freedom in many ways — not just the freedom to become wealthy by purchasing stock that we hope to sell to someone else for a higher price.

Professor Elton G. McGoun
William H. Dunkak Professor of Finance
Bucknell University

Prologue

The animals that depend on instinct have an inherent knowledge of the laws of economics and of how to apply them; Man, with his powers of reason, has reduced economics to the level of a farce which is at once funnier and more tragic than Tobacco Road.

— James Thurber[1]

Political finance? As in "political economy"? Who in his right mind would conjure up such a thing? The short, barely six-decade history as an academic discipline of what is called finance that later distinctively changed to "financial economics" or "modern finance" has been ruled by Friedmaninan instrumentalism (Friedman, 1953) and neoclassical economic dogma. Its elite vehemently argue that financial economics is value-neutral, ergo it is not and cannot be influenced by politics that is by definition ideology-laden.

If one subscribes to the notion that nothing that humans do is value-neutral, but rather based on ideology, be it creed, religion, politics or self-promotion, then one must consider financial economics' claim to value-neutrality as a farce at best and disingenuous at worst. Thus, modern finance[2] just might be a ruse with which academic research (what can be thought of the ontology and epistemology of the field) masquerades as an imitation of the natural sciences. Consequently, it is busy developing models and explanations — the more complex, the merrier — that fit compactly within the confines of equations and statistics, instead of dealing with economic realities that are suffused with politics.

This logic is to make sure that the movers and thinkers of academe will debate forever whether one paradigm or another can be supported by empirical evidence without the possibility of ever reaching a definite conclusion. It also ensures that finance academics are not engaged in the

---

[1] *The Columbia Dictionary of Quotations* is licensed from Columbia University Press. Copyright © 1993, 1995 by Columbia University Press. All rights reserved.

[2] I am using the term modern finance interchangeably with the term financial economics, as many of the practitioners of the latter argue that the two are one and the same.

process of discovery, the ultimate goal of science, because such process might bring an end to the ideology that rules the field.

This is why, for instance, academics in the finance discipline have been pondering close to 40 years the question of whether markets are efficient, and if yes, then to what degree. Informational market efficiency[3] was enshrined in Fama's efficient markets hypothesis (EMH) (Fama, 1965, 1970) as a quasi-religion and later was assigned three distinct forms:

- the weak;
- the semi-strong; and
- the strong.

The consequence of the EMH is the perception that markets are omnipotent (*de facto* the avatar of God), and Pareto optimal. So, anything that would replace them would be a deterrent to the welfare of some and possibly everyone without leaving anyone better off. This notion, lately, found for itself several new euphemisms for the benefit of the common man, the most popular of which are "free markets," "globalization," "new/space age," "the new world order," etc. Accordingly, everyone who sets out to interfere with the market, especially a government, is doing a disservice to any given society, and possibly to humankind as well.

Those who doubt my contention here that modern finance is ideology-laden are advised to read Frankfurter and McGoun (1999). If after doing so the reader is still convinced that financial economics is "pure science," although there is no such thing even in the natural sciences, then this manuscript is to serve as an additional charge to the contrary. I will argue, in the hope to convince the convincible skeptics,[4] that the financial world which financial economics tries to understand, explain, forecast and fashion is infused with politics to the point where the boundaries between economics and politics are totally muddled. Thus, finance as a discipline that is ideologically driven cannot possibly understand, explain, forecast and fashion this world.

---

[3] There are two other qualifiers of efficiency: liquidity (how fast the market can find a buyer for an asset), and allocational (how well the market allocates capital where it does the best). However, here as almost everywhere else I am dealing with informational efficiency only: how well prices reflect value.

[4] I learned that where beliefs are based on deep ideological convictions, no argument, fact or evidence would change the mind of those who, because of this deep ideological belief, will not accept anything inconsistent with their values.

Not that it ever wanted to, either. Fama (1998) argues that the EMH cannot even be criticized until or unless a better and more complete paradigm is proposed to replace it. This is in complete contradiction of Karl Popper's heeding that "the beginning of science is myths, and the criticism of myths." For how can we come up with a better paradigm than the EMH if one cannot criticize the EMH without offering a better paradigm?

One must also recall that the EMH is there because it was the first to arrive, and not because it unseated an inferior paradigm that preceded it.

To make my point, first, I let others speak for me. An editorial of *The Washington Post* that appeared in late May 2002, titled "After ENRON", has this to say:

> The past decade has been a strange, split-screen kind of period. On your left screen there was America the superpower, which triumphed over communism, created a new realm called cyberspace and outpaced rivals in Europe and Japan. On your right screen there was America the scandal power, plagued by an explosion in political money and insider lobbying and a decline of trust in government. Throughout the 1990s, these two screens seemed separate. But the Enron scandal, starring a firm that symbolized both America's economic dynamism and its political cronyism, brought the screens together. It showed how lobbying and campaign money can damage the economic system.
>
> This is why the Enron scandal is so potent. Its many tentacles are united by a sense that rich insiders are rigging the system at the expense of ordinary Americans. Enron's energy dealers ripped off California's consumers and got away with this behavior because of Enron's clout in Washington. Wall Street's analysts cynically promoted Enron's stock to unsuspecting investors because they coveted fat investment-banking fees — and got away with this conflict of interest because lobbyists and campaign dollars kept the regulators soft. Capitalism rightly rewards people who make life better by providing goods and services. But when rewards are distributed according to insider influence, that is cronyism.
>
> Accounting is where the economic costs of cronyism are potentially highest. Since the 1970s, the accounting lobby has fought off regulation and squashed opposition to its consulting ambitions — despite the fact that those ambitions sometimes turned outside audits into insider shams. As a result, corporate accounts have been distorted — in Enron's case, spectacularly, and investors are hard-pressed to know which companies deserve their money. Capitalism defeated communism partly because the apparatchiks directed savings to the wrong places. When cronyism undermines the information that investors rely upon, it damages capitalism's central nerve.

Then, the column goes on to describe how the Republican Party and the administration leaves the cure for the disease threatening capitalism's "central nerves system" to industry itself, as opposed to a Democrats' sponsored bill. The editorial makes the point that

> . . . the bill crafted by Senator Paul Sarbanes, Democrat of Maryland, is so important. Unlike the sham alternative backed by Senators Phil Gramm, Republican of Texas, and Michael Enzi,[5] Republican of Wyoming, the Sarbanes bill offers most of what is needed to make corporate numbers meaningful. It guarantees the financial independence of the accounting standards board, thus shielding it from moneyed lobbies. It creates a new regulatory board to watch over auditors, one that would be genuinely independent of the profession. It goes part way toward curbing auditors' conflicts of interest by banning some types of consulting.

The column concludes by making it clear what constitutes a better-informed market, and, consequently, better-informed investors, *vis-à-vis* the *laisseze faire* claims, and who sides with which:

> Now, precisely because Sarbanes has proposed tough legislation, the accounting lobby is pounding him. This week Thomas Donohue, president of the US Chamber of Commerce, sent out a letter accusing Sarbanes of a "knee-jerk, politically charged reaction" to the Enron scandal. But strong accounting reforms are not, as Donohue alleges, a threat to "informed market decision-making." On the contrary, they are a prerequisite for functioning markets. It is precisely because public policy ought to be pro-market that it must not be pro-business — not if pro-business means allowing companies to distort the accounting information upon which healthy capitalism depends. Lobbies such as the Chamber of Commerce appear to have lost sight of this, promoting cronyism in place

---

[5] NPR's Scott Simon, in an interview broadcast on July 13, 2002, asked Senator Enzi, who is the only accountant by profession in the Senate, whether he thought that the crisis in corporate America is endemic, or just a "few bad apples." Mr. Enzi replied that he thought it was the latter. He also indicated that shareholders were shirking their responsibilities. Quoting his father's wisdom, the Senator remarked, "If it looks too good to be true, it probably isn't." This is, of course, the well-known *caveat emptor* principle, which in this context and coming from an accountant sounds strange. How can the shareholder do his/her research when the data coming after certification by an independent accountant are fraudulent or other relevant information is dated? But one must know that Senator Enzi is coming from those politicians who, after 99 percent of the wealth of the nation is securely at the hands of the top 1 percent, would still ask for tax cuts to fix all our woes.

of capitalism. Those who care about the public interest have a duty to fight back.

For five decades, untold generations of business undergraduates and MBAs were raised on the religious belief that markets see all, know all and do all, and therefore one must keep the dirty hands of government away from them. Of course, it has been nothing less than a carefully nurtured myth, bolstered by corporate America and its support of research that "found" evidence to this "market efficiency" (see Soley, 1995), all the while making the rich richer, the big humongous, and the powerful mightier.

There is no research in existence that would deal with the fact that markets cannot be "efficient" because they are manipulated on a grand scale. This objective would be quite different if addressed seriously than the proof or rejection of the EMH. Depending on how one is slicing, dredging, sifting and otherwise manipulating data, one can prove either one of the two contentions. The untold numbers of papers in the milieu of "anomalies," work that show the existence of real or conjured effects, are no chinks in the EMH's armor. They are called no more than anomalies and treated as such. One can make notice of these without worrying too much, or God forbid, considering the replacement of the paradigm.

Indeed, the history of the "anomalies literature" is over 30 years now. It is still going strong, yet has not changed a thing as far as the paradigm goes.[6] As early as 1978, Ball (1978) allayed the doubts of the would-be bothered by anomalies:

> There is nothing that necessarily should be done because as argued by Kuhn (1969 *sic*),[7] no area of normal science can justify chasing all anomaly at the expense of more fruitful research. The one proviso is that, if the anomaly is judged to be sufficiently large to hinder normal research, then it must be resolved (*ibid.*, p. 117).

---

[6] This is in spite of the rumors floating around about how people actually made a bundle by exploiting these anomalies. If the rumors were true, then these alone should call into question market efficiency. For if one can take advantage of the anomalies, how come many others do not? Taking advantage of market imperfections is the driving force behind the arbitrage mechanism, the *deus ex machina* of modern finance that is always there when needed, yet never proven to exist.

[7] The reference is to Kuhn's *The Structure of Scientific Revolutions*. The first edition was published in 1962. The second edition that is usually quoted was published in 1970. In either case, Ball's reference is incorrect.

Without going into questioning what is "normal science" and "normal research" (as opposed to what? crazy science or crazy research?), it is sufficient to say that up to this very day no anomaly was "judged sufficiently large."

This treatise is a collection of 13 essays written in years 1999 through 2006, a prologue (you are reading, momentarily), an epilogue, and afterword. The first five essays are general in nature and deal with issues of the methodology of financial economics and its relation to neoclassical economics, the meaning of "market efficiency," and what other theoretical development in 21st century economics would be relevant for finance, albeit do not seem to purchase a foothold. To close out the somewhat more academic tone of this part of the book, two papers dealing with the academic publication process in finance explain, among other things, how editors and editorial boards control what is to be known, and what in fact more than half a million journal pages of half a century show, or do not show.

The first essay in this monograph deals with the methodology of financial economics/modern finance. It compares the methodology to a ziggurat, built on layers, each layer being solidly anchored to the one below it. In the ancient ziggurat, at the bottom as well as at the top there was a temple, yet the real purpose of the ziggurat is still shrouded in mystery. I argue in this essay that finance research mistakes method for methodology, where by sheer formalism one can forget about the philosophical underpinnings of what one is doing. The methodology and this blurring of the difference between method and methodology also serve as a vehicle to perpetuate the paradigm. The case in point I am discussing in this essay is the CAPM (Lintner, 1965; Sharpe, 1964; Black, 1972; and others), and its relation to the EMH to perpetuate the myth of market efficiency.

The second essay titled "What is All Efficiency?" deals with the concept/theory/hypotheses of market efficiency. With the simple possible storytelling and images, I am trying to clarify that market efficiency, although heavily ideology-laden, is just an imaginary construct that has nothing whatsoever to do with reality.

The third essay titled "Still Autistic Finance" compares and contrasts perhaps the most important development in teaching and research in the field of economics — the emergence of Post-Autistic Economics, or PAE for short. Following the call of a group of French students for a departure from the hegemony of neoclassical economics, students at Cambridge and later in the USA started a worldwide movement to make economic teaching and research more meaningful. Thus, a new movement got its start at the dawn of the third millennium that calls itself Post-Autistic Economics. In this essay I discuss the meaning of this movement for the methodology of finance and how one should hope that it would create a change in thinking of financial economists as it did in the other branches of economics. Or perhaps not?

The fourth and fifth essays in this book, titled "The Young Finance Faculty's Guide to Publishing" and "Prolific Authors in Finance," respectively, are about the publication process in academic finance. Contrary to naïve beliefs that ascribe to academe purity and impartiality, the publication process in the academic finance journals is very much ideology-driven. It is decidedly not designed to further the true mission of academe, which is discovery, but rather to safeguard an elite from any serious challenge as a result of redirecting the research program. The process is also very much influenced by the sociology of the field, where one's economic and reputational capital is almost totally dependent on one's publication record.

The next section is a collection of six papers dealing with the influence of politics on what should be, supposedly, a pure economic process. The first essay is about for-profit higher education. In the paper I discuss the perils of merchandising higher education: its effect on the real knowledge that is imparted on those who seek their degrees through these enterprises, and what it will or could do to academic freedom.

The next article, titled "Weep Not for Microsoft: Monopoly's Fatal Exception," is about the monopoly case the justice department brought against Microsoft, its resolution and what society is losing by supporting an enterprise that is peddling an inferior product by the crudest tactics of a ruthless monopolist.

The last four essays in this section are about the Enron scandal and its aftermath from different points of view. With these four essays I hope to bring to the fore the connections between ideology and reality, and between reality and politics in and of finance. If I were Henry Kissinger (who I am not), I would call it the *realpolitik* of financial economics. Instead, I call it *schlichtfinanzen*, which translates to simple finance, because instead of complex mathematics and sophisticated econometrics it reveals what finance *simply* is.

The belief in market efficiency as a dogma that had not been shaken by the market crash of 1987 that was, the crash of the market in 1998 that wasn't, the techno-bubble burst of Spring 2000, and the finally officially-confirmed economic recession of 2001, as it has been shaken by the Enron debacle, and its many tendrils that are being discovered as time goes by.

The first of the Enron "trilogy" is titled "The Socio-Economics of Scandals." I started thinking about the issue at the encouragement of Professor Manfred Holler of the University of Hamburg. I was sure that Manfred was joking when he asked me to write about the subject. The issue came about with the collapse of @home.com, the fast Internet service provider that turned to dust as it bit the dust. The demise of @home.com was because some of its partners wanted it to fail, so they could pick up the pieces at fire-sale prices. The end result was thousands of people out of their job, while some executives made a bundle. By that time, the Enron debacle was going on full force, with the possibility of tens of thousands of employees from both Enron and Arthur Andersen losing their livelihood and their retirement investment. The paper is about the paradox of not caring about the working man when mega-firm power plays cause thousands to lose their jobs which we call downsizing and mergers and acquisitions, yet trying to save a failing firm whose executives are caught with their hands in the cookie jar.

In this essay I also introduce the concept of "fair markets," to replace the myth of efficient markets. Fair markets are markets built on the tenets of Judeo-Christian ethics in which the weak is protected so as not to fall prey to the asymmetry of power that would give a distinctive advantage to the mighty.

The second member of the Enron trilogy is about what I call the "Enron encounters of the third kind." Its title, "Desperately Seeking Toto," reflects on the fact that because of politics and ideology, we are supporting a world not unlike the one created by the Wizard of Oz. Because Enron was a champion of the idea of free markets, all the while rigging the energy markets that turned to be devastating to the State of California, and using both unethical and illegal means to line the pockets of its chief executives, an administration sympathetic to these ideas and the real money that flew into its political coffers not only turned a closed eye on Enron activities, but practically let Enron dictate energy policy for the nation. Nevertheless, I point a finger at a special cabal of operators who enjoyed monetary benefits from furthering Enron's objectives, without taking any real risk of monetary repercussions, loss of reputation, or credibility. This kind of tradeoff, "reward without risk," cannot conceivably exist under the logic of neoclassical economics.

The last essay of the "Enron kind" is about free-marketism turning into a religion with its ceremonies and rituals, not unlike those of the Catholic Church during the period of the inquisition. The title, "And Now for Something Entirely Different," (admittedly borrowed from *Monty Python's Flying Circus*) is to refocus our thinking about globalization, the new world order, the new age, etc., in terms of a religion. This is the case of trying to save Andersen LLP, the CPA firm of Enron, from criminal prosecution on charges of obstruction of justice, with the help of one of Wall Street's "saints," former Federal Reserve Board chairperson Paul Volker. It is not the deeds of Andersen that should or should not be judged, but the purity of the man who is taking the side of a repentant sinner. The moral question of Volker's involvement is also discussed in this essay.

Following the Enron trilogy is what the post-Enron "cat dragged in." Many of the scandals that got their well-deserved limelight were already brewing before the Enron fiasco superseded our war on terrorism. Yet, on the coat-tails of Enron, these scandals — fleecing shareholders; falsifying corporate financial statements; insider trading; investment bankers grossly misleading, indeed, mocking investors — became a major source of devastating loss of nominal capital of the financial markets. It also reflects rather poorly on a president whose attempts, which are long on macho rhetoric but short on substance, are designed to calm investors and markets. This is a president who may be culpable of all the accusations leveled against top corporate executives today, when he was one of them. It rings hollow when he labels these executives today as corporate criminals. No wonder that markets do not take seriously his calls for new morality, and they keep following their downward spiral.

The penultimate essay is the scrutiny of the idea, propagated first by Friedman (1962, 1983) that freedom and democracy is possible only under the social order of capitalism. Because of the gross disparity of allocation of wealth and income pronounced especially during the turn of the century, American society is giving up more individual freedoms, and ultimately a democratic form of government one could have envisaged only under Stalinism.

Finally, one cannot escape the label "bleeding heart" without providing an alternative to the now ruling research program. In the last essay of this anthology I offer a new avenue of research, which perhaps is not a completely defined and focused paradigm, nevertheless represents a start of a journey of new empirical research that, eventually, might cause something of a "paradigm shift." The title of this paper is "The Theory of Fair Markets (TFM): Toward a New Finance Paradigm."

The epilogue is my pondering whether a change, even a marginally significant one, could come, especially in the ways and means of academic research. I am very sorry to conclude the collection on a not necessarily encouraging note.

In closing this introduction, a few words of well-deserved gratitude are in order. The first in line is Ms. Yvonne Lewis Day whose magnificent editing work gave true expression to my thoughts. Elton McGoun is by far the person from whom I have learned the most and I hope will keep on teaching me for many years to come. A thousand thanks, Skip.

There are many others to whom I am thankful, but do no want to mention by name, because they might be found guilty by association with a heretic. There is one, however, I am eager to mention by title, if not by name. I am grateful to my former dean at the E.J. Ourso College of Business Administration, Louisiana State University, who was too stupid to understand that progress in science as well as in anything else comes from nonconformists, but smart enough to make my life unbearable as to opt to retire. This gave me all the freedom and time to work on what follows herein.

References

Ball, Ray. 1978. "Anomalies in Relationships Between Securities' Yields and Yield Surrogates." *Journal of Financial Economics* 6: 103–126.

Black, Fischer. 1972. "Capital Market Equilibrium with Restricted Borrowing." *Journal of Business* 45: 444–455.

Fama, Eugene F. 1965. "The Behavior of Stock Market Prices." *Journal of Business* 38: 34–105.

———. 1970. "Efficient Capital Markets: A Review of Theory and Empirical Work." *Journal of Finance* 25: 383–417.

———. 1998. "Market Efficiency, Long-Term Returns, and Behavioral Finance." *Journal of Financial Economics* 49: 283–286.

Frankfurter, George M. and Elton G. McGoun. 1999. "Ideology and the Theory of Financial Economics." *Journal of Economic Behavior and Organization* 39: 159–177.

Friedman, Milton M. 1953. "The Methodology of Positive Economics." In *Essays in Positive Economics*, edited by Milton M. Friedman. Chicago: The University of Chicago Press.

————. 1962, 1983. *Capitalism and Freedom*. Chicago: The University of Chicago Press.

Lintner, John. 1965. "The Valuation of Risk Assets and the Selection of Risky Investments in Stock Portfolios and Capital Budgets." *Review of Economics and Statistics* 47: 13–37.

Sharpe, William F. 1964. "Capital Market Prices: A Theory of Market Equilibrium Under Conditions of Risk." *Journal of Finance* 14: 425–442.

Soley, Lawrence C. 1995. *Leasing the Ivory Tower*. Boston, MA: South End Press.

Contents

capitalism is the only social structure in which the individual can be truly free. In contrast I argue that in the Anglo-American strain of capitalism, individuals gradually give up their freedom because of the grossly skewed distribution of wealth.

Chapter 1

Method and Methodology[*]

I have studied now philosophy
And Jurisprudence, Medicine
And even, alas, Theology
From end to end with labor keen;
And here, poor fool, with all my lore
I stand no wiser than before — *Faust*.

— Johann Wolfgang Von Goethe

A. Introduction

Recently, as I was skimming through the papers in the journal of one of
the associations to which I belong, I noticed that all the papers had a section titled "Methodology," either alone or in combination with some other
term such as "Data and Methodology," "Research and Methodology," or
"Methodology and Results." Without exception, however, these sections
were about *method*, not *methodology*.

In a letter to the journal's newly appointed editor, I pointed out the
difference between the two words, first by quoting the definitions of methodology from my *Microsoft Bookshelf* dictionary, and then by quoting the following "usage note" found there:

> **Usage Note**[8]: *Methodology* can properly refer to the theoretical analysis of
> the methods appropriate to a field of study or to the body of methods and
> principles particular to a branch of knowledge. In this sense, one may speak
> of *objections to the methodology of a geographic survey* (i.e., objections

---

[*] The original version of this paper appeared in *Homo Oeconomicus*, 2002, Volume 18(3/4):
465–491.

[8] Excerpted from *The American Heritage® Dictionary of the English Language, Third Edition*
© 1996 by Houghton Mifflin Company. Electronic version licensed from INSO Corporation;
further reproduction and distribution in accordance with the Copyright Law of the United
States. All rights reserved.

1

dealing with the appropriateness of the methods used) or of the *methodology of modern cognitive psychology* (i.e., the principles and practices that underlie research in the field). In recent years, however, *methodology* has been increasingly used as a pretentious substitute for *method* in scientific and technical contexts, as in *The oil company has not yet decided on a methodology for restoring the beaches.* This usage may have been fostered in part by the tendency to use the adjective *methodological* to mean "pertaining to methods," in as much as the regularly formed adjective *methodical* has been preempted to mean "orderly, systematic." But the misuse of *methodology* obscures an important conceptual distinction between the tools of scientific investigation (properly *methods*) and the principles that determine how such tools are deployed and interpreted — a distinction that the scientific and scholarly communities, if not the wider public, should be expected to maintain.

To support my argument for replacing the word *methodology* by editorial fiat with *method* or *method of analysis*, I also quoted the remark Fritz Machlup (Machlup, 1963, p. 5) made as chairperson of the session on *Economic Methodology*; namely, that only semi-literates do not know the difference between the two words.

As a member in good standing, and as a matter of courtesy, I expected at least a letter of acknowledgment from the editor, if not a reply of substance. I got neither. More recently, while thumbing through the same publication, I found that only four of the eight papers used the word *methodology* when the authors described their *method of analysis*. Perhaps the change was not due to the editor's newfound understanding of the nature and seriousness of the blunder in logic, but stemmed from the enlightenment of the authors.

Bookshelf, nevertheless, is crystal clear in pointing out that ". . . the misuse of *methodology* obscures an important conceptual distinction between the tools of scientific investigation (properly *methods*) and the principles that determine how such tools are deployed and interpreted — a distinction that the scientific and scholarly communities, if not the wider public, should be expected to maintain." So, in a test of logical reasoning we may find the pairs:

Method–methodology is like

- tools–principles
- milk–dairy products
- shirt–clothes

Although I do not have empirical proof, I believe that an overwhelming majority of researchers in financial economics would correctly choose the parallel "tools–principles" in a Miller Analogies test, instead of, say, "milk–dairy products." Why then does this widespread misuse occur, even among some of the brightest in the profession? In Fama (1998), in fact, this misuse obscures the difference between what was to become known as the "anomalies literature" and "behavioral finance."

Being a conspiracy theorist, I think the misuse is not semi-literacy (or just semi-literacy), but is, rather, a device for preserving today's methodology of financial economics. In the next section, I discuss the methodology of financial economics (also called modern finance[9]). In Section B, I deal with methods, and, in Section C, with methods of preserving the methodology. Sections B and C each include a brief summary of points.

In the concluding section, I contend that we will all benefit by observing the distinction between *tools* and *principles*.

B. Methodology

An often-used description of the methodology of a scientific field[10] is that it is a confluence of ontology (what is to be known) and epistemology (how the what is to be known is known). In short, *methodology* is the sphere of interest and the methods by which we discover what is in the sphere. Although this definition covers all fields of science, whether natural or social, it is not an adequate operational description because it obscures the delicate details of each of the components. After many years of pondering the matter, I am proposing another description that is perhaps a blueprint for understanding the methodology of financial economics, as it evolved

---

[9] In recent papers, I have seen *modern finance* also termed *traditional finance*. This is, in and of itself, an interesting development because *traditional finance* was the term often applied to the pre-Modigliani and Miller seminal paper (Modigliani and Miller, 1958) literature. This shows that receptacles do not change much. We just put different contents in them.

[10] Although I argued elsewhere that *financial economics* is meta-science at best, or perhaps art or not science at all, for the sake of discussion here, I am accepting the loftier description of the field as science.

Figure 1. The Methodology Ziggurat

from the mid-1940s to present. I call this blueprint the *methodology ziggurat* of financial economics.[11]

Perhaps the most "shocking" aspect of Figure 1 is its foundation. Untold times, I have received the response to my claim to the contrary, mostly from reviewers, that financial economics is "value-neutral." I understand that the justification for this argument is in Friedman (1954), who declares unequivocally:

> But I continue to be unrepentant in believing that its acceptance or rejection has no bearing on the criteria by which we judge the desirability or undesirability of the predicted implications. Am I required to shift my moral, ethical, normative, welfare — or whatever the word one may use for such absolutes — position according as experience in using the hypothesis leads us to accept, reject, or modify it? Alternatively, should my willingness to accept, reject or modify an hypothesis about observable phenomena be determined or altered by my ethical and philosophical position? (p. 409)

> Science is science and ethics is ethics; it takes both to make a whole man; but only confusion, misunderstanding and discord can come from not keeping them separate and distinct, from trying to impose the absolute of ethics on the relatives of science.

> To put it in Humpty Dumpty's words again: "It is a–*most–provoking–thing*" he said at last "when a person doesn't know a cravat from a belt!" (p. 409)

---

[11] For those who might have missed the pun, the ziggurat, or temple tower, was the dominant feature of religious architecture throughout the history of Mesopotamia. From the late 3rd millennium BC on, a temple was placed at the base of the ziggurat as well as on the top. The significance of the ziggurat is not completely understood, but it was probably thought of both as an altar and as a sort of stairway to and for the gods (Source: Groliers 1998 Deluxe Interactive Encyclopedia).

But this was not the only contribution of Friedman to the methodology of financial economics and to the ways and means it should be practised. In this section of the paper, I discuss the layering of the ziggurat from the foundation up, which describes and circumscribes the methodology of financial economics.

1. *Ideology*[12]

The basis of the discipline we now call financial economics — at its origins, called simply finance — is undoubtedly in another seminal essay of Friedman's (1953) titled, "The Methodology of Positive Economics." In this paper, Friedman lays the foundation for, among other things, what is *de facto* the instrumentalist methodology that economics must follow. The three necessary conditions for economic theory, a la Friedman, are:

(i)   The primary requisite of a theory is to produce acceptable forecasts.
(ii) The secondary requisite of a theory is to be simple and fruitful.
(iii) The assumptions of the theory **must be** unrealistic in order to satisfy requisites (i) and (ii).

A few words to clarify these requisites/conditions seem to be in order. By "acceptable forecasts," Friedman means forecasts that are better than other forecasts. Because there is an infinite number of theories "out there" that can produce forecasts, a theory cannot be proven as true. One can only reject the idea that the theory is not true. As long as the theory/model produces forecasts that are ". . . sufficiently good 'approximation' for the purpose at hand" (*ibid.*, p. 15), one should be content with it.

What is "sufficiently good" is a matter of subjective judgment, of course, but the purpose is clearly social policy. Because Friedman is a devout believer in the righteousness of capitalism in its purest form (today called "free markets," or "market economy" since Marx gave a bad name to capitalism), it is clear how "the purpose at hand" would fit the qualifier "sufficiently good approximation."

The fact remains that Friedman (1953) is a philosophical treatise that is not value-neutral, but rather economics-neutral. It is the belief system

---

[12] For a more comprehensive discussion on the ideology of financial economics, refer to Frankfurter and McGoun (1999).

that underlay the research program which colonized economic thinking for the last half century, largely because of the financial and moral support it received from outside the academic community. We call this ideology "neoclassical economics."

I suspect that Friedman was not completely honest when he argued, ". . .[O]nly confusion, misunderstanding and discord can come from not keeping them separate and distinct, from trying to impose the absolute of ethics on the relatives of science." The reason for my suspicion is that several other giants of contemporary economics declared openly that the field is ideology-influenced. Both Mannheim (1949) and Schumpeter (1949) are clear about the influence of ideology on all science, including economics. Although Schumpeter justifies such influence, surmising that eventually truth will prevail over ideology, Mannheim is more critical:

> Hence it has become extremely questionable whether, in the flux of life, it is a genuinely worthwhile intellectual problem to seek to discover fixed and immutable ideas or absolutes. It is a more worthy intellectual task perhaps to learn to think dynamically and relationally rather than statically. In our contemporary social and intellectual plight, it is nothing less than shocking to discover that those persons who claim to have discovered an absolute are usually the same people who also pretend to be superior to the rest. To find people in our day attempting to pass off to the world and recommending to others some nostrum of the absolute which they claim to have discovered is merely a sign of the loss of and the need for intellectual and moral certainty, felt by broad sections of the population who are unable to look life in the face (p. 77).

It is inconceivable that Friedman was not familiar with these views, yet made his *relative* of ethics the *absolute* of his science. Franco Modigliani is a bit more "blunt" than I. Mackie (1998, p. 107), quoting from Klamer (1992), attributes this statement to Modigliani:

> Friedman is driven by the idea that whatever the government does is bad. He has a mission and seems to be willing to sacrifice some intellectual honesty for that (*ibid.*, p. 120).

In spite of this, or perhaps because of this, the consensus today is that financial economics is value-neutral. Now, this is what Adam Smith (whom Friedman was so eager to co-opt and reinterpret) calls "clamour and sophistry."[13]

Although the combination of ideology and instrumentalism dominates the many branches of economics, none is so obsequious to the Friedmanian dogma as financial economics is. I attribute this servitude to the vast economic influence corporate America has on this segment of academia (Soley, 1995, pp. 57–91) and to the commanding influence on the field by the Chicago/Rochester school.

2. *Axioms*

The American Heritage Talking Dictionary has three definitions for *axiom*. Of these, the third definition is the most apropos and inclusive for "the purpose at hand" (if Friedman could get away with this, why not I?):

> A self-evident principle or one that is accepted as true without proof as the basis for argument; a postulate.[14]

In fact, axioms in financial economics are not self-evident principles or truths. They are just assumptions that have gained the status of higher order than mere assumptions, because they are so widely used or because many found them either logical or conducive for work that could be deemed as "fruitful."

In the context of methodology, an axiom defines the boundaries of ontology. Anything that falls beyond such borders can then be termed an anomaly and dismissed as an unfortunate occurrence that should not overly concern anyone.

An axiom is, in fact, just a set of assumptions that originally had a degree of verity much weaker than the dictionary definition of the word, but which somehow became deeply entrenched in the field. Because of

---

[13] The full quote is:

> . . . the clamour and sophistry of merchants and manufacturers easily persuade . . . that the private interest of a part and of a subordinate part of society is the general interest of the whole (Smith, 1776, Book I, p. 101).

[14] Excerpted from *American Heritage Talking Dictionary*. Copyright © 1997 The Learning Company, Inc. All Rights Reserved.

this entrenchment, no one questions any longer the verisimilitude of these conjectures.

Axioms, then, become the foundations of theories, thus circumventing any need to prove whether the axioms themselves are veritable. In reality, many of the axioms upon which an economic doctrine is built are nothing more than hypotheses, deriving from some basic understanding of the state of the world as perceived by the creators and propagators of a particular paradigm, or as adopted by them as a matter of convenience for further theory building. That is, they are the preconceived behavior of an emotionally vacuous, economically astute, perfectly calculating entity.

In essence, most of the axioms that we take for granted are self-serving. Albert Jay Nock's observation, "It is an economic axiom as old as the hills that goods and services can be paid for only with goods and services," is an example of the efforts of many economists to portray human behavior as selfish and motivated only by rewards directly translatable into monetary units, or barter.

The axioms on which financial economics builds are those put forth by Von Neumann and Morgenstern (1967) (VM, subsequently). The six axioms of VM constitute the quantifiable psychological makeup of the financial-economic person and determine his/her mode of behavior. Many books and articles contain these axioms. For the convenience of the reader, I reproduce them here as they appear in Frankfurter and Phillips (1994).

The Von Neumann and Morgenstern Axioms

(i)   *Comparability.* For any pair of investment opportunities, A and B, one of the following must be true: the investor prefers A to B, B to A, or is indifferent between A and B.

(ii) *Transitivity.* If A is preferred to B, and B is preferred to C, than A is preferred to C.

(iii) *Continuity.* If investment outcome A is preferred to B, and B to C, then there is some probability P such that the investor would be indifferent between the certain event B and the uncertain event {P∃A + (1–P)∃C}.

(iv) *Independence.* If an investor is indifferent between the certain outcomes A and B, and C is any other certain outcome, then he is also indifferent between the uncertain events {P∃A + (1–P)∃C} and {P∃B + (1–P)∃C}.

(v) *Interchangeability.* If an investor is indifferent between two uncorre-
     lated risky income streams, then the securities that produce them are
     interchangeable in any investment strategy — simple or complex.

(vi) *Risk Aversion.* If securities A and B offer the same positive rate of
     return, R = X, with probabilities P_a and P_b, respectively, and other-
     wise R = 0 with probabilities $(1-P_a)$ and $(1-P_b)$, respectively, then A
     is preferred to B if $P_a > P_b$. Moreover, one's relative preference for A
     in this case is a (possibly complex) monotonic function of the rela-
     tive certainty coefficient P_a/P_b (*ibid.*, p. 7).[15]

Financial economics adopted these axioms without much question or criticism, from the early start of Markowitz (1952) and thereafter.[16]

    Although the VM axioms are the foundation of much work in other
fields of economics as well — and were parleyed into the expected utility
maxim (EU, subsequently)[17] — that is not to say that economists did not
question the reality of these axioms regarding the investment behavior of
individuals or, to use a sexier term, economic agents. (I must admit that
I can never figure out just when an *individual* becomes an *agent*.) One
must bear in mind that these axioms are, in fact, no more than questionable assumptions.

    The first such criticism is what is generally referred to today as the
"Allais paradox" (Allais, 1952), or the "Allais ratio." In essence, Allais

---

[15] These axioms may be true or false as applied to a particular investor. However, to the
extent that investors do calculate and are willing to acknowledge the existence of risk, the
VM axioms are restrictive only with regard to the continuity assumption, which is inconsistent with Roy's (1952) "safety-first" argument. It is hard to see how one can have Stochastic
Dominance without satisfying (i), (ii), (iv) and (v).

[16] Axiom (vi) is explicitly assumed by Markowitz (1952), and his portfolio expectation and
variance operators follow from (iii). But this, of course, is the normative model. Sharpe's
(1963) derivation is based on the Markowitz results, plus equilibrium restrictions that, except
for the borrowing and lending, have no other purpose but to make the homogeneous expectations assumption in Sharpe (1964) plausible.

[17] The EU combined with the Rational Expectation Hypothesis conjointly makes up both the
abstract and the pragmatic. As Muth (1981) defines the latter

> . . . that expectation of firms (or, more generally, the subjective probability distri-
> bution of outcomes) tend to be distributed, for the same information set, about the
> prediction of the theory (or the "objective" probability distribution of outcomes)
> (pp. 4–5),

de facto the empirical validation of the EU.

questioned the Comparability axiom of VM. The paradox is revealed by a certain decision scheme, obtained from experiments of preferences between pairs of lotteries that are based on similarity relations between prizes and probabilities.

The Allais paradox is resolved in Rubinstein (1988), and is known today as the "similarity maxim." In short, the maxim is a contradiction of EU, in that a choice is deemed rational when the probabilities are similar, but the choice with the lower probability has a dominating prize; or, equivalently, where the prizes are similar but the lower prize choice has an overwhelmingly large probability.

During the three decades following the first questioning of the VM axioms, several new theories of choice under uncertainty/risk[18] had been proposed. Regret theory shows rational violations of the first three VM axioms (Leland, 1994). Buschena and Zilberman (1995) count and test other alternatives to VM, such as "weighted utility," "disappointment aversion," "implicit EU," "rank-dependent EU" and, last but not least, "prospect theory" (PT, subsequently) of Kahneman and Tversky (1979). What is most puzzling is that among the alternative axioms, all showing inconsistency with the VM axiom's dictated pattern of choice, only PT had limited success in breaking the chokehold of the EU maxim on financial economics.

PT's importation to financial economics created, overnight, the behavioral finance literature, and the over-, underreaction hypotheses, both at variance with EU-predicted behavior. Because the empirical evidence showing lack of validity for the CAPM/EMH paradigm is labeled "anomalies" and because such evidence obtained from event studies is labeled "methodology" (*de facto*, a regrettable *method*), Fama (1998) succeeds in rejecting PT and behavioral finance as an axiomatic basis for an alternative (finance) methodology.

Why would one fight so vehemently to prevent emergence of a new finance paradigm? Is it, perhaps, that such a paradigm is based on PT, which has its roots in the experimental psychology of decision-making with uncertain prospects? Such foundation, of course, would divorce

---

[18] The common distinction between *risk* and *uncertainty* is that the probability distribution of outcomes and its parameter(s) are known in the case of *risk*, whereas neither the distributional form of outcomes nor its parameter(s) are known in the case of *uncertainty*. I am taking the liberty here, however, of using the terms interchangeably. In fact, the parameters of the distribution of rates of return are never known. For this reason, many call the case where neither the distributional form nor the parameter(s) are known, "uncertain uncertainty."

finance from economics, thus ending the hegemony called "financial economics." Is it possible that such divorce might irrevocably separate the union that succeeded in tying the subject to rigid, traditional and orthodox neoclassicism? And if so, is it possible that those who vehemently reject the emergence of new paradigms do so to avoid losing this domination?

3. *Assumptions*

Within the ideological confines of the axioms, the financial economist is free to make any assumptions necessary to ensure that the resulting theory is as plausible as he or she wishes it to be. This "freedom" to make such assumption derives, without a doubt, from Friedman's oft-quoted statement:

> The relevant question to ask about the assumptions of theory is not whether they are descriptively "realistic," for they never are, but whether they are sufficiently good "approximations" for the purpose at hand (Friedman, 1953, p. 15).

Note the two words in double quotation marks in this passage from perhaps Friedman's most important philosophical work. One must wonder at the significance of these double quotation marks. Are they signals from the author that these two words are never absolute, but rather subjective interpretations? Or are they Friedman's way to emphasize the importance of the two components in his view of economic model-building? Whatever Friedman's purpose, the statement, in its entirety, is subjective and has neither economics science nor philosophical universality.

When the quotation is deaggregated into the components that prescribe the assumptions needed for economic theory development, the subjectivity of Friedman's instrumentalism becomes self-evident:

(i) Assumptions should be questioned.
(ii) The questions should not pertain to reality, or a "realistic" description of the world the theory is designed to describe.
(iii) Assumptions are "never" (my double quotation marks) realistic.
(iv) Assumptions should be sufficiently good "approximations" for the purpose at hand.

(v)   What is sufficient and what is approximation is left to individual interpretation.

(vi) Assumptions are good approximations with respect to a purpose that happens to be at hand.

None of these components stand on objective grounds, but rather reflect the world of economic theory production.

But Friedman does not stop there in developing his thesis of the positivist methodology. After exempting economists from the necessity of building models that are anchored in observable reality, he continues:

> Truly important and significant hypotheses will be found to have "assumptions" that are wildly inaccurate descriptive representations of reality, and, in general, the more significant the theory, the more unrealistic the assumptions (in this sense) (*ibid.*, p. 14).

With all fairness to Friedman, I must point out that, in footnote 12 of his paper, Friedman makes it clear that the reverse does not hold; that is, unrealistic assumptions do not create, by themselves, "truly" important hypotheses.

Here, Friedman "kicks up a notch" the fire under the assumptions caldron. It is one thing to argue that assumptions should be "sufficiently good 'approximations' for the purpose at hand," and quite another to claim that the more significant economic theories are based on "wildly inaccurate" descriptions of the world. Thus, one must be fully cognizant of Friedman's intention to give a "00" license to assume on no other grounds than his subjective perception of the normative rules of economic model creation. Without question, Friedman's positive philosophy is subjectively normative.

Now, let us consider what is certainly the most influential work in financial economics (Sharpe, 1964) — a work that prompted the bulk of the literature in what is now called "modern finance." Many, in fact, consider this paper the foundation of the finance paradigm. In the paper, Sharpe argues that his doctrine should be adopted because of its internal logic (his assumptions "imply equilibrium conditions"):

> . . . since the proper test of theory is not the realism of its assumptions but the acceptability of its implications, and since these assumptions imply equilibrium conditions which form a major part of classical financial doctrine, it is far from clear that this formulation should be rejected (p. 434).

In one fell swoop, Sharpe suggests abandoning perhaps the most important and verifiable building block of the Friedmanian doctrine — the quality of prediction. So, there is no requirement for predictive ability, however
subjective that quality might be, as long as the theory/model is consistent
with the classical financial doctrine.

To move from Sharpe to Fama, with his two definitions of informationally efficient markets (Fama, 1965, 1970), is just a small step for the
financial economist, but a giant leap for financial economics methodology.
In combination, Friedman–Sharpe–Fama create an impenetrable and inde-
structible fortress, complete with moat, drawbridge and boiling oil on the
parapets.

More binding and exclusionary than the explicit assumptions are the
implicit ones — i.e., those silent acquiescences that, because of their sub-
liminal nature, are not, and can never be, disputed. Here are the strictest
of these:

- That arbitrage opportunities will be discovered and arbitrageurs by
  their activity will bring the market to equilibrium.[19]
- That the sum of the parts equals the whole. This assumption was the
  push behind the practice of decomposing a complex problem into arbitrary parts, solving the parts separately and then putting all back
  together for a solution of the whole.
- That processes which are without a doubt anchored in culture and language can be modeled by the same tools as physical processes.
- That the disproof of one thing is the proof of its opposite (whatever
  that opposite might be). This assumption is the genesis of the volumi-
  nous event study literature.[20]
- That the assumptions of one model which were not questioned at the
  time the model was proposed can be germane to a different model,
  without mentioning them.

Together, explicit and implicit assumptions immunize the methodological structure from any possibility of refutation (see Fama, 1998). One

---

[19] The presumption of arbitrage was the *deux ex machina* of Propositions I and II of
Modigliani and Miller (1958), and the heart of arbitrage pricing theory (APT) of Ross (1976).
[20] This is the absurd idea that if error terms of a regression are called abnormal returns, and
if these terms are aggregated across economic micro-units/agents to show a quantity that
is different than zero, then it is proof that an event took place independent of any other
circumstance and the learning curve of economic micro-units/agents.

non-falsifiable

must not forget, however, that the impossibility of refutation is the *causa causans* to disqualify a particular methodology as a scientifically productive process by the adherents of the Popperian philosophy of science and its many tendrils.

4. *Theory*

The final layer of the methodology substructure of the finance research program (financial economics' ontology) is the theory arranged on the first three tiers of the ziggurat. That is, if the theory is in line with the tenets of the previous three tiers and if its conclusions are consistent with the dogma stacked on these tiers, then it is considered an acceptable description of the world of finance. Again, reality does not count for much, and it is often sacrificed in the name of the ideology it represents. In this regard also, there is a great deal of data snooping. Theories are developed via observed data, and then the same data are used to validate the theory. More about that later.

But even with the latitude the three previous strata of the ziggurat offers, *ceteris paribus*, theories that are mathematically tractable (and the more complex the better) are preferred over theories of common sense. This is especially clear in the case when all empirical evidence points in the direction that the theory does hold, neither as a predictor, nor as an existing condition.

The prime examples of this departure from reality are theories on the corporation side (and where financial economics failed the most): cost of capital, capital structure, valuation and, perhaps foremost, dividend policy. Dividend and dividend policy theory have created the largest number of models, all mathematical, and all unverifiable by either empirical evidence or measurability of the theoretical variables, or both. In practice, there are no models per se of dividend policy, the only exception being agency theory's normative rule that the firm should be sucked dry of all of its current income. Else, managers who act from greed and nothing else will squander the shareholder's hard-earned wealth. Although this view of the world/theory has been known for quite some while (Easterbrook, 1984), as a practice, it is not observable.

The vast majority of the dividend research, however, is not about policy, but rather about what dividends do to value. There is, without doubt, a positive statistical connection between the act of paying dividends and the value of shares. However, none of the dividend theories/models can convincingly explain the connection. The empirical evidence is simply not there.

The other theories of corporation finance share the same lack of validity. First, most theories, especially the garden-variety type of agency theory, are not refutable. Second, either the empirical validity is not there, or it is only there for a subset of firms. After half a century, we still are not keen on how to measure the cost of capital, on whether capital budgeting should be performed by the net present value method (Stulz, 1999), and whether there is an optimal, or even target, capital structure. And if none of this is known for sure, how can one go about measuring value that would be, in any way, different from what accountants could do?

5. *Summary*

It is important to understand that the structure on which the method of modern science rests is multilayered. At the base of the ziggurat is a concrete ideological belief in beginning-of-the-century capitalism as envisaged by Friedman (1962). Piled atop this are ever-narrowing tiers of axioms, explicit and implicit, that limit intellectual freedom and force ontology to concentrate on what is dear to the builders of the ideological foundation.

In return for acknowledging the ziggurat, practising academics are granted a semblance of freedom, however small, to manufacture their own assumptions. This quasi-freedom allows them, first, to develop theories, and later, as I argue in the next section, to test models that will show what they set out to show.

C. Method

1. *Model*

Now, here is the trickiest maneuver on the ziggurat: the move from a theoretically plausible and appealing construct consistent with the ideology, to a statistically testable model. One must derive from one's theory a set of hypotheses that are empirically testable: the ultimate validation of one's model.

There are serious philosophical, statistical and practical problems involved — problems that are either overlooked entirely or nitpicked to a painful death. The most fundamental philosophical issue is how one can use mathematics as a proxy for cultural processes. From Wittgenstein to Popper, philosophers argued that mathematics — which is an interculturally cogent procedure — cannot be equated with rituals, customs and social habits — characteristics that explain the behavior of humans both individually and in organizations.[21]

Yet, modern finance flourishes on mathematics, the more obscure and unrealistic the better — art for art's sake. I suspect, however, that there is a close connection between mathematics and the neoclassical ideology of modern finance. The emphasis on mathematics and numbers and the

---

[21] A major void in the field is that Ph.D.'s in finance do not receive any formal education in philosophy, although their doctorate is *in* philosophy. Nor do most feel any inclination or need to consider philosophical views, much less accept them. The few who have heard of Thomas Kuhn, and the even fewer who have read him, accept his thesis without question as developed in *The Structure of Scientific Revolutions* (Kuhn, 1970).

Yet, Kuhn's view of science, its structure, functioning and growth is a placating view — a position that not only ignores the built-in institutional safety devices that protect the ruling elite, but also lulls his readers into believing that eventually a revolution will come.

Scientific revolution might be a historical fact, but the welfare costs associated with the existence of a less than truthful description of the world, for an indeterminant length of time, are completely ignored by Kuhn. Moreover, as elites become more sophisticated, they increasingly deploy tactics that perpetuate their existence. R.H. Coase points out this sentiment in his acceptance lecture for the Nobel Prize in economics:

> [But] a scholar must be content with the knowledge that what is false in what he says will soon be exposed and, for what is true he can count on ultimately seeing it accepted if only he lives long enough (Coase, 1992, p. 719).

It is amazing that, while the bulk of applied mathematics in finance is covered by two courses of college calculus and Brownian motion, mathematicians as of late question the limits of mathematics altogether. John Horgan, writing in the August 1994 issue of *Scientific American*, observes:

> Mathematics has had some success in delineating its own boundaries, Taub remarks. The most dramatic example was Kurt Gödel's demonstration in the 1930s that all moderately complex mathematical systems are "incomplete"; that is, they give rise to statements that can be neither proved nor disproved with the axioms of the system.

> Gregory J. Chaitin, a mathematician at the IBM Thomas J. Watson Research Center, sees darker implications in Gödel's theorem. He notes that this insight has been followed by similar ones, notably Chaitin's own finding that mathematics is riddled with truths that have no logical, causal basis but are simply "random." As a result of these difficulties, he says, mathematics may become an increasingly empirical, experimental endeavor with less of a claim to absolute truth.

reward system that favors everything quantitative are instrumental in translating emotions, psychology and the metaphysical to a quantity, turning value to a monetary entity. If value is a monetary entity, of course, one has no difficulty in translating risk to a monetary entity as well.

I submit that the term modern[22] finance is a misnomer. What we have is not modern finance, but "robo-finance." The latter robotically translates complex social/cultural systems for which no one has a comprehensive, or even a simple, theory into blips on the radar screen of price-volume changes. From these blips, shrewd operators extract "meaning" using an ever-increasing array of statistical models (see the next subsection for a demonstration). This is analogous to analyzing a patient's temperature chart with sophisticated statistical methods to find the cause of his/her illness. Our intellect is so poor that we do not even recognize we are being bamboozled.

We also tend to forget that reverse of the aphorism, "If it ain't soporific it ain't scientific," is not true. That is, just because the presentation of an idea sounds like the recording of a medical examiner's autopsy, the concept is not necessarily a scientific truth.

The next problem is to find observable variables. Many models — the most obvious being those of dividend signaling — are crammed with variables that exist conceptually, but are nowhere to be found empirically. The usual remedy is to resort to proxies which open a Pandora's box when the paper comes to be reviewed. If a reviewer does not like the research idea, the proxy is the sure-fire excuse to reject the paper. In this circumstance, the empirical findings are tantamount to the proverbial tree falling in the forest when no one is there: it does not make a sound.

Suppose we are lucky and find observable variables that are not proxies. We still have the problem of how to measure them. Consider, for instance, the ratio of debt-to-equity. Are we to measure all debt? At market? At book? At what unit of measure and at what date? Ditto for equity. The slightest manipulation of the data will produce results close to the heart of the researcher, though not necessarily anywhere near validation of his/her model. The caveat, "Keep one eye on the hypothesis and one eye on the data," is apropos here, and the guiding light of the *episteme*.

But, this is not all. The tsunami of event studies showed that, in the solicitous effort to mimic the natural sciences, quasi-laboratory experiments are unable to hold constant all factors, especially those affected by time

---

[22] I use the term "modern" in the sense of modernism — the belief that science and the scientific approach will solve all the ills of our lives.

and the learning curve. That is why many of these studies show results contrary to results some other studies of the same ilk showed before.

Let us not forget the delicate issue of assumptions made when the econometric models were originally put forth and whether those assumptions are reasonable or valid, given the data. This is different, of course, from the freewheeling assumption-making as per the Friedmanian doctrine that was needed to develop the theory. That is, in order to take the results of empirical tests seriously, regardless of what assumptions one made to develop the theory, one must strictly meet the assumptions of the statistical model used. These assumptions are rarely considered or mentioned anymore because the novelty of the econometrics covers up for the weakness of the statistical model. After many event studies of significant results had coefficients of correlation less than 0.05, the goodness of fit of the statistical model was not reported at all. Substance and economic significance are buried in the grave of superficial formalism.

2. *Tests*

In this tier of the ziggurat, one can find the capital accomplishments of modern finance. During half a century of econometrics, researchers have inexorably sifted, winnowed, pounded, churned, fermented and even tortured their data to concoct some sort of statistical significance for their respective model. As an alternative, some have dredged up arcane data sources to prove the validity or non-validity of earlier tests performed by others who, unfortunately, were not privy to the same data.

My estimate is that, over the last half century, modern finance has cranked out 60,000–65,000 papers and dissertations, published in refereed and unrefereed journals and conference proceedings, or papers presented at meetings of learned societies without leaving a trace in print in the public domain. The bulk of these papers dealt with the CAPM/EMH, which, as I argued before, turned out to be the major concern of modern finance.

For an earlier project, I sifted through hundreds of published papers on CAPM/EMH and found several astonishing regularities in this vast effort of academic research. Perhaps the most shocking was the fact that, although Fama's classical definition of informationally efficient markets,

> . . . a situation where successive price changes are independent is consistent with the existence of an "efficient" market for securities, that is, a

market where, given the available information, actual prices at every point
in time represent very good estimates of intrinsic values (Fama, 1965, p. 90),

leaves no doubt that prices are the averaged intrinsic values of all market
participants, the models of the CAPM's statistical tests are so complex
that only a very few academics could formulate their expectations accordingly. Even these specially anointed persons would need several weeks of
data collection and analysis to unlock the secrets of pricing, if indeed their
model was the correct one.

The econometric fireworks are blinding. Though the volume of papers
considered here is limited, it is nevertheless representative of what the
authors of these papers attribute to the process that "explains" prices, in
or out of equilibrium, the connections between return and risk, forecasting ability, and the properties of the ever-elusive beta for the "market"
en toto, or some of its arbitrary segments.

There are several ways to present this anthology, but I include it here
in alphabetical order, according to first author. The main reason is to
demonstrate the other perplexing phenomenon: the smoothness and ease
with which some authors move from one model to another, practically in
the same year, espousing entirely different belief systems regarding the
data. Judge for yourself.

Ang and Peterson (1985), after-tax, cyclical model, using maximum likelihood techniques; Bark (1991), application of the *methodology* of Fama and
McBeth (1973) to Korean data; Beedles (1984), non-stationarity, and the
amazing revelation that the CAPM is better for electric utilities than for
other firms; Best and Grauer (1985), time-series of mean vectors in risk-
return space; Bey (1983), stationarity; Bodurtha and Mark (1991), time-
varying risks and returns; Bower *et al.* (1984), comparing the CAPM with
APT; Branch *et al.* (1983), adjustment of alpha to zero beta; Brigham and
Crum (1977), the use of the CAPM in utility rate structure determination;
Brigham and Crum (1978), again the use of the CAPM in utility rate
structure determination; Brown *et al.* (1983), SURM and 2-step GLS applications to size related anomalies; Brown (1979), autocorrelation and the
relatedness of the CAPM; Bubnys (1990), simulation and the comparison
of the CAPM to APT; Casabona *et al.* (1983), duration and interest rate
risk in the CAPM; Casabona and Vora (1982), bias in the CAPM due to
interest rate duration; Cecchetti and Mark (1990), moment restrictions and
calibration methods; Cheng and Grauer (1980), invariance law; Conine and
Tamarkin (1985), skewness and the cost of equity capital of public utilities;

Connor and Korajczyk (1988), skewness in utility stock cost of capital; Corhay *et al.* (1987), international evidence of seasonality in the CAPM; Cox and Rudd (1991), to calculate underwriters' betas; Elton *et al.* (1983), the relationship between zero beta portfolios and dividend yields; Elton and Gruber (1984), the estimation of the CAPM using "smart source parsing"; Frankel (1985), maximum likelihood estimation of beta; Friend and Westerfield (1981), comparison of residual variances with the covariances of returns; Friend *et al.* (1978), two new tests of the CAPM, (1) substituting *ex ante* returns for *ex post* returns, and (2) the use of bond prices (?)[23] to calculate beta; Goldberg and Vora (1978), bivariate spectral analysis; Goldberg and Vora (1981), grouping based on historical betas; Gombola and Kahl (1990), Kalman filtering model to estimate the time-series utility betas; Grauer (1978), comparison of the mean-variance model to five forms of the power utility model; Haddad and Benkato (1989), intertemporal tests of beta stationarity; Harlow and Rao (1989), pricing in Generalized Mean Lower Partial Moment framework; Harrington (1983), the relationship between returns and several alternative measures of risk in the CAPM for life insurance firms;[24] Harvey (1989), time-varying conditional covariances; Harvey and Zhou (1990), Bayesian inference (!);[25] Homaifar and Graddy (1990), variance and lower partial moment betas as alternative risk measures; Jensen (1978), anomalies; Johnson and Lanser (1981), measuring the expectational value of the systematic dividend risk (?); Jorion (1991), Bayesian and CAPM *estimators* (my italics) of the mean returns of portfolios; Keim (1983), anomalies; Keim (1986), more about anomalies; Klemkosky and Jun (1982), monetary impact of market risk premia; Kroll *et al.* (1988), experimental tests, with subjects, of the separation theorem and the CAPM; Lakonishok and Shapiro (1986), anomalies; Lee (1976a), investment horizon; Lee (1976b), investment horizon and systematic risk; Lee and Lloyd (1976), the CAPM as a recursive system; Lee (1977), errors-in-variables estimation; Lee and Lloyd (1978), block recursive systems of estimation; Lee and Chen (1982), variable mean response regression; Lee (1984), random coefficient and errors-in-variables regression estimation; Lee and Wu (1985), kurtosis and stationarity; Lee *et al.* (1990), heterogeneous investment horizon; Levhari and Levy (1977),

---

[23] I have stated elsewhere (Frankfurter and Phillips, 1994) that it is absurd to lump together asset returns that are generated by distinctly different economic processes. Thus, returns of bonds determined by the fluctuation of interest rates and other type of risks, characterized by a finite horizon, cannot be aggregated with the returns on stocks.

[24] Observe again the segmentation of the capital market for testing a model that is equilibrium-restricted for *all* capital assets.

[25] Pray tell how Bayesian inference — which is totally subjective — can fit an equilibrium-based model. How on earth can subjectivity proxy for consensus?

investment horizon; Levy (1980a), investment horizon, inflation: the Israeli evidence; Levy (1980b), beta and market imperfection; Levy (1981), investment horizon; Levy (1982), a confidence level approach to the CAPM; Levy (1984), *ex post* selection bias; Litzenberger *et al.* (1980), CAPM for estimating cost of capital for public utilities; Long (1978), valuation of cash dividends; MacKinlay (1987), missing factors in multivariate tests; Mankiw and Shapiro (1986), consumption beta (?) and market beta; McEnally (1978), public utility rate cases; McEnally and Upton (1979), *ex post* risk-return; Mullins (1982), cost of capital estimation; Murphy (1990), Bayesian estimation of beta; Nagorniak (1982), the use of beta in interpreting risk adjusted equity performance; Ng (1991), multivariate GARCH tests of the time-series CAPM; Percival (1974), interest rate risk and default risk of bonds in the CAPM's framework; Peseau and Zepp (1978), public utility rate cases; Pettway and Jordan (1987), comparing APT and CAPM return generating functions for public utility rate cases; Reinganum (1981a), anomalies; Reinganum (1981b), returns of extreme portfolios; Roll and Ross (1983), APT, CAPM and rate calculations for public utilities; Sauer and Murphy (1992), comparison of several alternative models of the CAPM in Germany; Schmalensee (1981), dividends, risk adjusted returns and the CAPM; Schwert and Seguin (1990), time-series betas and heteroscedasticity; Scott and Brown (1980), biased and unstable betas, autocorrelation of residuals and intertemporal correlations between market returns and residuals in the CAPM; Shanken (1987), a multivariate proxy for the market portfolio, consisting of a stock and a bond index in validating the CAPM; Sharpe (1978), CAPM and public utility rate cases; Sharpe (1982), a factor analytic model to analyze past performance and to predict future returns; Shukla and Trzcinka (1991), a factor model to explain variability of returns in both the APT and the CAPM; Stambaugh (1982), testing the sensitivity of the CAPM for different indexes and for different subsets of assets; Stambaugh (1983), net rental return on real estate, using a broad market index and a two-stock index; Stoll *et al.* (1983), anomalies; Swidler (1988), heterogeneous expectations in financial analysts' forecasts;[26] Turnbull *et al.* (1982), critique of the Cheng-Grauer CAPM model; Udinsky and Kirshner (1979), predictive power of four models: the market model, the CAPM, the zero-beta model and the portfolio variance model; Vandell and Malernee (1978), utility equity returns and the CAPM; Watts (1978), systematic abnormal returns (?) after quarterly earning announcements — anomalies; Yawitz and Marshall (1977), the government bond market and the CAPM; Zhou (1991), eigenvalue tests of portfolio efficiency when there is no riskless asset.

---

[26] One of the less than a handful of papers in which the surreal assumption of homogeneous expectations is replaced by its more realistic opposite.

One may dismiss many of these papers on the grounds that they appear in publications other than the nobility press, and that their salient feature is their meticulous mediocrity. Yet, there is no denying that many of the most exotic ones are authored by the best names in the business and published in their favorite organs.

3. *Summary*

Magic, real or imaginary, is performed in six forms or any combination thereof:

(i)   Production: in which something appears or something multiplies.
(ii) Transformation: in which something changes in color, shape or size.
(iii) Transportation: in which something moves from one place to another.
(iv) Penetration: in which one solid object passes through another.
(v)   Mentalism: in which mind-reading and predictions occur.
(vi) Disappearance: in which something vanishes from sight.

Is it not true that modern finance's methods (its models and tests, its epistemology) have all these elements of magic? And, if the answer is yes, then is it not true that modern finance is not unlike an act of theatrical magic rather than real science?

But that is not the only dimension where the similarities between the paradigms of financial economics and magic are striking. Consider the careers of the short list of authors I cited here. Are the six forms of magic not present in their accomplishments? That is why a limited and cursory inspection of the literature shows how so many practised the elements of production, transformation, transportation, mentalism and disappearance, practically year after year, in their research. I am not making this remark in an accusatory or slighting manner. I am just reflecting on the nature and outer shell within which the methods of the paradigm develop, survive and flourish.

D. Concluding Remarks

It was not my intention in this paper to criticize the academic subject called financial economics (and sometimes, modern finance), neither for its accomplishments (which are numerous), nor for its intellectual one-dimensionality and paucity (an unfortunate fact). My purpose was to analyze the methodological construct of the field, and ascertain what the components of this construct really are.

In this process, I could not help wondering why the commonly used *methods of analysis* of financial economics are referred to as *methodology*. Although I am quite sure that hundreds, if not thousands, of the academics who write in the subject do not know the difference between the two concepts, many of the leading and, thus, influential ones do. Especially a writer so central to the most researched paradigm of finance, the EMH, must be well aware of the distinction. Yet, Fama (1998) clearly and deliberately refers to methods of analysis as methodology.

I suspect that this is done merely to replace substance with form. That is, by concentrating on the tangential issue of statistical correctness, what samples can and cannot show in random tests, and how all these relate to the accuracy of the hypotheses about the operation of markets, one can obscure the more central and important consequences of the profession. By devoting another 10,000 or so journal pages to arguing whether markets are efficient, researchers dodge the cardinal question of why we should care about market efficiency in the first place — especially before we discover how market participants actually behave and why they choose to behave the way they behave.

One also must make a resolution regarding the ultimate goal of science, inclusive of financial economics. Even if the goal is to provide better forecasts that will enable economic agents (I yield here to those who like to call individuals by this loftier term) to make better decisions, one should look for causes and effects deeper than skin.

I, however, believe — along with many philosophers of science (not that I am calling myself one) — that science is about the search for the truth. That is, it is a process of discovery that will lead us to a better understanding of what we are and what is around us. This does not mean, of course, that there is an ultimate truth "out there," or that we will find it any time soon, if ever. It just means that we must look deeper than the superficial combination of data and models, especially since science is deeply rooted in an ideology/religion that has in mind its own perpetuation rather than the search for truth.

Accordingly, attacks on behavioral finance of the kind one finds in Fama (1998) and Ball (1996) are for the sole purpose of protecting a religion from competing *memes*,[27] rather than for the sake of growth in scientific knowledge. All that these or similar attacks prove is that all truth is ideological.

This is not to say that the foundations of behavioral finance in its purest sense (not the anomalies literature) is without its faults. It is grounded in PT of Kahneman and Tversky (1979), which has its own share of critics and criticism. But at least it is not so fundamentally value-laden as the paradigms of modern finance, and deserves the chance to evolve to something that can be an alternative to the current methodology.

Instead of fostering a nascent tendril, "modern finance" fights behavioral finance with its heavy-hitters — if not with outright ridicule, then in ways of assimilation (McGoun and Scubik, 2000). This is definitely not in the interest of growth in scientific knowledge.

As unfortunate as it sounds, matters become worse when one also considers personalities and the reward systems involved. The four horsemen of academic inanity — hubris, self-importance, loftiness and cocksureness — have visited financial economics throughout its existence. One has only to read Reiter and Williams' (2001) careful analysis of how debates in finance are conducted to understand the severity of this problem.[28]

The only way to ease modern finance's grip on the profession and judge both its merits and its shortcomings is to understand its methodological structure. My hope is that this paper has been a step, however modest, in that direction.

Acknowledgments

Since I became the unofficial *enfant terible* of finance, I am not sure it is wise to mention the many that enriched my understanding of and broadened my views on what is called financial economics. Yet, I must give credit to two without whom I would have never written this paper. First, a fellow traveler, Skip McGoun of Bucknell University, whose wisdom and immense knowledge of the literature helped me for almost a decade to clarify my thinking. And, second but not least, Manfred Holler of the University of Hamburg who opened the door for me to the world of alternative theories

---

[27] See Lynch (1996) and Frankfurter and McGoun (2000).

[28] See also Frankfurter and McGoun (1996).

of utility largely ignored in the financial economics literature. I hope these words of gratitude will not hurt their career, and that they forgive me for any errors in this paper that are totally my responsibility. I am also grateful for the hospitality of the University of Hamburg where this paper was conceived and the bulk of it developed.

References

Allais, M. 1952. "Fondoments d'une théorie positive des choix comportant un risque at critique des postulats at axiomes de l'ecole américaine." Paper read at Memoire presente au Colloque International sur le risque. Centre National de la Reserche Scientifique, Paris.

Ang, James S. and David R. Peterson. 1985. "Return, Risk, and Yield: Evidence from Ex Ante Data." *Journal of Finance* 40: 537–548.

Ball, Ray. 1996. "The Theory of Stock Market Efficiency: Accomplishments and Limitations." *Journal of Financial Education* 22: 1–13.

Bark, Hee-Kyung K. 1991. "Risk, Return, and Equilibrium in the Emerging Markets: Evidence from the Korean Stock Market." *Journal of Economics and Business* 43: 353–362.

Beedles, William L. 1984. "Electric Utility Returns and the Market Model." *Journal of Business Research* 12: 463–479.

Best, Michael J. and Robert R. Grauer. 1985. "Capital Asset Pricing Compatible with Observed Market Value Weights." *Journal of Finance* 40: 85–103.

Bey, Roger P. 1983. "Market Model Stationarity of Individual Public Utilities." *Journal of Financial and Quantitative Analysis* 18: 67–85.

Bodurtha, Jr., James N. and Nelson C. Mark. 1991. "Testing the CAPM with Time-Varying Risks and Returns." *Journal of Finance* 46: 1485–1505.

Bower, Dorothy H., Richard S. Bower and Dennis E. Logue. 1984. "Arbitrage Pricing Theory and Utility Stock Returns." *Journal of Finance* 39: 1041–1054.

Branch, Ben, Alan Gleit and Harold B. Tamule. 1983. "Note on the Instability of Alphas." *Review of Business & Economic Research* 18: 78–80.

Brigham, Eugene F. and Roy L. Crum. 1977. "On the Use of the CAPM in Public Utility Rate Cases." *Financial Management* 6: 7–15.

———. 1978. "Use of the CAPM in Public Utility Rate Cases — Reply." *Financial Management* 7: 72–76.

Brown, Philip, Allan Kleidon and Terry Marsh. 1983. "New Evidence on the Nature of Size-Related Anomalies in Stock Prices." *Journal of Financial Economics* 12: 33–56.

Brown, Stewart L. 1979. "Autocorrelation, Market Imperfection and the CAPM." *Journal of Financial and Quantitative Analysis* 14: 1027–1034.

Bubnys, Edward L. 1990. "Simulating and Forecasting Utility Stock Returns: Arbitrage Pricing Theory vs. Capital Asset Pricing Model." *Financial Review* 25: 1–23.

Buschena, David and David Zilberman. 1995. "Performance of the Similarity Hypothesis Relative to the Existing Models of Risky Choice." *Journal of Risk and Uncertainty* 11: 233–262.

Casabona, Patrick A. and Ashok Vora. 1982. "The Bias of Conventional Risk Premiums in Empirical Tests of the Capital Asset Pricing Model." *Financial Management* 11: 90–96.

Casabona, Patrick A., Jack C. Francis and Ashok Vora. 1983. "Duration, Beta and CAPM: An Integration of Risk Measures for the Analysis of Security Returns." *Review of Business* 4: 14–20.

Cecchetti, Stephen G. and Nelson C. Mark. 1990. "Evaluating Empirical Tests of Asset Pricing Models: Alternative Interpretations." *American Economic Review* 80: 48–51.

Cheng, Pao L. and Robert R. Grauer. 1980. "An Alternative Test of the Capital Asset Pricing Model." *American Economic Review* 70: 660–671.

Coase, R.H. 1992. "The Institutional Structure of Production." *American Economic Review* 82: 713–719.

Conine, Jr., Thomas E. and Maurry Tamarkin. 1985. "Implications of Skewness in Returns for Utilities' Cost of Equity Capital." *Financial Management* 14: 66–71.

Connor, Gregory and Robert A. Korajczyk. 1988. "Risk and Return in an Equilibrium APT: Application of a New Test Methodology." *Journal of Financial Research* 21: 255–289.

Corhay, Albert, Gabriel Hawawini and Pierre Michel. 1987. "Seasonality in the Risk-Return Relationship: Some International Evidence." *Journal of Finance* 42: 49–68.

Cox, Larry A. and E. Ann Rudd. 1991. "Book Versus Market Underwriting Betas." *Journal of Risk and Insurance* 58: 312–321.

Easterbrook, Frank H. 1984. "Two Agency-Cost Explanations of Dividends." *American Economic Review* 74: 650–659.

Elton, Edwin J. and Martin J. Gruber. 1984. "Non-Standard CAPMs and the Market Portfolio." *Journal of Finance* 39: 911–924.

Elton, Edwin, Martin Gruber and Joel Rentzler. 1983. "A Simple Examination of the Empirical Relationship Between Dividend Yields and Deviations from the CAPM." *Journal of Banking and Finance* 7: 135–146.

Fama, Eugene F. 1965. "The Behavior of Stock Market Prices." *Journal of Business* 38: 34–105.

———. 1970. "Efficient Capital Markets: A Review of Theory and Empirical Work." *Journal of Finance* 25: 383–417.

———. 1998. "Market Efficiency, Long-Term Returns, and Behavioral Finance." *Journal of Financial Economics* 49: 283–306.

Fama, Eugene F. and Kenneth R. French. 1992. "The Cross-Section of Expected Stock Returns." *Journal of Finance* 47: 427–465.

Fama, Eugene F. and James D. McBeth. 1973. "Risk Return and Equilibrium." *Journal of Political Economy* 71: 607–636.

Frankel, Jeffrey A. 1985. "Portfolio Shares as 'Beta Breakers'." *Journal of Portfolio Management* 11: 18–23.

Frankfurter, George M. and Elton G. McGoun. 1996. "But It Looked So Good on My Vita." *Journal of Financial Education* 22: 14–25.

———. 1999. "Ideology and the Theory of Financial Economics." *Journal of Economic Behavior and Organization* 39: 159–177.

———. 2000. "Thought Contagion and Financial Economics: The Dividend Puzzle as a Case Study." *Journal of Psychology and Financial Markets* 1: 145–153.

Frankfurter, George M. and Herbert E. Phillips. 1994. *Forty Years of Normative Portfolio Theory.* Greenwich: JAI Press.

Friedman, Milton M. 1953. "The Methodology of Positive Economics." In *Essays in Positive Economics*, edited by M.M. Friedman. Chicago: The University of Chicago Press.

———. 1954. "What Is All Utility?" *Economic Journal* 65: 405–409.

———. 1962. *Capitalism and Freedom.* Chicago: The University of Chicago Press.

Friend, Irwin and Randolph Westerfield. 1981. "Risk and Capital Asset Prices." *Journal of Banking and Finance* 5: 291–315.

Friend, Irwin, Randolph Westerfield and Michael Granito. 1978. "New Evidence on the Capital Asset Pricing Model." *Journal of Finance* 33: 903–917.

Goldberg, Michael A. and Ashok Vora. 1978. "Bivariate Spectral Analysis of the Capital Asset Pricing Model." *Journal of Financial and Quantitative Analysis* 13: 435–459.

———. 1981. "The Inconsistency of the Relationship Between Security and Market Returns." *Journal of Economics and Business* 33: 97–107.

Gombola, Michael J. and Douglas R. Kahl. 1990. "Time-Series Processes of Utility Betas: Implications for Forecasting Systematic Risk." *Financial Management* 19: 84–93.

Grauer, Robert R. 1978. "Generalized Two Parameter Asset Pricing Models." *Journal of Financial Economics* 6: 811–832.

Haddad, Mahmoud M. and Omar M. Benkato. 1989. "Intertemporal Testing of Beta Stationarity." *Akron Business and Economic Review* 4: 23–32.

Harlow, W. Van and Ramesh K.S. Rao. 1989. "Asset Pricing in a Generalized Mean-Lower Partial Moment Framework: Theory and Evidence." *Journal of Financial and Quantitative Analysis* 24: 285–311.

Harrington, Scott E. 1983. "The Relationship Between Risk and Return: Evidence for Life Insurance Stocks." *Journal of Risk and Insurance* 50: 587–610.

Harvey, Campbell R. 1989. "Time-Varying Conditional Covariances in Tests of Asset Pricing Models." *Journal of Financial Economics* 24: 289–317.

Harvey, Campbell R. and Guofu Zhou. 1990. "Bayesian Inference in Asset Pricing Tests." *Journal of Financial Economics* 26: 221–254.

Homaifar, Ghassem and Duane B. Graddy. 1990. "Variance and Lower Partial Moment Betas as Alternative Risk Measures in Cost of Capital Estimation: A Defense of the CAPM Beta." *Journal of Business Finance and Accounting* 15: 677–688.

Jensen, Michael C. 1978. "Some Anomalous Evidence Regarding Market Efficiency." *Journal of Financial Economics* 6: 95–101.

Johnson, James M. and Howard P. Lanser. 1981. "Dividend Risk Measurement and Tests of CAPM." *Journal of Portfolio Management* 7: 50–54.

Jorion, Philippe. 1991. "Bayesian and CAPM Estimators of the Means: Implications for Portfolio Selection." *Journal of Banking and Finance* 15: 717–727.

Kahneman, Daniel and Amos Tversky. 1979. "Prospect Theory: An Analysis of Decisions Under Risk." *Econometrica* 47: 263–291.

Keim, Donald B. 1983. "Size-Related Anomalies and Stock Return Seasonality." *Journal of Financial Economics* 12: 13–32.

————. 1986. "The CAPM and Equity Return Regularities." *Financial Analysts Journal* 42: 19–34.

Klamer, Arjo. 1992. *Conversations with Economists: New Classical Economists and Opponents Speak Out on the Current Controversy in Microeconomics.* Totowa, NJ: Rowman & Allanheld.

Klemkosky, Robert C. and Kwang W. Jun. 1982. "The Monetary Impact on Return Variability and Market Risk Premia." *Journal of Financial and Quantitative Analysis* 17: 663–681.

Kroll, Yoram, Haim Levy and Amnon Rapoport. 1988. "Experimental Test of the Separation Theorem and the Capital Asset Pricing Model." *American Economic Review* 78: 500–519.

Kuhn, Thomas S. 1970. *The Structure of Scientific Revolutions.* Chicago: The University of Chicago Press.

Lakonishok, Josef and Alan C. Shapiro. 1986. "Systematic Risk, Total Risk and Size as Determinants of Stock Market Returns." *Journal of Banking and Finance* 10: 115–132.

Lee, Cheng F. 1976a. "Investment Horizon and the Functional Form of the Capital-Asset Pricing Model." *Review of Economics and Statistics* 58: 356–363.

———. 1976b. "On the Relationship Between the Systematic Risk and the Investment Horizon." *Journal of Financial and Quantitative Analysis* 11: 803–815.

———. 1977. "Performance Measure, Systematic Risk, and Errors in Variables Estimation Method." *Journal of Economics and Business* 29: 122–127.

———. 1984. "Random Coefficient and Errors-In-Variables Models for Beta Estimates: Methods and Applications." *Journal of Business Research* 12: 505–516.

Lee, Cheng F. and Carl R. Chen. 1982. "Beta Stability and Tendency: An Application of Variable Mean Response Regression Model." *Journal of Economics and Business* 34: 201–206.

Lee, Cheng F. and William P. Lloyd. 1976. "The Capital Asset Pricing Model Expressed as a Recursive System — An Empirical Investigation." *Journal of Financial and Quantitative Analysis* 11: 237–249.

———. 1978. "Block Recursive Systems in Asset Pricing Models: An Extension." *Journal of Finance* 33: 640–644.

Lee, Cheng F. and Chunchi Wu. 1985. "The Impact of Kurtosis on Risk Stationarity: Some Empirical Evidence." *Financial Review* 20: 263–269.

Lee, Cheng F., Chunchi Wu and K.C. John Wei. 1990. "The Heterogeneous Investment Horizon and the Capital Asset Pricing Model: Theory and Implications." *Journal of Financial and Quantitative Analysis* 25: 361–376.

Leland, Johnatan W. 1994. "Generalized Similarity Judgements: An Alternative Explanation of Choice Anomalies." *Journal of Risk and Uncertainty* 9: 151–172.

Levhari, David and Haim Levy. 1977. "The Capital Asset Pricing Model and the Investment Horizon." *Review of Economics and Statistics* 59: 92–104.

Levy, Haim. 1980a. "The Capital Asset Pricing Model, Inflation, and the Investment Horizon: The Israeli Experience." *Journal of Financial and Quantitative Analysis* 15: 561–593.

———. 1980b. "The CAPM and Beta in an Imperfect Market." *Journal of Portfolio Management* 6: 5–11.

———. 1981. "The CAPM and the Investment Horizon." *Journal of Portfolio Management* 7: 32–40.

———. 1982. "A Test of the CAPM via a Confidence Level Approach." *Journal of Portfolio Management* 9: 56–61.

———. 1984. "Another Look at the Capital Asset Pricing Model." *Quarterly Review of Economics and Business* 24: 5–32.

Litzenberger, Robert, Krishna Ramaswamy and Howard Sosin. 1980. "On the CAPM Approach to the Estimation of a Public Utility's Cost of Equity Capital." *Journal of Finance* 35: 369–383.

Long, Jr., John B. 1978. "The Market Valuation of Cash Dividends." *Journal of Financial Economics* 6: 235–264.

Lynch, Aaron. 1996. *Thought Contagion: How Beliefs Spread Through Society.* New York: Basic Books.

Machlup, Fritz. 1963. "Introductory Remarks." *American Economic Review* 33: 204.

Mackie, Christopher D. 1998. *Canonizing Economic Theory: How Theories and Ideas Are Selected in Economics,* Paperback ed. Armonk, NY: ME Sharpe.

MacKinlay, A. Craig. 1987. "On Multivariate Tests of the CAPM." *Journal of Financial Economics* 18: 341–371.

Mankiw, N. Gregory and Matthew D. Shapiro. 1986. "Risk and Return: Consumption Beta Versus Market Beta." *Review of Economics and Statistics* 68: 452–459.

Mannheim, Karl. 1949. *Ideology and Utopia: An Introduction to the Sociology of Knowledge.* New York: Harcourt, Brace and Company.

Markowitz, Harry M. 1952. "Portfolio Selection." *Journal of Finance* 7: 77–91.

McEnally, Richard W. 1978. "On the Use of the CAPM in Public Utility Rate Cases: Comment." *Financial Management* 7: 69–70.

McEnally, Richard W. and David E. Upton. 1979. "A Reexamination of the Ex Post Risk-Return Tradeoff on Common Stocks." *Journal of Financial and Quantitative Analysis* 14: 395–419.

McGoun, Elton G. and Tatjana Scubik. 2000. "Beyond Behavioral Finance." *Journal of Psychology and Financial Markets* 1: 135–144.

Modigliani, Franco and Merton H. Miller. 1958. "The Cost of Capital, Corporation Finance, and the Theory of Investment." *American Economic Review* 48: 261–297.

Mullins, Jr., David W. 1982. "Does the Capital Asset Pricing Model Work?" *Harvard Business Review* 60: 105–114.

Murphy, J. Austin. 1990. "Using Bayesian Betas to Estimate Risk-Return Parameters: An Empirical Investigation." *Journal of Business Finance and Accounting* 17: 471–477.

Muth, John F. 1981. "Rational Expectations and the Theory of Price Movements." In *Rational Expectations and Economic Practice,* edited by R.E. Lucas and T.J. Sargent. Minneapolis: The University of Minnesota Press.

Nagorniak, John. 1982. "Risk Adjusted Equity Performance Measurement." *Journal of Finance* 37: 555–561.

Ng, Lilian. 1991. "Tests of the CAPM with Time-Varying Covariances: A Multivariate GARCH Approach." *Journal of Finance* 46: 1507–1521.

Percival, John. 1974. "Corporate Bonds in a Market Model Context." *Journal of Business Research* 2: 461–468.

Peseau, Dennis E. and Thomas M. Zepp. 1978. "On the Use of the CAPM in Public Utility Rate Cases: Comment." *Financial Management* 7: 52–56.

Pettway, Richard H. and Bradford D. Jordan. 1987. "APT vs. CAPM Estimates of the Return-Generating Function Parameters for Regulated Public Utilities." *Journal of Financial Research* 10: 227–238.

Reinganum, Marc R. 1981a. "Misspecification of Capital Asset Pricing: Empirical Anomalies Based on Earnings Yields and Market Values." *Journal of Financial Economics* 9: 19–46.

———. 1981b. "A New Empirical Perspective on the CAPM." *Journal of Financial and Quantitative Analysis* 16: 439–462.

Reiter, Sara Ann and Paul F. Williams. 2001. "Scientific Conversations in Financial Economics." In *From Individualism to Individual: Ideology and Inquiry in Financial Economics*, edited by G.M. Frankfurter and E.G. McGoun. Hampshire, UK: Ashgate Publishing Limited.

Roll, Richard W. and Stephen A. Ross. 1983. "Regulation, the Capital Asset Pricing Model, and the Arbitrage Pricing Theory." *Public Utilities Fortnightly* 111: 22–28.

Ross, Stephen. 1976. "The Arbitrage Theory of Capital Asset Pricing." *Journal of Financial Economics* 4: 129–176.

Roy, A.D. 1952. "Safety-First and the Holding of Assets." *Econometrica* 20: 431–449.

Rubinstein, Ariel. 1988. "Similarity and Decision-making Under Risk." *Journal of Economic Theory* 46: 145–153.

Sauer, Andreas and Austin Murphy. 1992. "An Empirical Comparison of Alternative Models of Capital Asset Pricing in Germany." *Journal of Banking and Finance* 16: 183–196.

Schmalensee, Richard. 1981. "Risk and Return on Long-Lived Tangible Assets." *Journal of Financial Economics* 9: 185–205.

Schumpeter, Joseph. 1949. "Science and Ideology." *American Economic Review* 39: 345–359.

Schwert, G. William and Paul J. Seguin. 1990. "Heteroskedasticity in Stock Returns." *Journal of Finance* 45: 1129–1155.

Scott, Elton and Stewart Brown. 1980. "Biased Estimators and Unstable Betas." *Journal of Finance* 35: 49–55.

Shanken, Jay. 1987. "Multivariate Proxies and Asset Pricing Relations: Living with the Roll Critique." *Journal of Financial Economics* 18: 91–110.

Sharpe, William F. 1963. "A Simplified Model of Portfolio Analysis." *Management Science* 9: 277–293.

———. 1964. "Capital Market Prices: A Theory of Market Equilibrium Under Conditions of Risk." *Journal of Finance* 14: 425–442.

———. 1978. "On the Use of the CAPM in Public Utility Rate Cases: Comment." *Financial Management* 7: 71.

———. 1982. "Factors in New York Stock Exchange Security Returns, 1931–1979." *Journal of Portfolio Management* 8: 5–19.

Shukla, Raviv and Charles Trzcinka. 1991. "Research on Risk and Return: Can Measures of Risk Explain Anything?" *Journal of Portfolio Management* 17: 15–21.

Smith, Adam. 1776. *An Inquiry into the Nature and Causes of the Wealth of Nations.* London and New York: George Routhledge and Sons.

Soley, Lawrence C. 1995. *Leasing The Ivory Tower.* Boston, MA: South End Press.

Stambaugh, Robert F. 1982. "On the Exclusion of Assets from Tests of the Two-Parameter Model: A Sensitivity Analysis." *Journal of Financial Economics* 10: 237–268.

———. 1983. "Testing the CAPM with Broader Market Indexes: A Problem of Mean-Deficiency." *Journal of Banking and Finance* 7: 5–16.

Stoll, Hans R., Robert E. Whaley and Paul Schultz. 1983. "Transaction Costs and the Small Firm Effect: A Comment." *Journal of Financial Economics* 12: 57–88.

Stulz, Rene M. 1999. "What's Wrong with Modern Capital Budgeting." *Financial Practice and Education* 9: 7–11.

Swidler, Steve. 1988. "An Empirical Investigation of Heterogeneous Expectations, Analysts' Earnings Forecasts, and the Capital Asset Pricing." *Journal of Business and Economics* 27: 20–41.

Turnbull, Stuart M., Ralph A. Winter, R.J. Sweeney, Pao L. Cheng and Robert R. Grauer. 1982. "An Alternative Test of the Capital Asset Pricing Model: Comments and Reply." *American Economic Review* 72: 1194–1207.

Udinsky, Jerald H. and Daniel Kirshner. 1979. "A Comparison of Relative Predictive Power for Financial Models of Rates of Return." *Journal of Financial and Quantitative Analysis* 14: 293–315.

Vandell, Robert F. and James K. Malernee. 1978. "The Capital Asset Pricing Model and Utility Equity Returns." *Public Utilities Fortnightly* 102: 22–29.

Von Neumann, John and Oskar Morgenstern. 1967. *Theory of Games and Economic Behavior*, 3rd ed. Princeton, NJ: Princeton University Press.

Watts, Ross L. 1978. "Systematic 'Abnormal' Returns after Quarterly Earnings Announcements." *Journal of Financial Economics* 6: 127–150.

Yawitz, Jess B. and William J. Marshall. 1977. "Risk and Return in the Government Bond Market." *Journal of Portfolio Management* 3: 48–52.

Zhou, Guofu. 1991. "Small Sample Tests of Portfolio Efficiency." *Journal of Financial Economics* 30: 165–191.

Chapter 2

What is All Efficiency?

1 Twas brillig, and the slithy toves
2 Did gyre and gimble in the wabe;
3 All mimsy were the borogoves,
4 And the mome raths outgrabe.

— Lewis Carroll *Jabberwocky* from
Through the Looking-Glass and What Alice Found There

A. Imagery

"Have some wine" the March Hare said in an encouraging tone. Alice
looked all round the table, but there was nothing on it but tea. "I don't
see any wine," she remarked. "There isn't any," said the March Hare.

— Lewis Carroll *Alice's Adventure in Wonderland*

A while ago, I was reading a book of fiction[29] about one of the Cambridge
spies, a commie intellectual-aristocrat who, during the Cold War, spied for
the Soviet Union. This chap, who was an operative of MI5, lived under the
cover of art historian. In that capacity he was obsessed with a distinguished French painter: Nicolas Poussin (1594–1665).[30] The protagonist
owned one of Poussin's pictures (yes, pictures, not paintings), *The Death
of Seneca*, that at the end of the story, in a symbolic twist of irony, turns
out to be a fake as his whole life has been a fake, deceit and casuistry.

Fascinated by the story and the description of Poussin's work, I was looking in my Grolier Encyclopedia for works of the master. That is how I stumbled onto Poussin's *The Adoration of the Golden Calf*. It seems that Poussin
was not only a remarkable artist who created a school around himself, but
also a philosopher (a stoic at that) and a mathematician. Poussin believed

---

[29] Banville, John. 1997. *The Untouchable*. New York: Alfred A. Knopf.
[30] See http://www.wga.hu/frames-e.html?/bio/p/poussin/biograph.html

in reason as the key to beauty, and the existence in basic laws in nature. The painting I mention is the artist's rendition of the story from the *Pentateuch*'s first book, *Exodus*, Chapter 32.

According to the Bible, the Jews demand from Aaron, Moses' brother, to make a visible and touchable god, because the man Moses, who took them out of Egypt, fails to come down from Mount Sinai. There, as we know from Chuck Heston (way before he became the president of the accidental death industry), Moses was busy receiving the Ten Commandments.

Aaron collects all the gold earrings from the women, makes a mold in the shape of a calf (an Egyptian god of agricultural abundance), smelts the gold and casts it to create a statue. On completion of his work, the people of Israel declare the calf as the god that delivered them from slavery. Aaron also builds an altar and calls the following day a day of sacrifices and festivities.

What we see in Poussin's picture is this day of festivities. Situated in a typical Italian landscape with trees and grass in front of a huge golden statue on an even bigger pedestal, and with Aaron in the middle of the festivities (whose Semite features are summed up in a white beard), lily-white people of all ages dressed in Roman garb adore the calf.

Poussin, although French by birth and at one time the title holder of "First Painter" in the court of Louis XIII, spent most of his life in Rome. For him, the biblical times were of ancient Rome and its people. This was the reality of his set of expectations, never mind the fact that the Sinai desert is as arid as they come, and Semites, fresh out of Egyptian slavery, were neither white, nor were they dressed as Romans. Nor could they possibly have possessed the quantity of gold, earrings or otherwise, that must have been needed to smelt the statue we see in the picture. The point I am trying to make is that the way we see things is an amalgam of one's beliefs and the world that creates these beliefs: reality is a matter of ideology.

B. What is Market Efficiency?

The fact that a believer is happier than a skeptic is no more to the point than the fact that a drunken man is happier than a sober one. The happiness of credulity is a cheap and dangerous quality.

— George Bernard Shaw *Androcles and the Lion*

Market efficiency as a concept is the creation of a financial economist from the University of Chicago: Eugene Fama (1965, 1970). The designation "financial economist" is the catch-all name for academics that teach finance in business schools and do research relating to financial problems. It gives these people the status of economists who are faculty, usually, in schools of Arts and Sciences and look down on their colleagues in B-schools as intellectually inferior. Financial economics is also called, interchangeably, modern finance.

Fama coined the phrase "market efficiency" to characterize financial markets and enshrine the concept as a quasi-religion with the demigod being the efficient markets hypotheses (EMH). According to Fama's dictum, efficient capital markets are those where prices of assets reflect all available information at a given moment of time, independent of their prior history, and they are good approximations of "intrinsic values." This he deduced at the cost of a whole set of unrealistic axioms and assumptions regarding investment behavior, the existence of an imaginary being, called the *Homo Oeconomicus*, and the economics theory's flight of fancy of "equilibrium."

For the sake of covering all bases, I must mention that later the case was made for two other dimensions of efficiency: allocational (whether capital goes where it does the most good) and liquidity (whether it quickly brings together buyers and sellers). I have no intention of discussing these other dimensions here, because for the purpose at hand they are only tangential.

If one accepts the premise that nothing that humans do is value-neutral, but rather based on ideology, be it creed, religion, politics or self-promotion, then one must consider financial economics' claim to value-neutrality as a farce at best and disingenuous at worst. Thus, modern finance[31] just might be a ruse with which academic research (what can be thought of the ontology and epistemology of the field) masquerades as an imitation of the natural sciences.

Those who doubt my contention here that financial economics is ideology-laden are advised to read Frankfurter and McGoun (1999). If after doing so the reader is still convinced that financial economics is "pure science," although there is no such thing even in the natural sciences,[32] then this

---

[31] I am using the term modern finance interchangeably with the term financial economics, as many of the practitioners of the latter argue that the two are one and the same.

[32] In the words of Pope John Paul II, "Faith is the guiding light of science."

paper is to serve as an additional argument to the contrary. I will maintain, in the hope to convince the convincible skeptics, that the financial world which financial economics tries to understand, explain, forecast and fashion is infused with politics to the point where the boundaries between economics and politics are totally muddled. Thus, finance as a discipline that is ideologically driven cannot possibly understand, explain, forecast and fashion this world. This is the first paradox of financial economics.

Consequently, financial economics has been busy developing models and explanations for over 40 years now — the more complex, the merrier — that fit compactly within the confines of equations and statistics, instead of dealing with economic realities that are suffused with politics. This logic is to make sure that the movers and thinkers of academe will debate forever whether one paradigm or another can be supported by empirical evidence without the possibility of ever reaching a definite conclusion.

It also makes it sure that finance academics are not engaged in the process of discovery, the ultimate goal of science, because such process might bring an end to the ideology that rules the field. I call the search for the truth "discovery," because this way I am avoiding the pitfalls of trying to define what truth is, or whether there is such a thing as truth at all. Searching for the truth, on the other hand, is like searching for the holy grail — we do not have to know even what it is, much less where to find it.

There is also a hidden tale in the selection of the noun "efficiency" to describe the operation of the markets. In brief, it comes from the work of the 1990 Nobel Laureate in economics, Harry Markowitz (1952), who invented a mathematical and statistical method for selecting a stock portfolio. In that framework, all possible portfolio choices that should be selected by a risk-averse person, endowed with a quadratic utility of wealth function, are being said to be on the frontier of efficiency (also called second order stochastic dominance). Suffice it to say, however, that we despise inefficiency; thus, the opposite of inefficiency must be something we value. Accordingly, there is a positive implied meaning to the term, whether or not we know its mechanics.

In the context of Fama's work, efficiency means that the market does best and, thus, one cannot do better than invest in the market as a whole. A situation like this is what economists call Pareto optimality. The sublime meaning of market efficiency is that markets for capital assets are Pareto optimal.

This notion, lately, found for itself several new euphemisms for the benefit of the common man, the most popular of which are "free markets,"[33] "globalization," "new/space age," "the new world order," etc. Tinkering with markets, such as government regulations, means imposing inefficiencies — the bane of society.

Thus, market efficiency is a moral view of the world and everyone should subscribe to this view. I would like to emphasize the adjective moral, because there is a social policy hiding behind this theory of market efficiency. First, the notion that it is best for society to leave the market alone (do not regulate). And second, that everything which is done for the best interest of the shareholders of corporations is in the best interest of society as a whole as well.

Of course, those who are not shareholders (roughly 50% of the population in the US and a much higher percentage in Europe, or elsewhere) may take issue with this worldview, but in the big scheme of things they do not count (they do not vote, either).

Later, and it is not clear to me how and by whom, although I made an honest effort to discover it, three subcategories of *informational efficiency* were suggested:

- Weak;
- Semi-strong;
- Strong.

The weak form means that one cannot obtain information that would put one in advantage from tracking the history of price movements. If this form of efficiency were true, it would be tantamount to sending financial analysts, called chartists, to the unemployment line, because they sell, and for a good price too, worthless advice to the public. Right here there is the second paradox of financial economics' market efficiency, because if markets were weak form efficient, there would not be chartists and other gurus who can tell their clients what to do by looking at historical data. Yet, there is an untold number of statistical studies that show unequivocally the existence of weak form efficiency by studying large volumes of data. These studies show that price relatives behave as Brownian motion.

---

[33] According to John Kenneth Galbraith, "free markets" is just a kinder gentler term, because Karl Marx gave a bad name to capitalism.

The semi-strong form implies that prices, at any point of time, reflect all *publicly* available information (such as accounting data, publications in journals, analysts' forecasts, company announcements, Internet, etc.). I have seen mixed results of tests trying to prove the existence of the semi-strong form. Most instances, it depends on how the data are sliced, what time period they pertain to and what were the intentions of the researcher(s).

Finally, the strong form means that prices reflect *all* information, both published and unpublished, at any given point of time. I have not seen a single statistical test that could prove, convincingly, the existence of the strong form of market efficiency. To the best of my academic experience, only the ultra-orthodox believe in the existence of the strong form of efficiency, and those by definition do not need any proof.

What these three forms of "efficiency" gave to academia was an aperture to shuffle, mine, dredge, sift through, spin and torture data (until they confess) to prove or disprove, statistically, the existence of these forms. Thousands of pages for over three decades have been written, inconclusive at best, a matter of religion at worst, mostly showing no more than meticulous mediocrity.

The brief summary of this work is this, however: the weak form, given the data, cannot be disputed; the semi-strong form, sometimes yes, sometimes no; the strong form could never be proven. But there is a problem with empirical research using price data. Unlike in a laboratory experiment, where everything is carefully and painfully controlled, new data, and how they are sliced, may bring new results. Thus, nothing can ever be proven conclusively, especially a theory that is built on a plethora of unrealistic assumptions.

The EMH also sat well with several versions of the capital asset pricing model (CAPM) of Sharpe (1964), and its main derivative: beta. In fact, Fama (1998) declared the two to be inseparable. Chicago, although not its original inventor, embraced both the theory and the CAPM with religious fervor, and its faculty and acolytes became the "Knights Templar" of market efficiency. The school also developed a price database, called CRSP (Center for Research in Security Prices), that it mass markets to other academics and private enterprises in a rare showing of the applicability of Say's Law: supply generates its own demand.[34]

---

[34] Not quite! The demand for this database was created by the tenure and promotion process, because without these data, newly minted faculty had no chance in a prayer to publish.

Because of Chicago's influence on academic research, and its tight control of the publication process in finance (publish or perish!), for a while it almost wiped out any attempt to raise doubts about market efficiency. This went on until such time when overwhelming evidence started to surface to show the existence of "effects," also referred to as of late as "anomalies," that neither the theory of efficiency nor the CAPM could explain: in short, massive loss of predictive power, the ultimate nemesis of an otherwise appealing theory, and the litmus test, according to Friedmanian positivism/instrumentalism the usefulness of a model/theory.

C. And Then Came Behavioral Finance

The true science and study of man is man. *La vraye science at le vray étude de L'homme, c'est l'homme.*

— Pierre Charron De la Sagasse

At the beginning there were only the first sparrows indicating that markets were not as efficient as one must have thought reading the articles coming out from the schools where the orthodoxy had a stronghold, which was practically everywhere. There was the crash of 1987 which the Brady Commission (also referred to as the Brady Bunch, after the popular television program) investigating the causes of the crash found to be program trading with computers. Now, that was a silly if not deceitful explanation, because if nothing else a computer is supposed to make markets more efficient by instantaneously disseminating information. Yet, Felix Rohatyn, a major financial mover and shaker, was not ashamed to remark that the scourge of Wall Street was an MBA with a laptop.

Behavioral finance gained respectability with DeBondt and Thaler (1985, 1987) who based their overreaction hypothesis on the seminal works of Tversky and Kahneman (1974, 1979) of Prospect Theory (PT). PT was not just the basis for another paradigm, but it was an alternative to the Expected Utility Maxim (EUM) that ruled academic finance (and still does), in spite of the fact that the latter was largely discredited in economics as well as decision sciences as a faulty theory.

Since DeBondt and Thaler, there were scores of papers showing over- and underreaction, and statistically significant price behavior that were inconsistent with the EMH. There has also been a new decision-making dictum on the rise which basically and simply involves investing in anything that would be at variance with the EMH's market portfolio. These chaps call themselves contrarians (see Dreman, 1979, 1998).

Yet Fama (1998) refers to the total of the behavioral finance work of a quarter of a century as the "anomalies literature." This clever name-calling puts behavioral finance at a level below the EMH, because it is nothing more than observing some anomalies, quite inconsistently, which perhaps are noteworthy for future examination, but by no means are a replacement theory for the EMH.

Quite the contrary, Fama argues, with a logic that nonplussed me up to date and will baffle me for the future to come, that the fact that anomalies are found some time, but there are no unequivocal over- or under-reactions, is proof that the EMH hold. This is so because this is the kind of randomness the EMH posit to exist.

Then, is it not true that, if there are no consistent and unequivocal proofs that there are no over- and underreaction, then there is no unequivocal proof that the markets are efficient as well? Just because the EMH got there first does not make them true.

D. And Then Came Enron (and Post-Enron)

When he had explained these procedures, which had become common practice of American business, to his father, the great capo mafioso, Don Corrado Prizzi, the old man marveled with admiration. "You have *really* organized crime, my son," he said with awe. "Every year you skim off another two or three billion and the way you got it all figured out, nobody can call a cop."

"It is just the modern way, Poppa," Price had said. "There is no one to bother you. The Congress looks the other way, because there is also a big buck in it for them, and the Securities and Exchange Commission doesn't make any waves. There are private plaintiff suits, sure, but they are get settled using the stockholders' money — and we come away from every deal richer and cleaner."

"But you gotta tie up a lotta cash for that."

"No, Poppa. We borrow from the banks."

"But that's a lotta interest you gotta pay on loans like that."

"So sell off some of the companies and fire a few thousand people to pay the interest. The rest is not only clear to us, but we get it all free."

"Jesus," his father said, "and we used to have to use guns."

— *The Final Addiction*, 1991, Richard Condon

Enron was the biggest corporate fiasco of all time until some others followed, when the lies had to stop and everything came to the surface. Tens of thousands of investors lost all their holdings, not to mention employees whose ESOPs, which was their retirement portfolio largely in Enron stock, went up in smoke.

Vice President Dick Cheney, then CEO of Halliburton, remarked that Enron should be emulated by all as the model of the new age corporation.[35] Many did emulate Enron, whereby institutionalizing corporate larceny. This included Mr. Cheney's own firm, Halliburton, which reported $100 million in non-existent revenues and has been accused of bribing foreign officials under his CEO-ship.

But Mr. Cheney was not alone. Senators and Congressmen from both sides of the aisle fed on the campaign contribution trough of Enron. Dozens of financial analysts and investment gurus sang the praise of Enron. Yet, the chief executives of Enron were still cashing in on their stock holdings while the US was traumatized by 9/11, and Enron's demise was written on the metaphorical wall.

The only ones that did not know all this were the ever efficient markets. I take the liberty to personify here, just as all the academics who talk about the "behavior of the market" have been doing for decades.

On June 14, 2002, a Houston jury, after lengthy deliberation in the obstruction of justice case against Andersen LLP, returned a verdict of guilty in federal court. Although Andersen faced no more than five years' probation and a $500,000 fine, the verdict, for all practical purposes, was the kiss of death for the once-giant CPA firm.

But it is evident now that the Enron saga was just the tip of the iceberg that threatened to sink that Titanic myth called "free markets." From view-media reporting, we have learned of rampant improprieties among the ranks of the Fortune 500. The list includes, among others:

- Adelphia
- GE
- Global Crossing
- Halliburton
- HealthSouth

---

[35] Mr. Cheney also did commercials for Arthur Andersen, LLP, Enron's CPA firm that had a blind eye to Enron's off-book borrowings. Andersen LLP was found guilty of obstruction of justice in federal court.

- Microsoft
- Tyco International
- WorldCom
- Xerox

The ticking bomb at WorldCom exploded on June 26, 2002, when the telecommunications giant acknowledged classifying $3.8 billion in expenses as capital investment. The firm's CFO, Scott Sullivan, was blamed for this "strain" of creative accounting. The company's CPA firm (you guessed it), Andersen LLP, disavowed any and all responsibility, declaring with a straight face that the accounting decision that grossly inflated the firm's earnings — and thereby misled everyone about the true financial condition of WorldCom — was made solely by the CFO.

After the public revelations, the share price of WorldCom dropped 73% in a single day. Experts were all over the media asserting that bankruptcy seemed the only option for WorldCom.[36] In the wake of the $11 billion swindle, it took nearly two years (until March 3, 2004) to indict Bernard Ebbers,[37] the firm's CEO, on charges of conspiracy, fraud and other offenses. Ebbers, through his lawyer, pleaded not guilty to all charges. Because it is a zero-sum game, many investors suffered instantaneous losses cumulatively totaling $180 billion, more than the GDP of over a hundred countries.

Just three days after the WorldCom admission of creative accounting, the *New York Times* on June 29, 2002, reported that Xerox, as part of a settlement with the SEC, had to reclassify more than $6.4 billion in revenues, affecting losses in 1997, 1998 and 1999, and profits in 2000 and 2001.

The knee-jerk reaction of the market was an immediate drop of $1.90 in Xerox's share price, but the share recovered later that day when word got out that the restatement was not the result of ". . . phantom sales or earnings that might lead to fresh accusations of accounting irregularities or additional SEC action." Nevertheless, Xerox ended the day with a 12.9% drop in share price (to "demonstrate" how informationally efficient the market is).

The complicity of accounting firms in corporate scandals is but half the problem. In the case of Enron at least, political machination is the other

---

[36] On July 21, 2002, WorldCom filed for Chapter 11, the largest corporate failure in American history.

[37] Bernard Ebbers was convicted of fraud and conspiracy on March 15, 2005 and is currently serving a 25-year sentence in a federal prison in Louisiana.

half. Key political figures from both sides of the aisle had their fingerprints all over Enron. Those who waxed most wroth over Enron's felonious behavior, calling loudly and often for criminal investigations in every direction, up to and including the White House, were in fact the very same who in the past did everything they could to allay SEC investigations into the company's off-books dealings. The gallery of rogues is a crowded one, and their list of names has been discussed *ad infinitum.*

There were other strains of enronomics,[38] too. On top of corporate crime of the Enron kind came the Merrill Lynch case, perhaps the biggest sham in the meltdown of morality.[39] In late May 2002, newspapers across the country reported that New York Attorney General Eliot Spitzer had reached a settlement with Merrill Lynch after a year-long investigation of the firm. Under the terms of the settlement, Merrill Lynch agreed to a "modest" fine of $100 million, promised to separate Merrill Lynch research from brokerage, and it expressed, rather disingenuously, its regret for past practices, all without admitting guilt of any wrongdoing.

Overnight, Spitzer became a dragon-slayer,[40] although the $100 million fine for a firm of Merrill Lynch's size was scarcely a slap on the wrist. Nor was it the first time the firm had engaged in behavior of this kind. On previous occasions, it had recommended "buy" for a stock, thus creating a run-up of the price, all the while planning to unload its holdings in that security before the stock tanked.

The difference this time was that Merrill's security analysts had exchanged e-mails ridiculing the stock even as they were recommending that clients buy it. If the firm had been charged with and convicted of giving false advice to investors — which would have allowed cheated investors to sue — court costs and damages might well have totaled $5 billion. The mere possibility of this happening weighed "heavily on Merrill's stock price, which has dropped nearly 20 percent."[41] A $5 billion cash strain could have meant closing time for the firm.

---

[38] There is, at least, one thing we have to be thankful to Enron for: enriching the English language.

[39] Don't we all have a soft spot for alliteration?

[40] Next to villains we love to hate and fear comes the dragon-slayer, the white knight we adore, who saves the public. The latest in this line of folk heroes is Rudolph Giuliani, whose tireless work in the wake of the 9/11 catastrophe earned him a knighthood (a real one), became a symbol of the American spirit, and got surcease for his being the most racially divisive mayor of New York City. Interestingly, at one time Merrill Lynch contemplated asking Giuliani to be a spokesperson of the firm in an attempt to burnish its stained reputation.

[41] Quoted in the *New York Times.*

Caveat emptor? I don't think so. Larceny is larceny is larceny, whether you are robbed at gunpoint or at the hands of white-collar criminals.[42]

Although the President promised jail sentences for CEOs caught signing off on false accounting statements, there aren't many CEOs trembling in their corporate towers. The Sarbanes-Oxley Act of 2002, meant to tighten up the accounting practices of outside auditors, has been eviscerated past the point of viability. What remains is a gutless shell held up by the administration as an accomplishment. Nothing will change until politics is removed, at least to some degree, from corporate America. The first steps in this direction would be stiff campaign finance reform and the abolition of the lobby system, but that baby has not even begun to crawl, much less toddle. Don't hold your breath!

The two points I am trying to make with these selected, and by no means all-inclusive, examples is that:

(1) Politics and economics are tightly wound together; and
(2) Once one realizes this fact, one must understand that markets cannot be efficient by the very nature of things. Thus, researching whether they are or are not is an exercise in futility. But, perhaps that was and still is the hidden objective of the powers that be.

E. Final Musings

Knowledge is in the end based on acknowledgment.

— Ludwig Wittgenstein *On Certainty*

Today, in spite of mounting evidence and *a priori* logic, most academics still hold on to the belief of market efficiency, or pretend that they do (publish or perish!). The accent is on the word belief, however, because that is where the state of the art is. There is also a much smaller, yet increasingly growing, camp of opposition which argues that markets cannot be efficient, no matter what statistical tests may or may not show, because people do not behave according to the axioms and assumptions of the theory. And, perhaps more importantly, people together may behave differently than each individual alone would.

---

[42] Not by chance, Eliot Spitzer, who ran a campaign for change and against corruption in New York State, was sworn in on January 1, 2007 as the 54th governor of the Empire State.

The market efficiency agnostics come from a wide berth of the social sciences: sociology, psychology, anthropology, experimental and behavioral economics, accounting and psychiatry. I met one scientist of animal behavior, too — scout's honor! Come to think of it, there is a lot of the herd mentality in a multitude of investors: the Johnnies come late, and lose early.

The iconoclast academics established their institute and publication outlet: *The Institute/Journal of Psychology and Financial Markets*, renamed not long ago to *The Journal of Behavioral Finance*. There is no downside risk with this direction of research, and perhaps we can learn something we never knew before. Perhaps we can learn some basics, such as how people really form their expectations, and how they measure, relate and convert to monetary quantities (if they do) the risks they are taking. Or, we may study the social costs of nefarious deeds of corporate apparatchiks.

I have seen works which maintain that all the shenanigans and lawlessness that characterize the beginning of the 21st century are no cause for alarm, because markets did not crash, and eventually recovered. These works never take into consideration the social and other costs born by people whose life was ruined so the upper managerial class could carry conspicuous consumption to never-imagined heights and receive bonuses of astronomical sums. Ergo, there is no need for new legislation, tighter controls on corporations, and the systematic weakening of the SEC was justified.

I guess everything can be proven by cleverly designed statistical tests that use irrelevant data. That was the purpose of my quote of Carroll's Jabberwocky. Here is how Humpty Dumpty translates the first stanza to Alice:

1 It was four o'clock in the afternoon and little badgers
2 Gyrated and made holes with gimlets in the grassy sun-dials;
3 All mimsy[43] were the shabby looking birds,
4 And the lost green pigs whistled in the woods.

Explaining market efficiency is a slightly easier task then, but it makes just as much sense.

So, where is the truth (if there is such a thing as the truth)? Think of Poussin and *The Adoration of the Golden Calf*. Morale: When in the Sinai desert, don't do as the Romans do, because that is not and cannot be the real thing.

---

[43] A portmanteau word of flimsy and miserable.

References

DeBondt, Werner and Richard Thaler. 1985. "Does the Stock Market Overreact?" *Journal of Finance* 40: 793–805.

———. 1987. "Further Evidence on Investors' Overreaction and Stock Market Efficiency." *Journal of Finance* 42: 557–581.

Dreman, David. 1979. *Contrarian Investment Strategy.* New York: Random House.

———. 1998. *Contrarian Investment Strategy: The Next Generation.* New York: Simon and Schuster.

Fama, Eugene F. 1965. "The Behavior of Stock Market Prices." *Journal of Business* 38: 34–105.

———. 1970. "Efficient Capital Markets: A Review of Theory and Empirical Work." *Journal of Finance* 25: 383–417.

———. 1998. "Market Efficiency, Long-Term Returns, and Behavioral Finance." *Journal of Financial Economics* 49: 283–306.

Frankfurter, George M. and Elton G. McGoun. 1999. "Ideology and the Theory of Financial Economics." *Journal of Economic Behavior and Organization* 39: 159–177.

Markowitz, Harry M. 1952. "Portfolio Selection." *Journal of Finance* 7: 77–91.

Sharpe, William F. 1964. "Capital Market Prices: A Theory of Market Equilibrium under Conditions of Risk." *Journal of Finance* 14: 425–442.

Tversky, Amos and Daniel Kahneman. 1974. "Judgment under Uncertainty: Heuristics and Biases." *Science* 185: 1124–1131.

———. 1979. "Prospect Theory: An Analysis of Decisions under Risk." *Econometrica* 47: 263–291.

Chapter 3

Still Autistic Finance[*]

A. Le Movement Autisme Économie

In June 2000, a group of French economics students published a petition on the web protesting the teaching of economics in institutions of higher learning because of:

- Economics' "uncontrolled use" and treatment of mathematics as "an end in itself," and the resulting "autistic science,"
- The repressive domination of neoclassical theory and derivative approaches in the curriculum, and
- The dogmatic teaching style, which leaves no place for critical and reflective thought.[44]

The students' manifesto demanded that the economics curriculum be changed with regard to:

- Engagement with empirical and concrete economic realities,
- Prioritizing science over scientism, and
- A pluralism of approaches adapted to the complexity of economic objects and to the uncertainty surrounding most of the big economics questions.

They also demanded that their professors ". . . initiate reforms to rescue economics from its autistic and socially irresponsible state."[45]

Before I continue, it would be productive perhaps to define the term *autistic*. According to the American Heritage Dictionary's CD-ROM version:

Autism — Abnormal introversion and egocentricity; acceptance of fantasy rather than reality.[46]

---

* An earlier version of this paper appeared in *Alternative Perspectives on Finance and Accounting Web Journal*, 2001, Volume 1, http://www.departments.bucknell.edu/management/apfa/
[44] From http://www.paecon.net
[45] *Ibid.*
[46] Excerpted from *American Heritage Talking Dictionary*. Copyright © 1997 The Learning Company, Inc. All Rights Reserved.

The etymology of the word is from ancient Greek, a portmanteau word of *auto* = self, and *ismos* = referring — hence, self-referring. The word was first coined as *autismus* (the Latinate form of the Greek compound word) in 1911 by Eugene Bleuler, the Swiss psychiatrist, to describe a mental condition later called schizophrenia. In 1943, the term was used by the American psychiatrist Leo Kanner to characterize infantile autism (also called Kanner syndrome), a condition in which a child retreats into himself and stops to communicate socially.

So, "autistic" is the adjective derived from autism, which must mean abnormal behavior, as in egocentrism, and acceptance of fantasy rather than reality. Hmmm. One would have to look long and hard to find an adjective that would better describe the state of economics in general, and financial economics in particular. In fact, autistic is the word that describes also one of the three requisites of Friedman's (1953) positivist methodology,[47] much of which became the foundation of modern finance.[48]

Although I was not surprised that the revolt in economics (a subject almost totally colonialized by American universities) came from French students, for whom starting revolutions is a 500-year tradition, I was flummoxed by the immediate reaction of French economics professors to the petition. As it turned out,

> Almost immediately, a group of French economics teachers responded with a petition of their own, supporting the students' demands, adding to their analysis, and lamenting the cult of scientism into which economics has in the main descended. The professors' petition also called for the opening of a public debate (http://www.paecon.net).

In sharp contrast to the French "revolution" are the classroom attitudes in America concerning the central question of what financial economics is. These attitudes can be discerned from a letter I received some time ago from a former student. The writer became flustered when he

---

[47] That the assumptions of a useful theory must be "wildly unrealistic."

[48] It never ceases to fascinate me how a term that was invented to signify an utterly individual medical condition (through transference) is a well-thought out signifier of an academic movement. It is even more captivating that this movement is aimed — if not to replace — then at least to be a contender of a paradigm that is an outgrowth of the political movement called radical individualism.

tried to discuss some philosophical aspects of financial economics in a Ph.D. seminar:

> Earlier this year in my Theory of Finance course someone questioned why utility theory, because it is based on assumptions which we know to be false, is worthy of study. Professor *Tunnelvision* [my italics, because I changed the name to protect the guilty] implied that because of Friedman's admonition that assumptions are not important, and that all that matters is how a theory measures up to empirical evidence, we don't have to bother with such "philosophical" questions. I responded that Friedman's assertion was in itself the statement of a philosophical position. Another student commented, "This is a finance course and not a philosophy course." My response was that if we consider ourselves "scientists" we could not shrink from such philosophical questions. Dr. *Tunnelvision* responded that Friedman's position was THE philosophy of modern finance, and that if I hoped to get published it would be my philosophy as well. Everyone in the class laughed at this statement but me. I left the class wondering what self-respecting scientist would make a statement such as that . . .

Now, I must admit that the correspondent is a student in a doctoral program at a Southern state university. This particular institution indoctrinates and ordains priests likely to proselytize the Visigoths at the outer fringes of the academic empire demarked by *Pax Americana*. But, as I have learned from colleagues and some published material (Klamer and Colander, 1990), the situation is not too much different in the Ivy League, or anywhere else.

As the story in http://www.paecon.net unfolds, something that would have been totally unprecedented in America happened:

> That debate began on the 21st of June, when the French national newspaper, *Le Monde*, reported on the students' petition and interviewed several prominent economists who voiced sympathy for the students' cause. Other newspapers followed. As the French media, including radio and television, expanded the public debate, fears among students and teachers of persecution diminished and the number of signatories to their petitions increased. This fueled further media interest. Jack Lang, the French minister of education, announced that he regarded the complaints with great seriousness and was setting up a commission to investigate.

Thus did the movement that today is referred to in English as Post-Autistic Economics (PAE) get its start. The original signatories and their supporters met in October 2000 at the Sorbonne. Soon, other universities throughout France joined the fray. The movement became a groundswell, prompting widespread discussion of the reform of economics teaching and the direction of economics as a science (if one has the courage to call it that). The real possibility of escaping the straightjacket of neoclassicism was no longer the aspiration of a very few.

B. The Cambridge Proposal

In June 2001, a group of 27 doctoral students at Cambridge published a proposal on their website, asking economics students and economists everywhere who were sympathetic to their cause to endorse the proposal by corresponding to cesp@econ.cam.ac.uk. The Cambridge proposal raised the same points as the French initiative, and added other criticisms (all supporting the argument that contemporary economics is monopolized by a single approach which is formalistic, and that this approach cannot be conducive to understanding economic phenomena, etc.). The Cambridge students were keen on stating, however, that all they asked for was a debate, not the total 86-ing of neoclassical economics.

Specifically, the Cambridge students proposed:

(1)   That the foundations of the mainstream approach be openly debated. This requires that the bad criticisms be rejected just as firmly as the bad defences. Students, teachers and researchers need to know and acknowledge the strengths and weaknesses of the mainstream approach to economics.

(2)   That competing approaches to understanding economic phenomena be subjected to the same degree of critical debate. Where these approaches provide significant insights into economic life, they should be taught and their research encouraged within economics. At the moment, this is not happening. Competing approaches have little role in economics as it stands simply because they do not conform to the mainstream's view of what constitutes economics. It should be clear that such a situation is self-enforcing.

The students justified the merits of their proposal with four points. Firstly, it is harmful to students who are taught the "tools" of mainstream economics without learning their domain of applicability. The source and evolution of these ideas are ignored, as are the existence and status of competing theories.

Secondly, it disadvantages a society that ought to be benefiting from what economists can tell us about the world. Economics is a social science with enormous potential for making a difference through its impact on policy debates. In its present form, its effectiveness in this arena is limited by the uncritical application of mainstream methods.

Thirdly, progress towards a deeper understanding of many important aspects of economic life is being held back. By restricting research done in economics to that based on one approach only, the development of competing research programs is seriously hampered or prevented altogether.

Fourth and finally, in the current situation an economist who does not do economics in the prescribed way finds it very difficult to get recognition for his or her research. The dominance of the mainstream approach creates a social convention in the profession that only economic knowledge production that fits the mainstream approach can be good research, and therefore other modes of economic knowledge are all too easily dismissed as simply being poor, or as not being economics. Many economists therefore face a choice between using what they consider inappropriate methods to answer economic questions, or to adopt what they consider the best methods for the question at hand knowing that their work is unlikely to receive a hearing from economists.

The Cambridge proposal (letter) was published on June 14, 2001. By December 22, 2001, there were 569 signatures from all over the world posted on the website.

C. The Kansas City Proposal (KCP)

Not to be left out by the French and the British, the KCP letter/proposal was released on August 13, 2001. The KCP manifesto is the work

> . . . of 75 students, researchers and professors from twenty-two nations who gathered for a week of discussion on the state of economics and the economy at the University of Missouri–Kansas City (UMKC) this June 2001. The discussion took place at the Second Biennial Summer School of the Association for Evolutionary Economics (AFEE), jointly sponsored by UMKC, AFEE and the Center for Full Employment and Price Stability (see http://www.paecon.net).

The KCP opens with the caption, "Economics needs fundamental reform — and now is the time for change." It then repeats many of the points from the French and British proposals, which, incidentally, is an explicit purpose of the letter. The proposal suggests that the following seven ideas be included in the teaching of economics and in economics research:

- A broader conception of human behavior
- Recognition of culture
- Consideration of history
- A new theory of knowledge
- Empirical grounding (more effort to validate theory with empirical proofs)
- Expanded methods
- Interdisciplinary dialogue

The final two ideas recognize the neoclassical orthodoxy's aversion to criticism (to the point of totally stifling it) and globalization, the new world order, which, among other things, is ". . . of economic change, of inequality between and within societies, of threats to environmental integrity, of new concepts of property and entitlement, of evolving international legal frameworks and of risks of instability in international finance" — all of which are outside the domain of the neoclassical methodology.

D. Financial Economics, Where are Thou?

At the risk of being accused of tooting my own horn, I refer the reader to my writings over the last two decades. With my dear friend and distinguished colleague, Skip McGoun — or alone — I have devoted much effort to bringing to the forefront of finance the same issues raised by the three initiatives (e.g., Frankfurter and McGoun, 1993; Frankfurter, 1995; Frankfurter and McGoun, 1995; Frankfurter and McGoun, 1996a,b,c; Frankfurter and McGoun, 1999; Frankfurter and McGoun, 2000a,b; Frankfurter, 2002; Frankfurter and McGoun, 2002a,b). These are works that either are already published or are scheduled for publication. I can say with pride that none of these articles won first prize from the finance nobility press — but not for my lack of trying.[49]

The standard response to a paper dealing with the methodology of finance — which paper by its very nature must be critical of the field — is that it is "not good enough for publication in the top journals." The interested reader can easily verify whether this claim holds water by skimming through the material I cited above. Just as easily one can verify that no paper dealing with the methodology of the field (others' or mine) have been able to penetrate the phalanx of those guarding the runes — i.e., the editors of these journals.

The sad fact is that criticism is not welcomed in the bastion of financial economics, and is much less tolerated here than in any other branch of economics. Fama (1998) is very clear about this. According to Fama, until a new and better paradigm is put forth, one cannot criticize the EMH/CAPM. Through control of the publication and the promotion/ tenure processes, of course, the EMH/CAPM is sufficiently sheltered so that no other paradigm can be established in the foreseeable future.

In an interview with Fama, appearing on the CAPITALIDEASON-LINE.COM website (or go straight to link: http://www.ifa.tv/Library/Support/Articles/Scholarly/TextInterviewEugeneFama.htm), Fama reiterates his claims to be found in his 1998 article and expands his views on behavioral finance:

> Well, my good friend, Dick Taylor [*sic*, the reference is to Richard Thaler who moved a few years ago from Cornell to Chicago in the latter university's attempt to cover all the bases] is kind of the guru of behavioral finance and every time he walks down the corridor, I ask him a question. The question isn't a complete question, but a person on the street wouldn't know what was going on. My question is always the same: now what is it? He knows what it refers to. It's behavioral finance, and the reality is they haven't defined the top. They haven't defined the area. What it is at this point is, unkindly speaking, just dredging for anomalous looking things

---

[49] This is not the place to discuss my correspondence with the editor of one of the top finance journals. The reader, however, can get a clear idea of how papers questioning the methodology of finance are suppressed by the gatekeepers of modern finance by reading the history of such a paper in our book, *From Individualism to the Individual* (Frankfurter and McGoun, 2002a).

in the data. But the fact is that even in a perfectly efficient market, every dataset would be on the foremost phenomenon just on a strictly random basis. So that's not evidence for or against anything. If you don't have a specific view of what behavioral finance is in the way it manifests itself in the behavior of prices and returns, you don't really have anything to work with because everything you observe really can be rationalized in the context of an efficient market. For example, all of these studies on behavioral finance basically look at how prices react to different kinds of announcements. So sometimes, it seems to be the case that prices underreact, sometimes it seems to be the case that prices overreact, but that's exactly what you predict in an efficient market. You're going to see drift one way or the other, but it will be random. So if you don't have a theory that predicts when it's going to underreact and when it's going to overreact, you don't have anything. It looks to me like an efficient market, just a random price behavior. [Professor Fama has a paper coming out soon on the subject, Market Efficiency Long-Term Returns on Behavioral Finance (this is in effect the 1998 paper I am referring to here).]

Fama masterfully reduces behavioral finance to a pitiful attempt to dredge up anomalies. In the same swoop he also attaches to a fellow colleague the dubious rank of "kind of the guru of behavioral finance" which is not only an ill-concealed insult, but also an insinuation that Professor Thaler somehow stumbled into a major university straight from the ashram of behavioral finance (perhaps a Hindu cult?).

What Fama conveniently forgets is that behavioral finance is not just the anomalies literature, or over-/underreaction, but the realization that the assumptions of modern finance/financial economics on which his EMH is built is an autistic world. As far as prediction is concerned, by Fama's own research, the EMH's proxy, β, has no predictive power (see Fama and French, 1992). Then, what makes the EMH something above doubt, while behavioral finance is "just dredging for anomalous looking things"? I am also doubtful that Dick Thaler cannot answer Fama's question. This is the same Thaler who, in an article in the *Financial Analysts Journal* (Thaler, 1999), had this to say:

> I predict that in the not-too-distant future, the term "behavioral finance" will be correctly viewed as a redundant phrase. What other kind of finance is there? (p. 16)

The core problem is not a matter of prediction, but rather the matter of methodology. The question is: what is the role of science? Is it the invention of an ideology-based model out of some set of "rules" and then the search for predictive power, or the discovery of the machinery? How can one explain the "behavior of prices" without being able to explain the behavior of agents whose activity or inactions create prices?

That is why there is a clear and extreme prejudice against discussing the methodology of financial economics, because such discussion necessarily involves criticism. And criticism must be avoided at all costs at the church of modern finance. Karl Popper was both circumspect and succinct when he remarked that: "Science must begin with myths, and the criticism of myths." What we had so far was the myth of efficient markets, but we were taught not to criticize the myth or even look elsewhere. The result has been thousands of insubstantial and mediocre papers, and the warm and comforting feeling of not going anywhere.

It was not the case that we did not know any better. It was the case that we should not do better. As we observe in Frankfurter and McGoun (2002b) regarding the chance of behavioral finance to evolve as a new paradigm:

Finance itself is burdened with its large investment in the old paradigm, and no one, young or old, can get out from under it. How does one become interested in behavioral finance without it being featured in textbooks or presented in inspiring lectures? How does one write a Ph.D. dissertation in finance without a committee knowledgeable in and supportive of behavioral finance? How does one earn tenure and promotion at a reputable institution on the strength of behavioral finance research with so few conferences and journals in which it can be presented and published or without senior colleagues to argue its merit before a review committee? A dominant paradigm is by definition a frame upon which the profession is dependent, and it is made up of a hard-core of heuristic-driven biases on how things are to be done. But change may be coming, if for no other reason than that traditional finance has exhausted itself as a progressive research program. As implied by the brief description of the "effects" literature in Section II, there is a limit to how long aggregate data can be subject to statistical testing of essentially the same theories before nothing new is left to extract from it. This will have to be admitted, however reluctantly, and a fresh perspective and fresh methods adopted.

Wishful thinking? Fama certainly hopes so.

E. *Punkt und Contrapunkt*

What happened next in France is something quite unimaginable in America. A national debate had started in the pages of the most popular daily paper about a matter as obscure as the meaningful teaching of a subject as difficult to understand as economics. The plight of economics students in France started a national debate that turned into a real potboiler.

Soon, responses from academia followed, some dismissing the students' manifesto, others defending it. By year's end, two internationally-known economists had joined the fray on the side of neoclassicism. Olivier Blanchard, a Frenchman himself, who is the head of the economics department at MIT, made his defense in the October 13, 2000 issue of *Liberation*. Two months later, Nobel laureate Robert Solow (1987, economics) set forth his ideas in *Le Monde*. When it comes to economics, these two can hold the proverbial butter in their metaphoric mouths for long periods. I myself would give wide berth to such folk, but opponents in the other camp wasted no time and proceeded with bombarding the neoclassicist arguments with piratical glee.

The Solow response, carefully condensed with great veneration by James Galbraight (the *fils*), argues that it is the quality of teaching in France that must be addressed, not the claim that there is something wrong with neoclassicism. But how is this possible, asks Galbraight, when French economics academia have been educated in America? Thus, something else must be wrong, because economics could not cope with the changing times and circumstances of a new world order.

The critics of Blanchard were less deferential than Galbraight was. First, Joseph Halevi of Sydney University (Halevi, 2001a,b) and later Jacques Sapir of the *L'École des Hautes études en Sciences Sociales* of Paris (*PAECON Newsletter*, 5, March 2001) fired broadside. They accused Blanchard, in his efforts to save French neoclassicism, of making false claims or being completely ignorant, and being in cahoots with Jean-Paul Fitoussi (a prominent economist, according to the students who wrote the open letter).

The debate did not end with those two. It had been dragging on in the pages of *Le Monde* for the better part of the year 2001. What the French students achieved is not so much a reform of economics teaching as it is the creation of a heated international dialogue about the state of economics as a science, and an in-depth discussion of its methodology.

During the year 2001, the students met several times with Monsieur Fitoussi. He listened dutifully to the students and was amenable to including some of their suggestions in his conclusions — but at first Fitoussi seemed to be reluctant to end the hegemony of neoclassical microeconomics.

Surprise, surprise! In December 2001, the following report was posted on the PAENETWORK's website as the conclusion of Monsieur Fitoussi's charge:

> Fitoussi's report, *L'Enseignement supérieur de l'économie en question*, calls for the integration of debate on contemporary economic issues into both the structure and content of university economics courses. It means real debate, not neoclassical opinion presented on its own or with only token alternatives. Such an open environment would preclude the standard practice of keeping the ideological content of neoclassicism hidden from students. This change alone would radically transform economics teaching, with inevitable and incalculable effects to economics itself.

One may call me pessimistic, cynical or *the* consummate skeptic. Nevertheless, until a new cadre of Ph.D.'s step up to the plate, not much is going to happen in the steppes of financial economics. And the 40 years the people of Israel wondered in the desert until Moses could bring them to the Promised Land may seem short compared to what is before us in modern finance. But to quote a fellow entertainer (using the word in the Marshall McLuhanian sense; teachers and entertainers are the same, and who does not know the difference is neither): this is just my opinion and I might be wrong.

F. What is at the Heart of the Debate?

We learn about the issue at the heart of the imbroglio from an essay by Tony Lawson of Cambridge University (*PAECON Newsletter*, 6, May 2001), excerpts of which appeared in the March 27, 2001 issue of *Le Monde*, titled "Back to Reality." Lawson contends that the debate between the French students and the proponents of neoclassicism is about which research methodology is more appropriate to economics. Whereas the students argue for pluralism (i.e., research methodologies from the other social sciences), modern economics is restricted chiefly to mathematical modeling.

The response to the students' claim is that economics needs to be scientific and that without mathematics, it would not be scientific.[50] If one

---

[50] Note that the framing of the issue by Lawson is not that without mathematics economics would not be scientific, but that economics needs to be scientific; ergo, it must be a collection of mathematical models.

accepts this framing, then, according to Lawson, the responses to the students' arguments seem inadequate. It is so because Lawson questions both contentions hidden in the responses to the students; namely, that

- Economics needs to be "scientific," and
- Mathematics makes something scientific which *sans* mathematics would not be scientific.

Those who make the claim for the use of mathematics argue that event-regularities not only justify mathematical modeling, but also beg for it. Lawson then quotes Maurice Allais (1992) — 1988 Nobel laureate in economics — as an apropos (even French) authority formulating this claim:

> The essential condition of any science is the existence of regularities which can be analyzed and forecast. This is the case in celestial mechanics. But it is also true of many economic phenomena. Indeed, their thorough analysis displays the existence of regularities which are just as striking as those found in the physical sciences. This is why economics is a science, and why this science rests on the same general principles and methods of physics (*ibid.*, p. 25).

Lawson contends, rather convincingly, that event-regularities in the social sciences are hard to come by and that econometricians find correlations non-existent as soon as they find one as significant (are markets efficient?). More important, even in the natural sciences, event-regularities — with the exception of celestial mechanics — are restricted to controlled experiments. Now, the question is: what is the role of science? Is it to reproduce events in a laboratory, or to find the prevailing mechanics that create the events?[51] As Lawson (2001) makes clear,

> Gravitational forces may give rise to event-regularity in an experimental vacuum, but gravitational forces continue to act on autumn leaves wherever the latter may fly, and help us to send rockets to the moon. It is an

---

[51] I must interject here to kick finance event studies one more time. If one accepts Lawson's arguments, then one must reject *en toto* the so-called event study literature. In event studies, an artificial, non-realistic model is assumed to be the mechanics explaining the event, and the event itself is the proof or disproof that the event is the result of this artificiality. This is not to mention the fact that there is not a single finance event study that is a true laboratory experiment.

understanding of the mechanism, not the production of an event-regularity, that is the essential goal here (*ibid.*).

Lawson's argument, in a nutshell, is the basic difference between positivism and realism. Correlating surface observations is one thing, but the role of science is to find the mechanisms below the surface reality, even when observable correlations, for one reason or another, are not to be (immediately) present. Interestingly, neoclassical economics stuck with Friedmanian positivism (*de facto*, instrumentalism) instead of the more progressive approach of realism — it is axiomatic instead of being realistic. I can only speculate that the reason must be the sociology of academia, a topic too complex and more controversial than I would dare to approach here.

Mathematics does not make economics a science, and economics can be scientific without mathematics. In certain instances, mathematics may help (it is not hard for me to imagine where in finance, for instance), and it is for the common good, but mathematics by no means is a *sine qua non*.

In fact, Lawson sees a quite limited use of mathematics in the social realms, especially when one considers national, ethnic and cultural differences (Lawson, 1997). The French students' argument, therefore, that mathematics is not a goal by itself is well-taken.

G. Still Autistic Finance: Some Final Cogitation

In Zen Buddhism, *koan* is a riddle in the form of a paradox. Financial economics/modern finance has been a paradox within a riddle. How is it possible that perhaps the most applied form of economics, which concerns itself with the financial dealings of corporations and individuals, is bound by a methodology that is now openly being declared autistic? The jig is up not just in terms of vapid academic pride and reputation, but also in real dollars. The *mise en scene* is real and the actors are flesh and blood. So, however pragmatic, Dr. *Tunnelvision's* admonition that ". . . Friedman's position was THE philosophy of modern finance, and that if [one] hoped to get published it would be [one's] philosophy as well" could not have prevailed for 50 years. But it did, and it does.

Is it perhaps because of the influence of big business in MBA schools (see Soley, 1995), which has a vested interest in perpetuating the myth of efficient markets? But that would cut against the grain of efficiency, a logic that is the driving force for businessmen and hence for big business. Or is it because of an ideology that cannot and will not tolerate anything that is inconsistent with this ideology (see Frankfurter and McGoun, 1999)? Yet, the ideology alone does not preclude pluralism and the espousal of research methods widely used in other branches of the social sciences.

In my darker moods, I remind myself of an adage by the people of the Sahara: the dogs bark, but the caravan goes forward. In my more optimistic moods, I believe that change, however slow and however small, will eventually come. As ideas are institutionalized, change must come from the elite universities, because anything that does not come from there is either not credible or not science. Or at least that is the consensus.

Perhaps the interest in behavioral economics that flared recently at MIT, Harvard and even Chicago is a start. Also, one must take note of the fact that George Akerlof, Michael Spence and Joseph Stiglitz shared the 2001 Nobel Prize in economics. Akerlof and Spence are considered the forefathers of behavioral economics. Two out of three ain't that bad, now is it? In 2002, the prize went to Daniel Kahneman and Vernon Smith, behavioral and experimental economics, respectively. In fact, the bulk of Vern's work is about dividend behavior of individuals.

Perhaps the French experience is so significant that it cannot be disregarded in America. Perhaps the risk of losing the hegemony on financial economics is perceived to be so imminent that a re-examination of the field at home is inevitable. Perhaps this is the *Götterdammerung* (The Twilight of the Gods) of neoclassicism in finance. Don't bet the farm on it! Still, whatever it is, it is a start.

References

Allais, Maurice. 1992. "The Economic Science of Today and Global Disequilibrium." In *Global Disequilibrium in the World Economy*, edited by Baldassarri M. Basingstoke. New York: Macmillan.

Fama, Eugene F. 1998. "Market Efficiency, Long-Term Returns, and Behavioral Finance." *Journal of Financial Economics* 49: 283–306.

Fama, Eugene F. and Kenneth R. French. 1992. "The Cross Section of Expected Stock Returns." *Journal of Finance* 47: 427–465.

Frankfurter, George M. 1995. "The Rise And Fall of the CAPM Empire." *Financial Markets, Institutions & Instruments* 4: 104–127.

———. 1999. "What Is the Puzzle in the 'Dividend Puzzle'." *Journal of Investing* 8: 76–85.

————. 2002. "Method and Methodology." *Homo Oeconomicus* 18: 465–491.

Frankfurter, George M. and Elton G. McGoun. 1993. "The Event Study: An Industrial Strength Method." *The International Review of Financial Analysis* 2: 121–142.

————. 1995. "The Event Study: Is It Either?" *The Journal of Investing* 4: 8–16.

————. 1996a. "But It Looked So Good on My Vita." *Journal of Financial Education* 22: 14–25.

————. 1996b. *Toward Finance with Meaning: The Methodology of Finance, What It Is and What It Can Be.* Greenwich, Connecticut: JAI Press.

————. 1996c. "Toward Finance with Meaning: The Methodology of Finance, What It Is and What It Can Be." *The Journal of Investing* 5: 7–13.

————. 1999. "Ideology and the Theory of Financial Economics." *Journal of Economic Behavior and Organization* 39: 159–177.

————. 2000a. "Market Efficiency or Behavioral Finance: The Nature of the Debate." *Journal of Psychology and Financial Markets* 1: 200–210.

————. 2000b. "Thought Contagion and Financial Economics: The Dividend Puzzle as a Case Study." *Journal of Psychology and Financial Markets* 1: 145–153.

————. 2001. "Signaling and Semiotics: A Search For Meaning." *Homo Oeconomicus* 17: 347–369.

————. 2002a. *From Individualism to the Individual: Ideology and Inquiry in Financial Economics.* London: Ashgate Publishers.

————. 2002b. "Resistance Is Futile: The Assimilation of Behavioral Finance." *Journal of Economic Behavior and Organization* 48: 375–389.

Friedman, Milton M. 1953. "The Methodology of Positive Economics." In *Essays in Positive Economics*, edited by Milton M. Friedman. Chicago: The University of Chicago Press.

Halevi, Joseph. 2001a. "The Franco-American Neoclassical Alliance." *PAECON Newsletter* 4.

————. 2001b. "Three Observations on a 'Cultural Revival'." *PAECON Newsletter* 6.

Klamer, Arjo and David Colander. 1990. *The Making of an Economist.* Boulder, Colorado: Westview Press, Inc.

Lawson, Tony. 1997. *Economics and Reality.* London: Routledge.

————. 2001. "Back to Reality." *PAECON Newsletter* 6.

Sapir, Jacques. 2001. "A Rejoinder to James Galbraight." *PAECON Newsletter* 5.

Soley, Lawrence C. 1995. *Leasing the Ivory Tower.* Boston, Massachusetts: South End Press.

Thaler, Richard H. 1999. "The End of Behavioral Finance." *Financial Analysts Journal* 55: 12–17.

Chapter 4

The Young Finance Faculty's Guide to Publishing: Inspired By and After (Rather Loosely) Benjamin Britten*

So wonder on, till Truth make all things plain.

— William Shakespeare *A Midsummer Night's Dream*

A. Introduction

The purpose of this paper is to provide a set of guidelines and principles that may serve, especially for young and inexperienced faculty, both as a strategic and tactical tool to publish the results of their labor. Such a service should be coming forth from meetings of professional associations where there is, more often than not, a panel or round table of journal editors.

My experience with these sessions is a bit different, however. In my experience,[52] Journal Editor's Panels are usually an opening for lofty and formulaic statements by the members of the dais. They expound on how much they care about quality (which they are bent on increasing), how carefully they monitor the reviewing process, and how sorry they are that they have no control over its length. Then, the audience asks questions which range from how can reviewing and time to publication after acceptance be shortened, to how fast the editor can send a letter of acknowledgment of acceptance so they can put it in the file for promotion and tenure consideration.

This concern about the acknowledgment of acceptance as an overriding and principal factor came across loud and clear as well while I had the good fortune of editing *The International Review of Financial Analysis*. I got so many calls and letters from authors making attempts to implant

---

*An earlier version of this paper was published in the *International Review of Financial Analysis*, 2000, Volume 9: 299–314. The current version, with minor editing, is reprinted here with Elsevier's permission.

[52] I moderated two such panels and was an invited guest editor to a third one.

guilt feelings in me that, for a while, I was contemplating to change the name of the journal to *The Journal of Promotion and Tenure*. There I had the empirical evidence, so important in our "scientific" work, that the real impetus to write is for the purpose of fame and fortune, and not for the interest of discovery (a search for the truth). This is why I think that what follows might be useful for some, if not all, starting faculty.

In no way have I any intention to make the pretense that this is about how to *write* a publishable paper, although some benignly vague references will be made regarding style, content and language. One such cautioning is, of course, never to use the passive voice at *The Journal of Portfolio Management*, but use it exclusively everywhere else. The assumption is made throughout this paper that, based on [self] quality control, the work of the researcher or at least the topic, is first class and therefore, warrants publication.

The last three decades have seen a steady increase in the number of schools requiring a minimum publication record as a condition for promotion and/or tenure. Simultaneously, there has been a parallel increase of aging faculty, tired of fishing and boating and too old for skiing and contact sports. Accordingly, the volume of articles written by both the young and the old has been increasing at an exponential rate.

Concurrently, the number of new journals that may provide an outlet for the overflow of production is in no proportion to what is being offered for sale. According to my own estimates, based on rejection rates obtained from casual discussions with editors and from published statistics, the number of articles submitted to journals must have quadrupled, in comparison to the mid-60s. Undoubtedly, the situation that has evolved resembles an imperfect market, in which entrance is controlled (may I say rather questionably). First, by a thin layer of "railroad ticket takers," also called reviewers, and ultimately by a strip-joint bouncer, called, erroneously, the journal editor. I might have called this market the "market-for-promotion-and-tenure," if I did not think that a similar name, "the market-for-corporate-control," was not so utterly silly. Although I must admit that if the two are "markets," which they are not, the former is more of a "market" then the latter will ever be.

Clearly, this paper is normative and not positive (a fact that would, by itself, disqualify it for publication in many leading journals). It also does not beseech, or demand otherwise, any conditions of equilibrium. Further, the model that is proposed in the following is, at the best, an heuristic of strategies and decision rules with complete absence of mathematical formulations (another shortcoming that will make its publication potential close to nil).

Thus, do not look for an objective function *per se*, twice differentiable and a set of fancy constraints. The lack of all these attributes, *de facto*, creates the preconditions needed for a rejection. Yet, because I am writing this for my own amusement (something I badly need), I have no concern whether it ever gets into the public domain or not. In spite of all the equivocal qualifications of this work (and my own self-serving motives), as negative reinforcement this paper might have the value of public service and a useful example.

The first, and conceivably the most important, question to answer is where to submit one's paper. Section B is a brief outline of how to select the appropriate journal for a given topic and, consequently, what style to avoid in writing the paper.

Perhaps the most momentous lesson to learn early on in one's academic career is to live with rejection. We are so full of our intellectual capacity that when and if an authority of any kind finds it questionable, our feelings are hurt. This may cause many to retreat into a cocoon where pride and self-respect act as repellents of outside criticism. Unfortunately, this is also tantamount to retreat, the worst possible reaction, because the future of an academic is dependent on his publication record. Section C then is about what to do in case of and how to live with rejection.

Section D is an attempt, however incomplete and feeble, in categorizing reviewers. My taxonomy is by no means scientific, and thus, one must not take it as universally applicable, appealing or valid. My categorization is subjective and introspective. Yet, it is the summary of 30 years of dealing with (most of the time) anonymous "adversaries" with whom one can hardly argue, creating a feeling of hopelessness and certain cause for despair and frustration.

In Section E I make an *admittedly* incomplete effort to suggest improvements of the reviewing process and offer my conclusions.

B. Journals and Styles

Learn to write well or not to write at all.

— John Sheffield, First Duke of Buckingham and Normandy
Essay on Satire

It is almost as consequential to select the appropriate journal for one's toil as the significance of the topic and the quality of the work itself. In this selection process, there are some distinct and well-defined dimensions.

First, the topic itself. Although it is assumed throughout this paper that the journal under consideration is in the area of finance (or has the word "finance" or its many derivatives in its name), nevertheless, not every topic is suitable for every journal. This can be the case for several reasons. For example, it may happen that the journal published a disproportionate number of articles on a certain subject and now the editor is imposing either a declared or an undeclared moratorium on the topic.

It also may happen that the subject belongs to the "black sheep" topics of the finance family. For instance, several journals would prefer to be investigated by a special prosecutor for publishing articles with strong pornographic content without redeeming social values, than to publish a paper in normative portfolio theory, critical of the ruling paradigm, or God forbid, an article with philosophical content.

In other instances the way the topic is presented may not be acceptable, or the conclusions of the study might amount to apostasy. There are journals that would not even review a paper if it does not have substantial empirical research. In other journals, empirical work would increase the odds of rejection. There are journals where the findings and conclusions must be "in line" with editorial views. Quality notwithstanding, the paper does not have a chance in a prayer to be *reviewed*, much less to see the light of *publication*, if it does not support the validity of the right theory.

It is difficult to find which journal fits what topic and treatment without experience, sometimes, of several years. The best approach for young faculty to follow is to ask the advice of more battle-tried and -tired colleagues. Another source of orientation might be the list of editors and associate editors. Look for the names. Try to match the names with works published by these ladies and gentlemen in the past and reach conclusions about their possible likes and dislikes.

This approach by itself may not help, of course. It happened to me in the past that in a certain journal, a doctoral candidate reviewed my paper. One could not make any mistake that the reviewer was a doctoral student after reading the review.[53] In such case, the destiny of the author depends on whether the reviewer came to a conclusion after dealing with an especially difficult undergraduate class, or was the evaluator under the influence of the last seminar of Professor So-and-so? Yet, it is also quite

---

[53] The reviewer wrote that in his dissertation the treatment of the problem was better than mine, and that he was looking for a job.

possible that the doctoral candidate/reviewer simply got the paper from his professor with the explicit instruction of rejecting it, and writing some inconsequential remarks to satisfy a minimum standard (zero?) required by the journal from the referee.

Assuming that the publication process follows a submartingale, the first step is to read the last two or three issues of the journal, cover-to-cover. If there was no change in editors during that time, the content of these issues gives quite adequate indication of the direction of the journal, what type of material is being published and to what level of audience. Not long ago, a paper of mine was rejected in one journal. Two readers reviewed it. The review of the first[54] reader was long and was a masterpiece in the art of rejection, deriving from sheer ignorance. The second review was also a rejection, but much more terse. This reviewer's advice was just one sentence: send the paper elsewhere.

A brief inspection of the last issue of the journal without a doubt bears out this recommendation. In recent years, the quality of the journal deteriorated to the point where one would not want to see one's work published there, anyway. The reviewer actually did a service rejecting the paper for which one should be grateful forever. So, with the exception of death, there is no such thing as a *totally* negative outcome, and this wisdom pertains to the reviewing process as well.

Quite another dimension is the tradeoff between cost and expediency. The submission fee to a journal can be anywhere between \$0–\$370. Some argue that the slope of an OLS curve in the two dimensional space of Cost and Time (where Time refers to "time under review") is not downward sloping, but rather zero, with a great deal of white noise and with a Wilt Chamberlain effect. The decision then becomes one of need, *ceteris paribus*. When one considers the fact that in some schools submission fees are reimbursed, while in others they are not, one realizes that a two-tier market is being created on top of other imperfections.

The last dimension is the quality and reputation of the journal. I distinguish here among three classes. Class A is the top, most highly regarded group of journals: the nobility press. Class B is the group of journals that one selects as an alternative, after accepting the faith of not being able to publish the work in Group A. Class C is the group of journals in which we wish our enemies would publish.

---

[54] The reference here to "first" and "second" is completely arbitrary. Because of the anonymity of the process, I cannot find a better designation for the reviewers.

The reviewing process is usually (but not uniquely) better at the top. Readers are more critical, yet more knowledgeable in general, henceforth providing for a better review.[55]

Group B is both unpredictable and a paradox. This is so, especially when one's work is good, but one just could not put it through the reviewers of Group A. In such instance, because of the low quality of the reviewer (and the high quality of the paper), one cannot publish in Group B as well. The paper is too good for the (incompetent) referee! As much as it may seem so, this is not an incongruity. This is the paradox. Yogi Berra, the greatest living American philosopher, puts it differently: "The place is so crowded that nobody goes there anymore."

Group C is immaterial, because we would not want to publish there anyway. Yet, some may opt to go to a Group C journal, nevertheless. This, for two reasons:

- In certain schools every publication counts, and
- One wants to see one's work published, no matter where.

Style is a major issue, the importance of which cannot be emphasized enough. My reference is not to typing, bibliography, section headings, footnotes, etc. — style that is explicitly discussed in the submission instruction sheet of the journal. My assumption is that those directions are followed to the letter.

I am referring to writing style, which can be a major problem, given the right (wrong) reviewer. There are some universal rules to follow, however, presented here as Lemmas.

Lemma 1.   *The paper must be written in totally boring and cotton-dry language.*

Lemma 2.   *It cannot be cynical, sarcastic or offending, even when the subject or previous work on the subject not only justifies scorn, but also demands it.*

Lemma 3.   *It must describe the topic, sometimes totally trivial, as serious, however difficult such task may be.*

Following these Lemmas by itself is, of course, no guarantee for acceptance and eventual publication.

---

[55] To be defined in the next section.

The next plateau to be reached is the "well-written" mark (which, incidentally, is no guarantee of acceptance, either). Here again one is totally at the hands of the reviewer. It happened, and not just once, that one reviewer argued that my paper is well-written, while the other thought it was very poorly written. Needless to say, both rejected the paper just to be on the safe side. (I am mentioning this only in passé to make it clear that the paper being "well-written" is a necessary, but not sufficient condition.) The discrepancy in evaluating writing style is especially pronounced in a journal where reviewers "grade" a paper in a matrix of, say, six by five, copied directly from the editor's school Promotion and Tenure Form.

In some journals the editor deplores a certain word, say, "which." In another publication, passive voice gives him the willies. Although the latter can clearly be a deterrent, it is by itself no ground for rejection. However, it will require serious efforts to rewrite the paper. Although it is difficult to know which editor dislikes what, once one has evidence of distaste of any particular kind, one must try to avoid it everywhere.

The advent of the personal computer, the evolution of artificial intelligence and the development of powerful parsers may open a new era in the writing and style category. It is quite conceivable that in addition to the Word Processor, Spell Checker and Thesaurus, in regular use now, together with ENDNOTE™, an extremely diverse and powerful referencing software with practically hundreds of journal styles in the social sciences alone will emerge.

I would not be surprised to see in the future a Windows or Apple-based "text duller": software that will interpret the content and context of a paper that presents only the bare idea and then translates it to the style of the journal of one's choice. Of course, the better text duller software packages will have a broad choice of journals.

I do not think that this idea is far-fetched. It is similar to today's choice of printers or bibliography softwares' journal style selection options. That this possible development is not a quixotic or futuristic notion is spotlighted by the following story, appearing in the August 1993 issue of *Harper's*. *Harper's* reproduces a questionnaire ". . . completed after each game by the coach of the Monroe City, Missouri Panthers high-school football team." The questionnaire has about 15 items. Some items are simple statistics (name of the opponent, game date, weather, etc.), some multiple choice, and some brief descriptions of team and individual performance of the Panthers and their opponents. The questionnaire may take the coach anywhere between five to ten minutes to complete (depending on his mood after the game) after which it is sent to the sports editor of the *Monroe City News.*

The *Monroe City News* developed the software that to the best of my knowledge is a first in our latest efforts to replace professional work with machinery. The program, using the input from the questionnaire, done by a low-paid operator, produces a cover article for the game. Imagine the "efficiency" to be gained from this development to make the resubmission of the paper elsewhere, in case of rejection, automatic! (Such a program may have yet unimaginable potential in writing up event studies as well.)

If these packages will be sold on the basis of site licensing, a strong economic incentive would be offered to both the developers and to future potential customers. In such case, reviewing by journals can be handled by a similar software package, too. The opportunities offered by this evolution are so far-fetching that it makes it the topic of a companion paper and hence I will not discuss it here any further.

If no such expedience and efficiency will be forthcoming, language has to be considered by the young faculty, writing alone or with other young faculty. The use of shop-worn metaphors is not only permitted, but also encouraged, because it pleases the orthodoxy when they see their *word-smithery* repeated by others. In many instances, their metaphorization makes the concepts they signal ring true as well. Thus, use lavishly expressions such as "economic agents," "neutral mutation," "heuristics," etc., even when those wordings do not have real meaning, cover up for an ideology, or can be safely replaced by much simpler phrasing. As a starting writer, never, ever invent your own metaphors, however.

C. The Resubmission Process

All who taught me enlightened Me.

— Talmud

Definition:

A bad review is a review that rejects the paper and at the same time provides neither clues nor help for improvement or correction.

A good review is a review that may or may not reject a paper, but it provides ground for improvements and corrects obvious errors present in the paper.

Paradoxically, the reviewing process, even though it has reached in recent years record lows of quality, is the best ally of an author. Throughout 30 years of publishing, I have been "saved" from embarrassment by fastidious and fussy reviewers who found errors in my work. And because there is always a chance that someone will carefully read your paper (very slight chance, I may add), it is good to be on the technically correct side.

But one cannot always expect conscientious referees. Better put yet, one must never expect conscientious reviewers. Accordingly, in case of acceptance (a minute minority of the cases), one is at one's own peril. In case of rejection, one has to fight one's own battles.

Arguing with referees involves many dimensions. If one is lucky (as I was), one starts out under the guidance and tutelage of one of the profession's elder statesman. This person will guide the young faculty as if and how to argue with the referees. In some instances, even though the reviewer is wrong and the review is clearly erroneous to the point of derision, it does not pay to protest because: (1) the editor will side with the reviewers anyway; and (2) it will create the image that the author is a troublemaker, jeopardizing future submissions. I know of but one journal in the field that specifically mentions in its submission instructions the possibility of an appeal in case of a negative decision.

Yet, in many cases it is a good idea to argue with an incorrect review. It has to be done in a polite and circumspect manner, with great care to detail explaining where the reviewer is wrong. The Roman aphorism *"quod licet Iovi non licet bovi"*[56] applies here as one would suspect, because there are benefits to fame and seniority. Or as one of my statistics professors put it once, the rich and the powerful may not always get their wish, but that is the way to bet. Resubmission is a time-acquired art, to be perfected with wisdom.

One must know, however, that resubmission, whether it is a result of arguing with referees or by invitation in the first place, is no guarantee for acceptance. In my experience, I resubmitted a paper three times to one journal, based on the reviewer's encouragement. Although I followed the reviewer's advice, with each submission the review was less enthusiastic than in the previous submission. After the third attempt the paper was rejected. One may get the impression that in order to publish, one is required to jump through hoops and one is perfectly right.

Looking at an invited resubmission from another angle, one might consider it akin to "hostage-taking." The referee writes that if the author

---

[56] What is permissible for Jupiter is not permissible to the ox.

acquiesces to do this and/or that, then the paper will be accepted. Just as in the case of hostage-taking, the author never knows for sure whether fulfilling the last demand of the reviewer/terrorist is a guarantee for the publication of the paper. Also, one runs the risk of one not recognizing one's own work after the referee's demands were met. Yet there are several types of hostage-taking, each with variable degrees of severity.

A simple situation is when the reviewer asks for additional material to be included in, or material included taken out of, the paper. In some instances these demands/conditions are justified. In many other cases, what the reviewer asks for is redundant or excessively space-consuming.

Yet, in other situations, adding to the paper what the reviewer wants is against the best judgment of the author to the point of conflict of the latter's belief system. I am not writing this to preach or to give advice regarding uprightness, rectitude and academic integrity. This is something the individual has to deal with when and if the time comes. Nevertheless, I would like to state for the record that I withdrew several papers from consideration when my co-authors or I felt that we could not do something we did not believe in. And they are my witnesses!

A much stronger form of "extortion" is what I call the "in your dreams" review. This is the case when the reviewer redesigns the study and makes acceptance conditional on yet unseen and unknown outcomes. A prime example of this type of "hostage-taking" is a former colleague's experience in one journal. His work was rejected, but the referee indicated that if he used another (entirely different) model, and if the coefficient estimates of that model were significant, and if the correlation coefficient was high enough, then he would recommend the publication of the paper.

The most extreme form of hostage-taking is the "if I wrote this paper" review. A while ago I had the pleasure of reading such a review. The reader notes that I am very knowledgeable in the subject and, consequently, I would have no problem to write a different paper. Mystifyingly, he then goes on to describe a project that has nothing to do with my work, which I never intended to do and would not have done even if all he recommends would be readily available at my fingertips. Clearly, this review is not about the quality of my work, but what the reviewer would have done if he had the know-how, the discipline and talent he expects from others to possess. Of course, here again the editor should intercede and dismiss the review and the reviewer. Editors, however, are so pleased with space-saving rejections that they do not think twice when their appointed referees recommend such course to follow. Frankly, there is too much paper floating around, anyway.

The core of the problem is in the ambiguity of the role of the review and the reviewer, and the lack of standards for rejection. Although some journals provide instructions for the reviewer, most do not, and there is no proof that not following the instructions would be cause to invalidate a negative review. Although Robert Merton (the pére) called the reviewing process organized skepticism, I doubt that either this definition uniformly holds or that it is a fitting one in the first place.

Some referees reject every paper they get to review for reasons that are more consistent with their own inadequacies than with scientific rigor. Others believe that if they do not find something wrong with the paper, they are not performing their duty. Yet others think that a paper should be in line with their own thinking on the subject, whether they are right or wrong, or whether a different dimension of the problem might also exist. Perhaps that dimension is more valid than the one with which they concur at the present.

Sadly, after 50 years of history and experience, we are no closer to the establishment of standards as to what constitutes growth in knowledge and a legitimate search for truth, than we were in the mid-1940s when all this started. I do not expect any improvement soon, unless a panel of editors will establish some basic standards for review. The official journals of our professional associations should lead the way in this endeavor. But they do not! Accordingly, everything is swept under the rug of the "sour grapes" syndrome and the scientific process is the ultimate loser.

While I am speaking of editors, it should be clear that their role is critical. First, they decide who will review the paper. Right there more than half of the decision process is completed, for if they send a paper they consider "revolutionary" to ultra-orthodox reviewers, the destiny of the work is sealed the moment it leaves the editorial office en route to the reviewer(s). All that has to be done is to wait for the rejection recommendation to come back and send the negative comments together with a "Dear Professor" letter indicating that ". . . due to the large volume of papers the journal receives, etc., etc." your work cannot be published, ". . . and hopefully the attached reviews will help in revising the paper for submission elsewhere."

Next, the *"quod licet Iovi. . .* , etc." factor (that I will call, subsequently, QLINLB) I alluded to above. A paper of Fama submitted to the *JF*, the *JFE* or the *Journal of Business* is not going to be reviewed by a "$35 reviewer."[57] Also, I suspect that many editors do not read carefully the reviews, the paper, or both.[58] If they did, they would not send to authors two reviews that are totally contradictory, yet take an unequivocal stance. Or as it happened in the case of a good friend, the review of another author's different paper.

With all fairness, there are also editors who will publish a paper against the reviewers' recommendations. This happens when they realize that the reason for rejection is not substance but ideology. Naturally, these editors indeed read both the paper and the reviews and exercise their editorial prerogative and calling. Unfortunately, such editors are few and they are the exception, not the mode. (I was lucky to come across three such chaps during a 30-year career.)

This is both a pity and a shame, especially when it concerns questioning ruling dogma. Reiter and Williams (2002) quote Longino (1990) on the importance of criticism in scientific discourse:

> Scientific communities will be objective to the degree that they satisfy four criteria necessary for achieving the transformative dimension of critical discourse: (1) there must be recognized avenues for the criticism of evidence, of methods, and of assumptions and reasoning; (2) there must exist shared standards that critics can invoke; (3) the community as a whole must be responsive to such criticism; (4) intellectual authority must be shared equally among qualified practitioners (*ibid.*, p. 76).

Then they add their interpretation (p. 11):

> Expanding on the points noted above, the first criteria means that criticism must be valued, not repressed, and there must be some way for criticism to interact with accepted theories. The second criteria relates to the standards and values of the scientific community that are needed to make attention to criticism possible. These types of shared standards could include values such as empirical adequacy, truth, expansion of the existing knowledge framework, reliability as a guide to action, relevance or satisfaction of social needs, or consistency with theories from other domains (*ibid.*, p. 77).

---

[57] A reviewer who is to be paid the sum of $35 (hardly the cost of a decent dinner for one), if the review comes back within a time limit.

[58] As I mentioned earlier, I organized two round-table sessions at professional meetings. Without exception, all editors argued that they read everything (paper and reviews), and that they carefully evaluated the reviews. One editor had the temerity to claim that he rejects papers to "maximize his journal's wealth."

The third criteria is that "the beliefs of the scientific community as a whole and over time change in response to critical discussion taking place within it" (*ibid.*, p. 78). The fourth criteria relates to equality of intellectual authority. This criteria is "intended to disqualify a community in which a set of assumptions dominates by virtue of the political power of its adherents" (*ibid.*, p. 78). The central characteristic necessary for "good conversation" is that criticism must be encouraged and taken seriously. It is not just that criticism must be produced and heard, it must also be incorporated, in some way, into the research program:

"When critical discussion becomes repetitive and fixed at a metalevel, or when criticism of one set of assumptions ceases to have or does not eventually develop a connection to an empirical research program, it loses its relevance to the construction of empirical knowledge" (Longino, 1990, p. 79).

It is regrettable that those are not the ways and means of the reviewing process in financial economics, and that editors of journals do not make these criteria their primary responsibility.

Then, there are also editors who feel obliged to take their task as seriously as any of their other professional tasks. After not hearing from the *Journal of Finance* for two years, I got a letter from the newly appointed editor that my file was vacuous and he needed a fresh copy of my paper. It turned out that the previous editor sent the paper out to review to someone who put his copy on the refrigerator, and by an unfortunate accident the paper fell behind said appliance. Beside the opportunity to ruminate how clean the reviewer's household must have been, it also reflected on how thorough a job the previous editor was doing, or how much he cared to consider my professional needs, if not the journal's. The new editor promised and delivered a quick review after which the paper was accepted and published.

1. *The QLINLB factor — A digression*

Every public action, which is not customary, either is wrong or, if it is right is a dangerous precedent. It follows that nothing should be done for the first time.

— F.M. Cornford *Microcosmographia Academica*

I mentioned the QLINLB (pronounced as climb) in two contexts so far. It has some more dimensions that are needed to be discussed for reasons that will become clear, shortly. I wish to start with the most influential aspect of the QLINLB. Reiter and Williams (2002) analyze the discourse of a conference on corporate takeovers with participants from elite schools and a wide range of interests. The proceedings of the conference that appeared in print,[59] including in addition to the papers the ensuing discussions as well, is the subject of their analysis as to how scientific discourse in financial economics is conducted. They observe:

> The powerful, elite figures, such as Jensen and Roll, played the role of rallying the troops and authoritatively dismissing doubts about the rightness or relevance of financial economic theory. In the academic discipline of financial economics, a handful of powerful elite figures are in charge of theory production, setting methodological rules, and interpretation of empirical results.

For young faculty, the critical part of this quote is that the elite figures — the high priests of the field and their handpicked sycophants, minions and acolytes — are the only ones "in charge of theory production, setting methodological rules, and interpretation of empirical results." Accordingly, both unknown and starting faculty persons (the two are not mutually exclusive) should not try their hand in any of these, because it would be considered sacrilegious.

A good example of the Reiter and Williams claim is Fama (1998). In this paper, Fama not only calls a method, methodology, and declares his EMH above criticism until and unless a new methodology is proposed and proven empirically superior, but also hand-picks the papers that may or may not show post-event proofs as to the validity of the EMH. Truly, this is the hallmark of a great mind that accomplishes all that is regrettable in one swoop. It is also reflective on the system that publishes a paper of that sort in the journal after which the field is named.

But Reiter and Williams do not stop here. They continue:

> The stories told by elite economic storytellers like Jensen and Roll are not generally subjected to critical scrutiny from within financial economics. In fact, such questioning is soundly discouraged from the beginning in many economics classrooms as students learn that it is considered bad form to question fundamental assumptions (Strassmann, 1994; Strassmann and Polanyi, 1992). Emphasis on analogic reasoning leads students to view the

---

[59] Columbia Law School's Center for Law and Economic Studies. 1985. "Conference on Takeovers and Contests for Corporate Control."

core material as the "valuable and unchallengeable consensus of experts" (Strassmann, 1993, p. 152) (Reiter and Williams, 2002, p. 18).

The morale is: never question axioms or assumptions other, better-known persons made, unless you co-author with one of them.

But the QLINLB factor has another dimension as well — do not use a method of analysis that has not been used already by someone more recognized than the starting academic. I cannot count the number of times my work has been returned with the reviewers' comments not to use Analysis of Variance, or God forbid, Analysis of Covariance (*de facto* a much richer method than regression), because the readers in finance are used to multivariate regression. Never mind that either one of the two other methods would have been both more revealing and more informative.

In another occasion I was totally frustrated in dealing with a reviewer who wanted an event study where there was no logic, excuse, or place for one. His reason: everyone was doing event studies.

But the documented proof I have with respect to this claim is, again, the earlier reference to my experience with the *Journal of Finance*. It was no coincidence that the paper was lost for two years by the editor-reviewer combo. In this paper we applied the method of random coefficients regression that was just then developed by Swamy, a gifted econometrician, under whom I studied in Buffalo. The new editor sent the paper to Barr Rosenberg who appreciated the fitting of the method to the problem and recommended prompt publication. However, the editor asked us to thank Barr by name in our acknowledgments, to which request we merrily obliged. Although he was the editor of the journal, he needed the official stamp of approval of a leading figure in order to publish a paper that invoked a yet uncommon method of analysis.

Then, luckily, QLINLB has its flip side as well. Once the door is open, then everyone is welcomed to follow, whether the method is appropriate or not. The deluge of event studies and cointegrations, whether needed or not, bear out my contention. So, be an early follower, and may the gods smile on you!

D. Reviewers

You can't step twice into the same river. — Heraclitus
Yes, you can. — George M. Frankfurter

In general, reviewers fall into three categories:

(1) The good;
(2) The bad; and
(3) The ugly.

One may find a more specific and apt taxonomy, in which the three major groups of the species are divided into further subspecies. Nevertheless, in the interest of economy and simplicity, I will concentrate on the three outlined above.

1. *The good reviewer*

The good reviewer is one that reads the article carefully, and then provides an "honest" opinion. Honest in this context means unprejudiced, divorced from the reviewer's own religious beliefs. For example, suppose that the reviewer is a firm believer of the notion that agency theory solves all problems in financial economics, and will solve even those that have not yet been stated. The article under review is, however, very critical of some aspects of agency theory's way of financial thinking. Nevertheless, the work has its own academic merits, together with some shortcomings. The good reviewer will not use these shortcomings to disqualify the article, or even to daunt the writer from making further amelioration of the work. A good reviewer, thus, has professional and human qualities that are rarely found; he is the member of a small subset of an elite group.

A young writer may never come across a good reviewer at the start of his career. The place to find such a person is at the better journals. This, of course, does not mean that all or most of the reviewers of better journals are good. Quite the opposite! One may often find a reviewer at a better journal who is professionally well-qualified, yet clearly flunks the test on human qualities. Nevertheless, the odds of being evaluated by a good reviewer are in favor of the better journals.

2. *The bad reviewer*

The bad reviewer may or may not be professionally qualified. But this minor detail does not matter at all, since this reviewer does not read carefully the article, because of predisposition, disinterest, or absolute laziness. All this reviewer wants to accomplish is to write something that will look intelligent in the eyes of the editor, yet bad enough to prevent the article's publication.

Of course, if all editors would read the reviews carefully and perhaps also read the paper *after* the review, the deck would be stacked somewhat against the bad reviewer. I say "somewhat," because no one would expect editors to be equally knowledgeable in every subject of the field. Accordingly, bad reviewers would still slip by. Nevertheless, editors do not read the article if the reviewer recommends rejection, and many read only the rejection recommendation and not the review itself.

Unfortunately, the system works in favor of the bad reviewer. Journal space is limited and the risk to the editor to publish a bad or mediocre paper is considerably higher than based on the reviewer's recommendation to reject a fairly decent one. One should also remember that articles do not carry with them their history. We do not know how many and what journals rejected the paper before it finally got published. As an accomplished author in the field remarked: the *Journal of Finance* would have had a perfect record of missing all the seminal papers if it were not for Markowitz's "Portfolio Selection."

Of course, the system of multiple reviews should theoretically reduce, if not totally eliminate, the existence of the bad reviewer. In practice, however, nothing is farther from the truth. The likelihood of "pulling a pair" of bad readers is quite high (especially at lower-level journals). Editors tend to reject articles, even if just one of the critics suggests rejection (and the other one is just mildly favorable). Also, many good reviewers can be bad reviewers some of the time.

There should be no place for bad reviewers in our (or for that matter in any) profession. Naturally, it is the duty of an editor to "weed out" bad reviewers. In practicality, this is not the case. I know of no editor today who has made the improvement of the reviewing process the primary policy matter of his journal.

3. *The ugly reviewer*

The ugly reviewer comes in many forms and shapes. In general, however, it is a small and insecure person, who is suddenly called upon to cast judgment on someone else's work (which is more often than not superior to the reviewer's own work). This fete is a great chance to control the life of someone else, an opportunity that may never present itself again. The goal of this reviewer is to crush and devastate the author, possibly to the point where the writer of the article will never try to write another paper again.

One has to remember that after the premiere of Sergei Rachmaninoff's second piano concerto, the composer, upon reading the critiques, was hospitalized with nervous breakdown for two years. I know of no such case in the finance profession, possibly because most in the field are less sensitive and emotionally vulnerable than a musician, and not because of reviews of works being less acrid.

The lesson to be learned is that one should immunize oneself from the bad side effects of such a review. This is conceivable if one does good work and has a strong belief in one's own ability. In such cases, the young faculty has to write on their foreheads (or, alternatively, tattoo it to their brains) that in spite of the review, they are right and the rest of the world is wrong. With these qualifications and attitude, one can rest assured that, eventually, the work will get published. At this juncture, what I suggest to remember is that it took Auguste Rodin, arguably the greatest sculptor of the 20th century, 30 years to get his work accepted by a French museum. Thus, we are not alone.

I have heard mediocre professors bragging about the fact that they never, ever recommended a paper for publication whenever they were called upon the duty of reviewing someone else's work. God is my witness that I have seen many bad papers both as an editor and as a reviewer, but I also have come across quite a few papers that were either outright publishable, or publishable with some help.

E. Suggestions for Improvements and Conclusions

> The ultimate truth is penultimately always a falsehood. He who will be proved right in the end appears to be wrong and harmful before it.
>
> — Arthur Koestler *Darkness at Noon*

I have been working on this paper on-and-off for quite some time. The impetus to write this bagatelle has been my belief that I had seen every review. As the work progressed and as I got back more commentaries about my work, I realized that I was dead wrong. Each time there is another twist on and a new reason to be mad about the process. Yet, I cannot suggest an alternative. If one wants to be productive, there is no other way but to fight the system from within.

My goal was to provide practical advice to young faculty from a professional lifetime's experience and not to criticize the reviewing process. Nevertheless, such criticism is inescapable, and the conclusion must be reached that something is wrong with the way we disseminate knowledge. Thus, unless steps are taken to improve our ways of communication, the very purpose of academic writing is in question.

As I have argued elsewhere, the basic problem is the connection between promotion and tenure and a publication record. That is, the gauging of one's academic quality and productivity with the number of articles one has published in journals of "recognized" rigor. It is almost guaranteed that such connection is neither for the benefit of growth of scientific knowledge, nor is it a proper gauge of intellectual excellence.

In a recent article, McGoun and Skubic (2000) emphasize this concern:

> This also has implications for us as researchers. The mind has evolved to find order, and does so even where there is none. Coupled with the tendency to structure statistical tests themselves in forms predisposed to finding significance, we must question whether what we think we have found in our empirical research is really there. And because the memory encoding process; that is, the way in which we impose order upon our perceptions, is itself a consequence of our preexisting memories, once we are conditioned to look at things from a certain point of view, we are literally unable, not simply disinclined, to look at them in any other. We have a built-in intellectual conservatism inclining us to immunize our cherished theories against refutation, and we must admit this and make determined efforts to counteract it (p. 20).

In their paper, McGoun and Skubic argue, and rather convincingly, that when we interpret the behavioral finance literature correctly,[60] we have not freed ourselves from "built-in intellectual conservatism." So, the most convincing challenge that has been mounted against the ruling paradigm of finance is just a minor detour by way of assumptions and not a cardinal departure from both method and methodology. This is the direct result of the connection of promotion and tenure's output requirements and a reviewing process that favors the orthodox thinking.

---

[60] And not just lump into it papers that find the CAPM/EMH inconsistent with empirical evidence, as Fama (1998) does, calling it the "anomalies literature."

A substitute must be found therefore to separate the objectives of growth of knowledge and the measure of academic excellence. One possibility, although at first might sound paradoxical, is to limit output to a fixed number. Say, starting faculty will get 10 coupons of publishing, and they must give up a coupon each time their work is accepted by a predetermined list of journals. Of course, coupons could be bought and sold in an auction market, as to provide for the needs of both productive and unproductive faculty. After the coupons are used up, work can be published only in books, where the decision to accept such effort will rest with a publisher specializing in treatises.

Yet, until this happens (if it happens), careers have to be made, and thus, one cannot wait for a miracle. If this paper proves to be some help for finance faculty at the beginning of their academic lifecycle, then my goal has been achieved. If not, the reader is welcome to write a bad review and send it to me through electronic mail. My e-mail address is pitypalaty@cox.net

References

Fama, Eugene F. 1998. "Market Efficiency, Long-Term Returns, and Behavioral Finance." *Journal of Financial Economics* 49: 283–306.

Longino, Helen. 1990. *Science as Social Knowledge: Values and Objectivity in Scientific Inquiry*. Princeton, New Jersey: Princeton University Press.

McGoun, Elton G. and Tatjana Skubic. 2000. "Beyond Behavioral Finance." *Journal of Psychology and Financial Markets* 1: 135–144.

Reiter, Sara Ann and Paul F. Williams. 2002. "Scientific Conversations in Financial Economics." In *From Individualism to the Individual: Ideology and Inquiry in Finance*, edited by George M. Frankfurter and Elton G. McGoun. Hants, UK: Ashgate Publishing.

Strassmann, Diana L. 1993. "The Stories of Economics and the Power of the Storyteller." *History of Political Economy* 25: 148–165.

———. 1994. "Feminist Thought and Economics: Or, What Do the Visigoths Know?" *American Economic Review* 84: 153–158.

Strassmann, Diana L. and Livia Polanyi. 1992. "Shifting the Paradigm: Value in Feminist Critiques of Economics." Working Paper, Rice University.

Chapter 5

Prolific Authors in Finance[*]

To be absolutely frank, I came across the Heck and Cooley (2005) (HC, subsequently) paper, titled "Prolific Authors in the Finance Literature: A Half Century of Contributions," unintentionally, and by coincidence. I do not read the *Journal of Finance Literature*, and I found the paper on the internet, because it came up with a reference to my name.

The stated objective of HC is the updating of Heck and Cooley (1988). Thus, there is no attempt of evaluating the real-substance contribution of the most prolific to the field of finance by the massive production of journal papers of these "most prolific" authors. It is rather, as they state in their abstract (*ibid.*, p. 40), the demonstration of the durability of the authors listed by name and rank-ordered in the appendix in "navigating the vagaries of referees and the demand of editors." I find this illumination a bit (perhaps unintentionally) cynical. A much more direct, albeit cruder, *bon ton* I used to hear repeatedly at the start of my academic career was: "The use of complex mathematics was to confuse the reviewer into accepting the paper."

The first of finance authoring compilation was by Heck and Cooley (1988). So the current paper was (kind of) long overdue. I remember meeting Jean once or twice a year during the 1990s. In those occasions I nagged him for a follow-up to the Heck and Cooley (1988) paper. My reasoning was that quite a few new journals had joined the public domain within which we communicated, and in which the important process of growth of scientific knowledge must take place. Jean dismissed my overtures saying that he did not have the desire to do it. I am glad that Jean and Phil did it this year, and their present effort should be welcomed.

The data HC collected for the paper are massive (and I am sure they may serve as an inexhaustible source of valuable information): in 72 finance journals — 17,573 are the authors of 29,717 articles published from 1953

* The original version of this paper was published in *The Journal of Investing*, 2005, Volume 14 (Winter): 5–8. The paper here has undergone minor editing and is reprinted with the *Journal*'s permission.

to 2002, an even half century. An average of 20 pages of text and tables per article, as a reasonable first approximation, would amount to a staggering half a-million plus journal pages. Nevertheless, as HC make it clear, this volume is no reflection on quality, nor is it a yardstick of the scientific growth that might distinguish finance as a field of science.

Also, the numbers should be taken with the understanding that many of the one- or two-article authors are freshly minted Ph.D.'s who are still struggling to publish a few papers from their dissertation. Then, there are authors whose field is not finance, but might have co-authored a paper with someone whose primary bailiwick is finance. And some left the profession either by natural attrition or in seek of greener pastures. When all this is taken into consideration, the number of authors would be significantly reduced.

Let us just say that 9,000 professionals have been the core cadre of finance as it is taught in B-Schools. The authors at the top of the coveted seven journals of the field represent just 0.55 percent (yes, percent) of the 9,000 I assumed. To get to that list, one had to publish better than with three or more co-authors, because the adjusted number (sharing equal credit for a "hit" and dividing it by the number of authors) had to be more than 11.33.

HC decided to stick, nevertheless, to some basic compilation and some explanation preceding the four exhibits which are the critical mass of their anthology. Exhibits 1, 3 and 4 include by-name listing of authors in seven, 16 and 72 finance journals who had at least nine, 14 and 18 papers, respectively, in these journals. Accordingly, there are: ". . . 332 prolific authors in seven leading finance journals, 350 prolific authors in sixteen core finance journals, and 367 prolific authors in all of the 72 journals. . ." (HC, p. 40) listed by name. The "meat and potato" segment of the appendix is clearly Exhibit 2, where the Panels A–C are the top 50 names, adjusted for multiple authorship,[61] of the three categories of the seven, 16 and 72 journals, respectively.

Perhaps using some basic compilation by others is for the better, because this way HC can keep themselves above scorn and criticism. I, nevertheless, am not so constrained, being in the enviable position of retirement. If I learned one thing from my academic experience of 30 plus years, that is to live with criticism and rejection. Thus, I feel free to make some observations apropos to what I see in the four appendices of HC.

---

[61] More about adjustment later.

When it comes to growth of scientific knowledge (see Popper, 1979), I would be in dire straights if I had to name 10 articles in finance. Perhaps not everyone would agree with my list, but I would be very much surprised if someone else's alternative assemblage looked much different than the following papers:

- Markowitz's portfolio selection (Markowitz, 1952)[62]
- Modigliani and Miller's irrelevance of capital structure (Modigliani and Miller, 1958)
- Miller and Modigliani's irrelevance of dividends (Miller and Modigliani, 1961)
- Sharpe's CAPM (Sharpe, 1964)
- Fama's efficient markets (Fama, 1965, 1970)
- Black and Scholes' and Merton's option pricing (Black and Scholes, 1973; Merton, 1973)
- Jensen and Meckling's agency theory (Jensen and Meckling, 1976)[63]

Because Modigliani and Miller already had in mind the second irrelevance paper when the first was published, and one cannot stand without the other, I consider the two papers as one effort. Thus, my list is just five works.

I am sure some would add market micro-structure too, but I am not so certain that it was a primary contribution. The thought-provoking thing is that out of the six Nobel Prize winners authoring the papers I mention, only Merton and Sharpe (49th) make the cut in the nifty fifty that is Panel A of Exhibit 2 in HC. Of course, Fischer Black would have made it too, but sadly, the Prize is not awarded posthumously. Merton Miller is named only in Panel C of Exhibit 2 (*ibid.*).[64]

---

[62] This paper is not credited to Markowitz by HC, because it is before their lower bound year of 1953.

[63] I consider signaling and free-cash flows just an outcrop (and not a too glorious one, either) of the agency theory literature. Signaling caught on because of the seminal paper of Michael Spence, "Job Market Signaling," *The Quarterly Journal of Economics* 87 (1973) that created the foundations of behavioral economics and for which the author shared the Nobel Prize in economics in 2001. The job market signaling modeled by Spence was in no way comparable to the different signaling scenarios that were presupposed in the finance literature, grossly violating Spence's model assumptions.

[64] Modigliani never makes the cut, because Franco's *oeuvre* was hardly in financial economics or core finance journals *per se*.

The rest of the finance literature is repackaging the truly seminal works I cited — hundreds, possibly thousands of even studies, or simply imitating knowingly, or unknowingly. Imitation is not a bad thing. A Paul Gaugin scholar once argued that imitation is the highest form of flattery. Nevertheless, when one imitates oneself by repeating the same study with different data or different models or both, it is more the sort of research that is for publishing sake.[65]

Thus, volume is not necessarily equal to accomplishment or progress. It seems, in fact, that publishing is the name of the game and not as HC argue that "*Publish or perish* [their italics] may be a hyperbole, but it still conveys a simple cogent message to academicians." If this contention were true, we would not have 10,275 (okay, 9,000 minus the most prolific) authors who published just one article in 72 core journals!

I believe the truth to be quite the opposite. It is *publish and publish* for the sake of building up a lucrative career. I would strongly contend that this "paper chase" is not necessarily what is good for the growth of scientific knowledge. May I just mention that Markowitz, who single-handedly created modern finance (the amalgam of scientific methods and an axiomatic principle), never makes any panel of HC's Exhibit 2. Perhaps this should be construed as an extra feather in Harry's cap (not that he needed one).

Despite the entire half a-million plus pages, we still do not know too much about the cost of capital, and capital structure. Dividends and dividend policy puzzles are yet to be solved. We have no idea whether markets are efficient or not, or whether we care at all beyond the ideological and evangelical meaning of market efficiency: leave the market alone to the mischief of those who manipulate it, and to rob those who are naïve enough to believe the pundits.

Arbitrage, the *deus ex machina*[66] of the two irrelevance theories and the relatively short-lived arbitrage pricing theory, has never been shown to exist in the real world, what we call "out there" and what is supposed to be the only justifying existence of academic finance.

Does anyone still remember stochastic dominance? Quite a few authors did very well in publishing papers about a concept that empirically was neither provable nor useful as a normative theory. But this is okay, because every science, even pseudo-science, has its false starts.

---

[65] I have found some authors who published the same idea, in the same year, using the same data in two different journals with diametrically opposing conclusions.

[66] God from the machinery, to "explain" the otherwise unexplainable.

Fama (1998) still calls behavioral finance that might develop into an alternative paradigm "the anomalies literature" (*ibid.*) in an effort to nip it before it has a chance to bud. And agency theory has the answer to everything and to nothing.

Although HC are quite circumspect to qualify that they do not cast judgment about quality and rather use others' work to group into the three groups of the magnificent seven, the sweet 16 and the 72 "all finance journals," one like myself, who spent an academic lifetime in the profession, notice two distinct undercurrents:

- Just 19 of those included in Panel A of Exhibit 2 are not in Panel B, and just eight authors in Panel C of the Exhibit are not in either Panel A or C. So this is a very "tight" grouping no matter how one broadens the including set.[67]
- Quite a few members of the three panels are, or were at some point of time, editors/associate editors or members of the Board of Editors of the respective journals where they are grouped.

Albeit my experience is anecdotal, and anything anecdotal, i.e., supported only by common sense and not by massive volumes of market data squeezed into mathematics, is frowned upon by true researchers. I can safely argue that I was not too lucky with papers asking the "*Quo Vadis*"[68] question. When I presented these papers at meetings, the unequivocal response of the audience was that going with this material to the so-called leading journals of the field was an exercise in futility.

My friends and colleagues argued that the proverbial camel will pass through the eye of the needle before the top outlets of the field will publish a paper that critically examines the methodology (the ontology and epistemology) of the profession. Indeed, those were great words of wisdom, as I learned when I did not heed the warning.

I was much luckier with journals that are designated as the 72 core journals and even luckier with some that are not in any of the three panels of Exhibit 2. Does this say anything about quality? I am not sure, because I find some in the 16 journal group I do not consider particularly rigorous as I find many in the 72 group, also.

---

[67] If one eliminates authors who are either not with the profession anymore, or are inactive for the last 20 or so years, the number of appearances in Panel A is further reduced.

[68] "Where are you going?" the Lord asked Peter on his way to Damascus.

Yet no progress in science, what I call discovery — the search for truth — can come when work that Cooley (1994) defined as *metafinance*[69] is not published in the perceived leading journals of the profession. In the words of one of my anonymous reviewers at the *Journal of Finance*: "An unexamined profession is not worth practicing." This was a clever twist on Socrates,[70] who was given the alternative by the good burghers of Athens to voluntarily drink hemlock, or to be put to death (and not by lethal injection either, but by a much more drastic method) because of poisoning the minds of young people. To make the paraphrasing and metaphor work to perfection, naturally, the reviewer rejected my paper.

We are but our past experiences. Consequently, what I learn from HC reflects on my life as an academic. I submit that someone else might have learned a different lesson or nothing at all. For whatever it might be worth, here are my final thoughts about "what is seen and what is not seen"[71] in HC.

Many years ago, over a glass of some brew (I am not sure what exactly the libation was), I jokingly suggested to my then colleague, Bill Lane, the awarding of 10 certificates to each newly anointed Ph.D. Each time the chap had a paper accepted in journals we consider to be of academic stature (and the list can be updated every year), the aspiring faculty must surrender one certificate. Of course, if one wanted to write in journals that were not included in the list, or God forbid, books, where a more complete expression of ideas and theses can be brought to public attention, one can do it. In such case, this effort would not count toward promotion and/or tenure.

If, however, the faculty was hell-bent on doing research and publishing papers that were limited by space availability and restrained to the passing fancy of referees, then such researchers could buy, in an open market, certificates from other Ph.D.'s who either did not have the drive or the talent for doing such work. Let the market rule the academic scene, and as we already have a market for corporate control, why not a

---

[69] In Cooley's (1994) definition, metafinance is "the nature, structure, and behavior of finance."(?). Forgive my fussiness, but fields of science do not behave — people or animals do.

[70] An unexamined life is not worth living. Attributed also to Plato.

[71] I confess I borrowed the phrase from Claude-Frédéric Bastiat.

market for promotion and tenure? The idea was a lunacy and, obviously, a joke, but Bill and I spent an afternoon escaping the terribly boring presentation of one of the profession's prime meetings by discussing fascinating possibilities.

Looking back on the 50-year production of finance, perhaps our "modest proposal," if adopted, would have solved some of the major issues of the field, or at least would have come closer to what one considers truth, with perhaps 15,000 papers instead of 29,717 (which did not bring us closer to the truth). In the good old days of normative theory making, we would have called this Occam's razor, or efficiency, compared to what we actually accomplished. And is it not efficiency the religion we worship at no ends?

References

Black, Fischer and Myron Scholes. 1973. "The Pricing of Options and Corporate Liabilities." *Journal of Political Economy* 81: 637–654.

Cooley, Philip L. 1994. "Survival Strategies for the Fledging Finance Professor." *Financial Practice and Education* 4: 8–17.

Fama, Eugene F. 1965. "The Behavior of Stock Market Prices." *Journal of Business* 38: 34–105.

———. 1970. "Efficient Capital Markets: A Review of Theory and Empirical Work." *Journal of Finance* 25: 383–417.

———. 1998. "Market Efficiency, Long-Term Returns, and Behavioral Finance." *Journal of Financial Economics* 49: 283–306.

Heck, Jean and Philip L. Cooley. 1988. "Most Frequent Contributors to Finance Literature." *Financial Management* 17: 100–108.

———. 2005. "Prolific Authors in the Finance Literature: A Half Century of Contributions." *Journal of Finance Literature* Winter 2005: 40–47.

Jensen, Michael C. and William H. Meckling. 1976. "Theory of the Firm: Managerial Behavior, Agency Costs and Ownership Structure." *Journal of Financial Economics* 3: 305–360.

Markowitz, Harry M. 1952. "Portfolio Selection." *Journal of Finance* 7: 77–91.

Merton, Robert C. 1973. "Theory of Rational Option Pricing." *Bell Journal of Economics* Spring: 183–242.

Miller, Merton H. and Franco Modigliani. 1961. "Dividend Policy, Growth and the Valuation of Shares." *Journal of Business* 34: 411–433.

Modigliani, Franco and Merton H. Miller. 1958. "The Cost of Capital, Corporation Finance, and the Theory of Investment." *American Economic Review* 48: 261–297.

Popper, Karl R. 1979. *Truth, Rationality, and the Growth of Scientific Knowledge.* Frankfurt am Main: Klostermann.

Sharpe, William F. 1964. "Capital Market Prices: A Theory of Market Equilibrium under Conditions of Risk." *Journal of Finance* 14: 425–442.

Spence, Michael. 1973. "Job Market Signaling." *The Quarterly Journal of Economics* 87: 355–374.

Chapter 6

For-Profit Education: An Idea That Should be Put to Rest?

Edward Wyatt of the *New York Times* wire service recently quoted Michael Milken of the junk bond calamity fame. Milken was said to bully the president of Teachers College of Columbia University that Milken's Knowledge Universe, a for-profit educational enterprise, will "eat alive" the not-for-profit private institution. Milken? Wasn't he dying from prostate cancer just after he was sentenced in criminal court and facing suits amounting to $3 billion in civil courts? If he was, thank God he is recovering, at least to the point that he is able to turn his predatory talents towards education, the latest public good to be ripe for new age entrepreneurs.

Milken is not alone. ¡LAMAR! Alexander — yes, the two-time presidential aspirant, who used to play the piano in plaid flannel shirts[72] to show his down-to-earthiness — has become the latest imitator of his friend and mentor, Chris Whittle. Whittle's Edison Schools were perhaps to first to create corporate automatons and docile consumers of mass marketing from grade through high school students as the newest product of the free markets. Not to be outdone, another former governor, William Weld, the ex-chief administrator of the Commonwealth of Massachusetts (and failed contender of the Mexican ambassadorship — I knew that Jesse Helms was trouble), is part of a group that is raising $150 million to invest in for-profit education.

A repeat of the healthcare debacle suggests Mr. Wyatt. It is far deeper than that, say I! The first time I learned about the educational forprofs was through an eye-opening piece, titled "HIGHER EDUCATION OR HIGHER PROFITS$," in *In These Times* (September 20, 1998), researched and written by Lawrence Soley of Marquette University. Soley sees grave danger in the separation of design and delivery of higher education, *de facto* the end of academic freedom. It means that course development and delivery are

---

[72] Mr. Alexander's television ads brought back memories of the Monty Python song, "I am a lumberjack and I'm okay, I work all night and sleep all day."

done by different entities. While development is at the hands of the notfor-prof, delivery is by cheap labor, more often than not people without a terminal degree (Ph.D.).

The usual sloganeering applies: privatize education because as a business enterprise, it is of higher quality than the faltering public system and is more efficient. The word "efficient" makes me recoil and feel very wary and suspicious, because more often than not, it puts a positive facade on a questionable proposition. This is one of these instances, because efficiency here translates to cost-cutting. "So what is so bad about cost-cutting?" one may ask. Well, let us do the numbers, as Lou Dobbs used to say.

According to Soley, the Apollo Group owns Western International University of Denver and the University of Phoenix, which enrols 49,000 degree-seeking students. Last year, enrolment at the University of Phoenix surpassed that of New York University, the nation's largest private, non-profit university. The University of Phoenix accepts 99 percent of applicants and is classified as "noncompetitive" by *Peterson's Guide to Four-Year Colleges*, meaning that "virtually all applicants are accepted regardless of high school rank or test scores."

To make its services more attractive to a working, over 23 years of age market (not the traditional student), the University of Phoenix schedules classes on a one night per week basis for six weeks. This is in contrast with 14 weeks, three contact hours per week of the usual notforprof university course. The "physical plant" is a store front and rented office space, off a highway ramp, for easy in and out access, but also to eliminate the exorbitant costs of the facilities of a legitimate university campus. Now, that is efficiency!

But this is not all. The forprofs do not have libraries, another bottomless pit of spending for any university with just a hint of self-respect, because without a decent and up-to-date library, neither students nor the faculty can grow. The cynical answer to the claim that without a suitable library there cannot be a proper university is that today libraries are far less critical than years ago, and besides, one would not have enough books for everyone, now would one? Is Harvard totally inefficient for spending $35 million a year on books?

Labor is also dirt cheap for the forprofs. Since adjunct lecturers masquerade for professors who do not lecture but "facilitate" — a euphemism for uncritical delivery of the course content designed and proscribed by the corporation — consequently, their wages are way below that of adjuncts in a notforprof university. As Soley remarks,

> Until two years ago, Phoenix had seven full-time and 3,400 part-time faculty. Because of questions raised by accreditors, the university increased the size of its full-time faculty. It now has 45 full-timers on board.[73]

There is no problem, then, with tenure, fringe benefits and regular salary increases to keep up with the rest of academe so retiring faculty could be replaced with newly minted Ph.D.'s coming out of decent programs, not to mention that the expenditure on research of the forprofs is exactly nil. Since the corporation pipes course content in, there is no need for and cannot be new accumulation of knowledge — the primary responsibility of an academic institution, private or public.

But this is just one side of "efficiency," the new age nice-nellyism for maximum profits. (Precisely, as "free markets" is a better-sounding idiom than capitalism. After all, what is free cannot be bad, now can it?) Well, here are Soley's numbers:

> For-profit universities, which sell themselves to students as bargains, actually charge higher tuition than most community colleges, state universities and some nonprofit private colleges. Tuition and fees at the University of Phoenix come to $6,500; Strayer University charges $8,100. In contrast, tuition and fees at state universities average about $2,500.

No wonder then those who got early into the game do well (they are efficient?).

> The profit growth of these companies comes from growth in enrolment, tuition increases and low labor and overhead costs. Between 1993 and 1997, Strayer nearly doubled its revenues, while its profits tripled. The Apollo Group did even better. Its revenues increased from $97 million to $283 million during the same period, but its net revenues or profits went from $1.1 million to $33.3 million (*ibid.*).

---

[73] The AACSB (American Assembly of Collegiate Schools of Business) requires the maintenance of a 60 percent terminal degree faculty rate, or else the school is put on probation, risking the revocation of accreditation.

As I argued at the start, education, like healthcare, is a public good. As such, for the interest of the society as a whole, it cannot be left to the marketplace, where the profit motive and the maximization of shareholders' wealth reign supreme. That is why the word "efficiency" is not just inappropriate, but also comes handy to camouflage a fraud — a deception perpetrated by those who are bent on making a profit by means that in the long-term might have dismal consequences for generations to come. So, although I agree with Mr. Wyatt's prophecy that forprof education will travel down the healthcare industry road, my ratiocination is different.

The demise of privatizing healthcare was not in the fact that as the HMO's grew, they had to increasingly cover the unhealthy members of society, as Mr. Wyatt claims. It has been a failure because the whole idea of the profit motive was, is and forever will be in a fundamental conflict with the Hippocratic oath. That is, as the primary deliverer of medical care, the physician's first responsibility is to the patient, and not to a profit center. In a roundabout way, it also goes against the basic tenet of free markets, because it enslaves labor in dead-end jobs (fearing the loss of health insurance), instead of moving to where it can get the highest return on its effort.

Similarly, education, at all levels, is a public good as well. Mary Burgan, general secretary to the AAUP (American Association of University Professors), writes this to prospective members of the professors' union:

> For one thing, we have been fractionalized by the erosion of tenure over the past ten years. Invoking the economics of downsizing both as a rationale for critique and as an excuse for practice, many institutions have systematically narrowed the range and security of faculty positions in higher education.

Because of that, untenured faculty are looked upon as academic entrepreneurs. Yet, the biggest danger of the erosion of tenure is erosion of academic freedom (the only reason for which it was hard-fought and achieved), because untenured faculty are at the whim of administrators. Thus, the pincer move on academic freedom is complete. Loss of academic freedom is tantamount of intellectual stagnation, the devastating consequences of which have to be born by future generations. That is why free markets cannot perform their usual function with respect to a public good. Perhaps better put: that is why a public good is different from a market good. And that does not bode too well with regards to our future as the intellectual leaders of the world.

So, what is the solution? The solution lays somewhere in the direction of licensing. The Association of Independent Colleges and Universities opposed Phoenix's request for a license in New Jersey on the grounds that they do not provide the same academic services (teach fewer hours, worse library facilities and too many part-time instructors). Accordingly the for-profs are not in compliance with state law. As usual, in the case of a public good, big, bad government has to step in and save us from the blessings of free markets. Until "markets" wake up, both our trading partners and competitors will surpass us, and we risk losing our hard-earned academic superiority achieved with academic freedom and massive spending on research.

Chapter 7

Weep Not for Microsoft: Monopoly's Fatal Exception

The words of A.J. Liebman, "The press is free for those who own it," usually ring true whenever one comes across third-rate or ideology-saturated journalism masquerading as objective analysis. But they are apropos as well when one stumbles into inane reporting. A case in point is a column written by one Mr. Paul Farhi for the *Washington Post* that the *International Herald Tribune* (November 11, 1999, p. 9) in its august wisdom cared also to share with its readers.[74]

In the column titled "Why Windows Is Like McDonald's," Farhi comes to Microsoft's defense that our big, bad government is picking on it for reasons big, bad governments pick on anyone that happens to become rich and successful in our free marketplace. In a pitiful effort to exculpate Microsoft from the charge of monopolizing the PC software business, this writer compares the software behemoth to McDonald's and Holiday Inn. On his way to his objective, Mr. Farhi succeeds to extol the virtues of the American psyche that under the deceiving surface of individualism, it strives, relentlessly, for the standard and standards.

Perhaps I start with my agreement with Mr. Farhi that Microsoft's WINDOWS is an inferior product. One of my students put it best when he said that WINDOWS is simple but bad. (I would have preferred the exposition "simply bad" but will settle for simple and bad, too.) This is my second point of agreement (that WINDOWS is simple) with the author of "Why Windows . . . , etc." But this is where we part course.

How on earth Mr. Farhi came to mass psychoanalysis and equate the manufacturer of software to the fast food and hotel business, respectively, is beyond my imagination. (He owns the press and thus his speech is free?) Indeed, McDonald's standardized its product, which created its success, but at the same time it did not limit the entrance of Burger King, Wendy's,

---

[74] The *Washington Post* and the *New York Times* conjointly own the *International Herald Tribune*. Thus, they serve as the fulcrum for leveraging overseas bad journalism.

Sonic and the half dozen chicken places, not to mention the pizza fast food chains, to that particular market. On the contrary, it established a standard for others to live up to. After all, it catered to the desire of the public not as much for standards, but for gobbling up fat and unhealthy food, which had to do with bad taste and an urban lifestyle. Yet, if one went to Burger King, one could have had it one's own way.

Neither did McDonald's require the purchaser of a big Mac to subscribe to its in-house recipe book at inflated prices, lest one is not allowed to bite into one single french fry. And no guest at the Holiday Inn was ever coerced to buy a lawn mower, or else one had to sleep under the king-size bed.

Have you tried to purchase lately a computer without either WINDOWS or WINDOWS NT? Moreover, if you have, say, PC-DOS on your computer and decide to load WINDOWS 95, 98, 2000, XP, and on and on,[75] it will destroy the better part of your DOS. So, in my opinion, Microsoft is a monopolist bundling a product that some, or many, neither like nor would want to pay for. Neither McDonald's nor Holiday Inn bundles anything with its product or service.

Farhi's claim that WINDOWS is the maestro of portability and compatibility is not exactly accurate, either. Every program that runs under DOS is portable to any computer running DOS. The reverse is not true with respect to WINDOWS, because not every DOS program runs under WINDOWS 95 and 98, and even fewer are compatible with NT or later versions of not NT WINDOWS. More often than not, one cannot figure out why.

But this is not all. WINDOWS did not just emerge in a wet dream of Mr. Gates. Both WINDOWS 2.0, and then 3.xx, were utterly useless imitations of Apple's — light years ahead of WINDOWS — operating systems. Then came WINDOWS 95, full of bugs, to be replaced by WINDOWS 98 that is not bug free, either. But while we, the users, complained about WINDOWS 95 going to La La Land at every other keystroke, and Microsoft fixed some of the obvious problems, we still had to pay full price for WINDOWS 98 that we helped to fix.

Imagine a Sunbeam toaster is the only toaster on the market, which one day toasts and the next day does not for no apparent reason. You send it back to the service center designated on the warranty card. You get, in return, a postcard from Sunbeam telling you that based on your complaint

---

[75] Each successive WINDOWS is in fact getting a fix on some of the bugs that have been written in earlier editions, in addition to preserving the monopoly power of Microsoft. This has been the cleverest and most sinister way ever invented by a monopolist to make the consumer pay for defects in its product.

they now have a better toaster, but you have to pay full price for it or else you get the old one back, unrepaired. So, Microsoft was neither innovative, as many argue without really considering its history, nor did it live up to minimum product warranty standards.

Sharing with you my nightmares with either WINDOWS 95 or 98 would fill a small brochure. But there is one story I want to get off my chest. After WINDOWS 95, I yielded to my own curiosity and the hope that WINDOWS 98 would have less or perhaps no bugs, and I bought the upgrade. Indeed, it seemed that I had less problems, until I had to reformat my hard disk. Unfortunately, my WINDOWS 98-based tape backup system failed to restore a full hard drive backup. So, I started with restoring with WINDOWS 98.

"Not so fast," the operating system informed me. "This is an upgrade, and you cannot install me from scratch." So, I went back to WINDOWS 95, and after installing it, again, I loaded WINDOWS 98 on top of it. Everything was going well, until I found out that some of the device drivers originally loaded under 95 were shut dead! The biggest problem was the driver for my HP scanner. After hours of trying to select the driver from WINDOWS or the original setup disk I received from HP without success, I called HP's technical support for a $25 consultation (because the scanner was out of its one-year warranty).

The HP support person informed me that I was in luck, because I could get from them the new driver that would work under WINDOWS 98 for just the cost of shipping. Needless to say, the new driver did not work according to its own installation instruction, and it took another $25 call to HP to get matters straightened out. Yet, the actual out-of-pocket costs in this case are dwarfed by the loss of productive hours I had to spend to fix the problem. My monitor is still not recognized by its name, but as generic, giving me less than its full potential.

On another unrelated occasion, I spent one hour with a Microsoft technical support person on the phone (a call for which I had to pay, under warranty!), who for all I know could have been in Calcutta, without ever solving my problem. Finally, I gave up, because life with a PC is full of compromises. It was either live with a puzzle, or spend untold number of hours dawdling in the maze of voice mail.

And, pray tell, how many times I got to the point where my screen came up with the message:

```
AN UNEXPECTED ERROR OCCURRED AT LOCATION E0, etc.
```

after which I could hit any key, or Ctrl+Alt+Del. This, for no known, at least to me, reason, as I did not do anything different when the message appeared. At this juncture I could hit any key which activity turned the screen black, or try the cold boot key combination, which either worked, rebooting the system, or else the system froze more than the inventory at a sperm bank. This kind of system freeze could have never happened with the Apple operating system.[76]

But this is just the tip of the monopoly iceberg. Microsoft became the manufacturer of the (practically) only operating system, force-fed to us, and at the same time the maker of major applications (word processor and spreadsheet). Accordingly, they have a year or year-and-a-half lead time, which in the software business is equal to a lifetime. That is how they replaced the lead of WORDPERFECT, clearly a superior product, with WORD. Ditto, LOTUS 1-2-3 with EXCEL. This is monopoly power, and this why I have my government and anti-trust laws to stop it for the welfare of society as a whole. It is wise for us to heed Adam Smith's idea that:

> It is not from the benevolence of the butcher, the brewer, or the baker that we expect our dinner, but from their regard to their own interest (*Wealth of Nations*, Book I, Ch. II, p. 11).

The endorsement of the benefits of self-interested behavior depends, crucially, on the existence of competition. Competition is precisely what monopolists try to allay. And when and if they are successful, it is the duty of our government to interfere. This is so, because competition is at the very basis of what we call the "free market system."

With all the hues and cries to save it from a cruel and unappreciative government, I doubt that any real economic harm will come to Microsoft. After all, it contributes, and rather generously, to both political parties. When the dust settles, my bet is that Gates and Co. will get off with a *slapchik* (a tiny slap) on the wrist, or nothing at all. In the meantime, my WINDOWS 98, the only operating system authored by Microsoft I am willing to pay for again, is shutting down whenever it feels like it. The reason: an illegal operation was attempted (by whom, for God's sake).

---

[76] Not that Apple, even if it was more widely spread, or even Linux, would have made a great deal of difference. Instead of a totally uncontrolled monopoly, we would have had an oligopoly on our hands. That is exactly why we need laws and the enforcement of laws so the oligopolists cannot take advantage of the market.

And what do you know? An appeals court overturned Judge Jackson's decision that would have required the breakup of Microsoft Operating Systems and Microsoft Applications, a first obvious move in the direction of reducing raw monopoly power. The government could not fight the battery of high-priced lawyers Microsoft could throw in the legal battle. When I hear next time, in connection with the death penalty given to an innocent man who could not pay for the right legal representation, that in spite of occasional mistakes the system is working, I will remember Microsoft as well.

Reference

Smith, Adam. 1937. *The Wealth of Nations.* New York: Random House.

Chapter 8

The Socio-Economics of Scandals[*]

The Arthur Andersen partner was on the phone when he said,
"Ship the Enron documents to the feds."
But his secretary heard,
"Rip the Enron documents to shreds."
It turns out that it was just a case of bad cellular.
SPRINT PCS The clear alternative to cellular[SM]

— Advertisement

A. To Set the Stage . . .

In the March 29, 1996 issue of the *Wall Street Journal*, Jensen and Fagan (1996) (JF, subsequently) assure the reader that capitalism is not broken. The opening paragraph sets the tone for what follows:

> AT&T is a sick company, and CEO Robert Allen is a courageous man for trying to fix it. AT&T's announced breakup into three companies and the layoff of 40,000 people is the beginning, not the end, of a difficult, painful process. If the company is not fixed, most of its current 300,000 employees will be out of a job over the next decade or so. AT&T is not alone in this challenge.

Sure enough, Allen "saved" sick AT&T. Allen the Savior exercised his stock options right after the market responded favorably to his divine intervention and earned a miraculous $20 million for his "trouble."[77] We heard nothing about the fate of the multitude — i.e., the 40,000 painfully downsized employees — nor any guess as to what the loss of their livelihood cost society as a whole.

---

* The original version of this paper was published in *Homo Oeconomicus*, 2002, Volume 19(2): 257–267.

[77] Another icon of Wall Street, Warren Buffett, argued that if the firm were managed properly, there would be no need to downsize it in the first place.

This made-to-order article is transparent in its attempt to play up to the readers of the *Journal*, but there is a hidden agenda here as well. The darker purpose is to attack Pat Buchanan, then a third-party presidential candidate. Buchanan's mortal sin is that he had become a socialist — a *national* socialist, to be exact. The reader is quickly given to understand that Mr. Buchanan's "national" bent is the least of JF's worries. And so, it would appear, are Mr. Buchanan's racism, anti-Semitism, homophobia, xenophobia, and his views on abortion and the NRA. These, apparently, are venial transgressions. What JF truly cannot forgive is Buchanan's "socialism."

According to JF, socialism (or communism, for that matter) is passé. They view the collapse of the Soviet Union not as the demise of a corrupt, repressive and inefficient *administration*, but as proof-positive that socialism as a *system* is dead. I will not burden the reader with examples to the contrary from both past and present, nor comment on the historical inaccuracies and revisionism in JF's text. These exercises are best left to historians, who, perhaps in a century or two, may decide, if the world is still turning, whether we had a third industrial revolution and, if so, whether it started June 13, 1973, at 2:30 p.m., Chicago time.

The gospel according to JF, however, proclaims that a third industrial revolution is indeed underway, and posits both proverb and parable to comfort the poor. Proverb #1: Putting multitudes of workers on the street is a painful, yet inevitable, fact of the revolution. Parable #1: Like grain before the scythe, workers mown down in the revolution provide seeds that in future will bear fruit for the benefit of their progeny. In other words, unemployed workers should suffer their fate with glad hearts, knowing that their children may live a better life 30 years down the road.

Though it be heresy, I say that JF are false prophets. What they call the third industrial revolution is nothing more than a conspiratorial doctrine devised by corporate America to redistribute income from the "have-nots" to the "haves." Their purpose is to ensure that the top 2 percent of the population will receive an increasingly larger share of the wealth, both in real and nominal terms, at the grievous expense of the rest of us. This scheme has many synonyms, among which "globalization," "free markets," "information/new age," and the "new world order" are the most popular and the least offensive to our senses.

Mr. Buchanan's mortal sin, according to JF, is that he trumpets the resentment of the "have-nots" — and the multitudinous middle-class in danger of becoming so — and, in so doing, foments class warfare. To JF,

Buchanan's effrontery is tantamount to inciting the working masses to revolt against this new order. Whenever the "have-nots" unite in opposition to income reallocation, the "haves" cry out with one voice, "Class warfare! Class warfare!" — the equivalent of a technical in basketball.

B. Are Markets Free or What?

But let us return to the gospel according to JF. Downsizing, they preach, is *good* for America. "Downsizing," of course, is a devilishly clever term for the massive layoff of wage and salaried workers. It is an act calculated to goad the stock market to a quick price increase, thereby creating inflated, short-term accounting profits that accrue gloriously (and lucratively) to those at the helm.

If we are to believe JF, however, when the CEO of AT&T orders downsizing, he is "fighting" for the "life" of the company, not for the glory or monetary benefit of management. Right. His blood and tears are all over every dollar he pockets from the transaction.

That was then. But what is now? Now it is Enron, the energy giant in bankruptcy, sprawled coyly atop a dozen or so congressional committees and subcommittees, flirting with full, frontal exposure. It is something of a spectacle, given that about half of the 535 members of Congress received campaign contributions from Enron (yes, it was *that* kind of power company), and are now seemingly astounded to learn that deregulated corporations cannot always be trusted to police themselves after all. Who would have guessed? Half of Enron's top executives — having spent years claiming to spin straw into gold (Rumpelstiltskins that did not possess any straw to begin with) — now insist they have "no recollection" of either straw or gold, nor any inkling of what either term could mean. The other half are "Fifth Amendment Capitalists" (to borrow a term from Daniel Shorr, senior political correspondent of National Public Radio). Shorr paraphrases the late Senator Joseph McCarthy, who, half a century ago, called the witnesses who took the Fifth Amendment before his committee on un-American activities "Fifth Amendment Communists."

The third half, mostly women executives who never saw light above the glass ceiling, are telling what they know — as little as it is — about what the good old boys were up to in the boardroom and their own lofty sanctums. The dirtiest laundry thus far is the role of the public accounting firm, Arthur Andersen (as of this writing, just Andersen), which not only turned a blind eye to the firm's "aggressive accounting practices," but also soiled its hands with the destruction of evidence, *de facto* obstructing justice, a felony by all counts. Now, this may not be the third industrial revolution, but it is certainly revolting.

With each new scandal, there is a tendency — particularly in the media — to draw comparisons. Hence, Enron is today's Watergate, Iran-Contra or Whitewatergate. These comparisons heighten the importance of unfolding events, dramatizing the magnitude of the crisis for the apathetic multitudes who are loath to pay attention at all until two or more of the miscreants are found together in bed or in an out-of-the-way closet. (Movie, rated X for sex, will follow shortly.)

For the most part, of course, these comparisons are meaningless. The Enron debacle, for example, is not Clintonesque. There is no evidence (yet) that anyone from Enron paid to sleep in the Lincoln bedroom. And though it appears that the company simultaneously screwed its entire workforce *and* thousands of investors (an admirable feat under capitalism), there is not a shred of evidence that anyone had sex with an intern (an impeachable offense if one does it just for the hell of it, without monetary gain). The Enron cesspool makes Whitewater look like a pure mountain stream, and a mere trickle of one at that.

Though mammoth, Enron is no Watergate or Iran-Contra either. Both of those crises were constitutional, striking at the foundation of a free republic. Enron, on the other hand, is a socio-economic catastrophe — an implosion of the house that greed built, injuring hundreds of thousands in the United States and the "global community" as its structure of cards cratered. So far, the only (and what a big "only") political aspect of the disaster is Enron's largesse to ranking members of both parties, the current occupant of *la Casa Blanca* (pssst . . . we dare not say White House), and, as rumor has it, even the royals of the UK.[78] Since Enron's patronage was meant (selfishly) to further the economic

---

[78] Because my concern is with socio-economics, and because I do not want to be accused of partisanship, I pretend not to notice the elephant in the living room; i.e., Vice President Dick Cheney, the patron saint of fossil energy, who sends down missives from his undisclosed location disavowing any familiarity with the company that paid less in taxes than the average person flipping burgers at McDonald's, that was able to rewrite key legislation to its own liking, and whose CEO was a key player in Cheney's secretive task force that developed this nation's energy policy. I leave parody to partisans like Senator Fritz Hollings (D-SC.), who put these words in the collective mouth of this administration: "I did not have political relations with that man . . . with Mr. Lay."

interests of Enron itself (which should have been tantamount to maximizing shareholders' wealth), the dimensions of this disaster are economic rather than political.

From a report by a special committee appointed by Enron's own board of directors, we learn that the firm "cratered" as the result of a chain reaction triggered by the nefarious deeds of senior executives. It would appear that Enron's top brass included an anthill of senior vice presidents, each in charge of one or more premeditated felonies — from making up totally ridiculous balance sheets, to masking off-balance-sheet shenanigans, to hiding the true nature of Enron's "leverage" (i.e., financial risk) from investors and lesser employees, to shredding possible evidence, to passing all the blame on to company lawyers and auditors, to making increasingly desperate calls to every power broker in DC (except, we are told, those at 1600 Pennsylvania Avenue), *ad nauseam.* The report describes a "revenue model" so complex that it led to the diversion of untold millions into the pockets of Enron's senior executives. A columnist for the *New York Times Services* intimates that the report contains enough information to keep the US Department of Justice busy handing out indictments for years to come, or who-knows-for-how-long, whichever comes last.

On the heels of the report comes the spectacle of Kenneth "Kenny Boy" Lay, under subpoena, assuming the mantle of Chief Fifth Amendment Capitalist before a congressional committee. Reading from a prepared text, he assures listeners that he really wants to tell all, but is constrained from doing so by counsel (who presumably were still counting the ways other Enron executives had perjured themselves before the same committee). This is the same Kenneth Lay who, on September 26, 2001, used an online chat to assure Enron employees that he really had their best interests at heart, and to prove it, urged them to buy company shares because the stock was "an incredible bargain." Well, it took a few weeks, but he was right. Turns out, it is a huge bargain now.

C. Who is Minding the Store?

If Enron was a shell game, was its "independent" auditor the pimp, and its legal counsels the "ladies of the evening"? The role of an outside auditor, under the law, is to protect public interest by certifying the accuracy of a company's financial statements and assuring that such reports are based on standard accounting principles (GAAP[79]). It is no secret now that CPA firms, small and large, are not exactly vestal virgins. They peddle their wares on street corners (albeit in pricey neighborhoods) and in the alleys of commerce where current regulations allow them to couple (i.e., sell consulting services) with the clients they are expected to censure. Even unbedded, they are often seduced or pressured by the client to perform any number of "unnatural," if not illegal, acts. The bigger the client, the greater the temptation; the wealthier the client, the greater the reward for acquiescence. From what is known at this point, it appears that Andersen not only climbed into bed with Enron management, succumbing to the firm's lewdest brandishments, but, when caught in the act, helped management attempt to burn the bed and shred as many dirty linens as time would allow. Andersen's role is akin to the police officer who not only lets the thief into the store, but stands at the door as well holding the flashlight.

As the Enron scandal unfolds, several columnists and pundits ask whether Andersen *could* survive the fiasco. Wrong question! The point, really, is whether Andersen *should* survive. From an ethical standpoint, my answer is a resounding no. It appears the firm violated its most basic trust past the point of redemption, without benefit of excuse or mitigating circumstance. The immediate impulse is to shut the firm down until it can prove its innocence — in essence, foregoing the American legal principle "innocent until proven guilty."

The impulse is admittedly a powerful one, with many adherents no doubt, but what of the 85,000 employees who work for Andersen worldwide? Is it ethical to peremptorily deprive them of work because of the illegal actions of a few at the top — actions they knew nothing about and were powerless to control even if they knew? The astute reader will note, surely, that this difficult question never arises when a firm announces large-scale downsizing, which has precisely the same effect, i.e., throwing tens of thousands out of work around the world because of mistakes by a few who mostly benefited from those mistakes. (Here is a good point to read again the opening paragraphs of this paper.)

As mentioned earlier, a major flaw of the current system is that the big five CPA firms are allowed, under the law, to serve as management consultants to firms they audit. The inherent conflict in this arrangement — and

---

[79] Generally Accepted Accounting Principles that, according to Lawrence Summers (former Secretary of the Treasury and current President of Harvard University), is at the very foundation of a free market system.

the opportunity for abuse — is apparent in the following imaginary conversation between a firm and its CPA, which also serves as the firm's management consultant:

CPA person: "What is this?"

Management person: "This is a shady deal."

CPA person: "Say what?"

Management person: "We want to keep our shady deals off the books."

CPA person: "No can dooooo."

Management person: "Let me think this over." Goes to see management consultant person.

*

Management person: "Your CPA person doesn't want to go along with keeping debt off the books."

Management consultant person: "Let me think for a moment." Thinks for a moment. "Tell our CPA person that I okayed this." Management person goes back to CPA person.

*

Management person: "Your management consultant person okayed this."

CPA person: "Then I apologize, and will sign off on this. Keep on piling unreported debt. And put me down for a couple of thousand shares in the offshore/off-books partnership, will ya?"

In the opinion of this writer, the Justice Department should look at the possibility of bringing anti-trust suits against all CPA firms that are also management consultants, forcing them to break up the two operations. This may not help, because of the generous political contributions of all big CPA firms to both political parties, and may result in the same outcome as the Microsoft suit, but it is a start, and it will focus attention on the socio-economic issues involved, just as the Microsoft case did.

D. *Cui Bono?*[80]

From the smattering of evidence available to date, we learn that the inner circle of Enron management, knowing that the company was about to

---

[80] Who benefits?

tank, exercised their stock options on the eve of destruction and dumped their shares in the company's myriad offshore, off-books partnerships, walking away with $1.1 billion in their capitalist pockets — indisputable proof, to them at least, that the system works. Senator Joseph Lieberman (D-Conn.), whose Governmental Affairs Committee is investigating Enron, said at a press conference on February 11, 2002, that Enron executives gave themselves $55 million in bonuses just two days before the energy giant filed for bankruptcy. And why not? Had they not grown the company to the 7th largest in the US (never mind that they did so by making up totally ridiculous numbers)? According to those executives not pleading the Fifth, however, there is a perfectly logical and rational explanation for this "suspicious" behavior. They were not trying to stiff the stockholders or their employees, but were merely selling a few pesky shares they had meant to get rid of years ago but somehow had never found time to trade until a slow afternoon in August 2001. That was all.

As for company shareholders and employees who lost more than the executives gained (this is not a zero-sum game), whose fault was that? They themselves, that's who. It is a tough world out there in this great free-market system of ours. Everyone knows investment is risk-taking. It was not management's fault that they foolishly chose to "believe in" their CEO or in the infallibility of, say, their retirement system, which alone lost $1.2 billion when the company crashed and burned. Now, this gargantuan sum may be an illusion, as all "values" are; nevertheless, this was the retirement fund of tens of thousands of workers. The Enron executives, when cashing in, took whatever they took in real dollars — also called cold, hard cash.

Of course, both shareholders and employees of Enron are outraged. And furious. And bitter. No one likes to lose. And lose they did — "big time," to borrow a phrase from Mr. Cheney. The losers here are employees and stockholders alike — two sets of people with a large intersection, i.e., employees who are also shareholders. The intersect set suffered doubly because Enron's ESOP and many of its employees' 401(k)'s were invested in company stock, now worth less than the coins it would take to make a payphone call telling the broker to sell.

As one mid-level manager has been quoted as saying, the people who worked for Enron "believed" in the company because it was different and "new age." And why not? Enron's Chief Financial Officer, one Mr. Andrew Fastow, who decamped in October 2001 with up to $60 million in his pocket after allegedly cooking the books, was selected as CFO of the Year by *CFO Magazine* in 1999 for his "innovative approach to financial management." Now *there's* indisputable proof that the system "works"!

Rational observers (of the capitalist persuasion) agree that government (meaning you and I, the taxpayer) should bail Enron out of its "financial setback," much as it did with the thrift institutions in the early 1990s when an entire industry — basking in deregulation under the Reagan–Bush "let-the-markets-alone" policy — went out of its way to prove that for-profit entities cannot always be trusted to police themselves. (How many times must we learn this lesson?) Up to that point, the savings and loan meltdown was the largest redistribution of wealth in recorded history, shifting, conservatively (no pun intended), up to $500 billion from the "have-nots" to the "haves." After the dust settled, the wealthiest of the "haves" circled to pick the bones clean, buying up the assets of failed thrift institutions for 10 cents on the dollar. The heads of a few high-profile "haves" (a la Charles Keating) rolled as a sop for the evening news. And a few "haves" got a slap on the wrist, a token fine (which some, believe it or not, are now suing to be refunded to them!), and a week or two of confinement in their cavernous mansions. As for the rest, they have moved on to bigger and better things in the "new economy" — indisputable proof, again, that the system "works."

Rational observers (of the conservative persuasion) agree that some sort of "economic stimulus" is warranted for poor Enron Corp. (which paid no income taxes four of the last five years). Even before the company collapsed — when it was still riding higher than the tail end of the orbiting space station — wasn't there a line item in Mr. Bush's ill-fated stimulus package to "kick it up a notch" with a gift of $254 million in taxpayer dollars? The same stimulus proponents, however, decry even the whispered suggestion that taxpayer dollars be used to compensate taxpayers, i.e., those who lost everything or close to it when Enron imploded. Hey, this is capitalism, and capitalism is risk-taking. Take a pill (playing now to the powerful pharmaceutical lobby), and get over it.

To which I say: wait just one darned minute. I may be willing (sort of) to respect the *caveat emptor* principle, but where in the tomes of neoclassical economics is it written to be on the *qui vive* for super-criminals? We were taught for four decades — and thus passed on to our students — that markets are informationally efficient. Almost everyone accepted the semi-strong form of efficiency (that market prices reflect all publicly available information), and some even believed in the strong form of efficiency (that market prices reflect all information, whether it is public or not). And so it was that "market efficiency" achieved sanctity. One must not tinker with efficient markets because any meddling with the market (specifically, government interference through regulation) would destroy the sacredness of efficiency.

Not surprisingly, Harvey Pitt, head of the Securities and Exchange Commission (SEC), though outraged by and critical of the Enron debacle, is stymied when it comes to suggesting any solution other than continuing to allow the industry (i.e., securities industry) to regulate itself. Equally unsurprising, the SEC decided in January 2002 — as Enron began to unravel on camera — to call off a suit that the National Association of Securities Dealers planned to file against a member dealer suspected of violating securities laws. As Gretchen Morgenson of the *Times Wire Services* reports, we are entering a new world "where accountants do not account, managers manipulate, and corporate disclosures conceal." Are the barbarians at the gate? No. Hell, they are inside the city manning the gates. Whence, then, do we get a new theory of nefarious neoclassicism?

In the meantime, the AT&T that Allen the Savior brought miraculously back from the brink showed its gratitude by joining with Cox Communications and Comcast to bankrupt @Home.com, the fast-speed internet provider, in order to cannibalize @Home.com's business. There are no congressional investigations of this matter, although many thousands lost their investments and an even greater number lost their jobs. This scandal, apparently, is a non-starter. It is just business as usual, part and parcel of old-world-style capitalism (what we now call "free markets" because Marx gave a bad name to the former).

E. *Que Sera Sera*

What will come of the Enron debacle? You tell me. How likely is that any of the congressional investigating committees, half of whose members received campaign contributions from Enron, will be able to form a quorum to even consider an indictment? How likely is it that an independent investigator with Kenneth Starr's zealous myopia will be appointed to sniff out the evidence and examine the facts, when the current administration stoutly asserts there is "no conflict of interest" in having its own Justice Department (or, as the Chief Executive likes to refer to it, "my Justice Department") handle the case? How likely is it that the Justice Department, rife with Bush appointees, will aggressively pursue the matter when the Attorney-General's Office has recused itself? I will go out on a limb and suggest that ultimately everyone in DC, except for poor Chandra Levy and possibly Monica Lewinsky, will

recuse themselves from this investigation. What is more likely to happen —
and even that is iffy — will be enactment, perhaps, of the Feingold–McCain
campaign reform bill that passed the House on February 13, 2002. I say
"perhaps" because the bill now has to pass the Senate as well, and who
knows? It may be that the political implications of Enron's contribution to
the nation's lawmakers are sufficiently damaging to embarrass them into supporting the bill. But do not count on it yet.

The White House is certainly talking tough about "evildoers" right
and left, so to speak, but do not hold your breath waiting for them to mar-
shal the Commerce and Justice departments to hunt down Enron's top
executives with smart bombs and tomahawk missiles, rout them from their
"caves," and send them running "through the bushes [no pun intended]
where a rabbit couldn't go" (borrowed from Johnny Horton's ballad,
"Battle of New Orleans"). Nor are there any preparations that I know of
at Guantanamo Bay to accommodate Enron's still-dangerous management
team and the "shredders."

In the meantime, the White House sent its chief occupant to China —
absent the proverbial slow boat — taking, in the literal sense, its mission
to distance the incumbent from any suggestion that he knows Kenneth
Lay from Adam's off ox, much less that he had any knowledge of the
$700,000 in token good wishes that this casual acquaintance forced upon
his campaigns over the years. (Oops! Here I am being political again!) In
the meantime, congressional investigators yelp with outrage on C-Span
as the scandal mill grinds on, reminiscent of an observation by the people
of the Sahara: "The dogs bark while the caravan moves on."

What *should* come from the Enron debacle? Is it too much to hope
that the myth of "market efficiency" will be debunked or forsaken? In a
system that enables the "haves" to do whatever they will until and if they
are caught doing the worst (remember the Nixonian advice: "Don't get
caught"?), there is no "market efficiency," regardless of what statistical
studies show or do not show.[81] We are entering a new world "where accountants do not account, managers manipulate, and corporate disclosures conceal." This means that the unprotected needs protection, because markets
are not efficient enough to be fair.

---

[81] At the time of writing this paper, I came across several television reports that show "creative accounting" being practiced by Fortune 500 and other firms for the sake of showing the
Balance Sheet/Income Statement in a light which is more favorable than the true financial
state of the company, grossly misleading investors. I am also eagerly waiting for the Tyco
scandal to unfold, where the CEO and the CFO of the company pocketed $500 million from
selling their shares an eye-blink before the stock started its long journey into the tank.

Instead of efficient markets, perhaps we should think about "fair markets," a concept consistent with the Judeo-Christian tenets (see Nelson, 2001) on which the utopia of perfect markets as an ideology was built. Fair markets would mean tighter regulation and an increase in the number of executive power tools in the hands of regulatory agencies. In a fair market, a CPA firm suspected of destroying documents, for example, would be suspended from operating until the firm is cleared of the charges. In a fair market, CPA firms would not be allowed, for example, to provide consulting services to the companies they audit.

Fair markets should provide security to both investors and employees of the firms on which the stock is traded. This is necessary because information is not free, and because the stewards of the firm control the flow of information — and many of them grossly abuse their control. Measures to protect employees should take into consideration the fact that, although employees may not be shareholders or just marginally so (and perhaps against their better judgment), they are risk-takers just the same. Despite the fact that the expected future income of employees is tied to the fortunes of the company, they have no control over, nor even influence with, company management. This would bring up issues such as executive compensation, stock options and stock appreciation rights (SAR), and the protection of ESOPs. It may make the proponents of privatizing Social Security ponder the logic of that scheme.

Another requirement of market fairness would be uniform accounting for all purposes. That is, the firm must show the same Balance Sheet/Income Statement to the tax authorities as it shows to other audiences (shareholders, financial analysts, lenders, etc.). Though efficiency is a religiously treasured concept, nevertheless, *fairness* must come before *efficiency*.

Are "fair markets" incongruous with capitalism? Will fair markets break capitalism as we know it? Are fair markets even a possibility? I see no reason why they cannot be. But are they going to come to pass? I seriously doubt it.

References

Jensen, Michael C. and Perry Fagan. 1996. "Capitalism Isn't Broken." *Wall Street Journal*, March 29: 12A.

Nelson, Robert H. 2001. *Economics as Religion*. University Park, PA: The Pennsylvania University Press.

Chapter 9

Desperately Seeking Toto[*]

TRADITIONAL CAPITALISM: You have two cows. You sell one and buy a bull. Your herd multiplies, and the economy grows. You sell them and retire on the income.

ENRON-STYLE CAPITALISM: You have two cows. You sell three of them to your publicly-listed company, using letters of credit opened by your brother-in-law at the bank, then execute a debt-for-equity swap with an associated general offer so that you get all four cows back, with a tax exemption for five cows. The milk rights of the six cows are transferred via an intermediary to a Cayman Island company secretly owned by the majority shareholder, who sells the rights to all seven cows back to your listed company. The annual report says the company owns eight cows, with an option on one more. Sell one cow to buy a new president of the United States, leaving you with nine cows. No balance sheet provided with the release. The public buys your bull.

We have hardly scratched the surface of the Enron scandal, arguably the biggest corporate failure in the history of American capitalism, and already the case has generated enough heat to qualify as a source of renewable energy. Although the debacle is complex and does not fit easily into soundbites for the 30-second attention span, the airwaves shimmer (more from heat than light) as both the left and right get in their licks. Even those only remotely connected to the failing firm are chewing the scenery at center stage as they emote their deep consternation and wail for "sweeping reforms" in financial disclosure, client-accountant relations, accountant-management consultant relations, protection of retirement and pension funds, 401(k)'s, yada, yada, yada. Even the President quipped, "Ken who? I hardly knew the man!"

Public acrimony and scorn are heaped on greedy and ruthless executives, corrupt politicians (always a good target), and even not-so-corrupt

---

[*] The original version of this paper appeared in *Practical Financial Economics*, 2003, Ed. Austin Murphy, London: Praeger, and is published here by permission.

politicians (whose only fault was accepting soft-money campaign contributions without which they could not have run for office). Perhaps there were no strings attached; perhaps there were. It is unclear what they did or did not do to help promote Enron's economic welfare at the expense of the rest of us.

There are other voices as well, usually conservatives, who argue that:

(1) The name of the game is risk-taking, *sans* which there is no reward, and if you invested in Enron stock, you should have known that you could lose some or even all your investment; and

(2) The market, after all, did not crash, which proves investors' confidence in the system.

I especially fancy the second argument. When the market crashed and burned in October 1987, not one of these people said that the system is bad and that it was time to replace it. No, we had the Brady bunch back then, and they sang us a chorus: program trading and its accomplice — in essence its *sine qua non*, the computer — were to blame. Felix Rohatyn, a Wall Street high-flyer, opined that the worst thing to happen to the financial industry was an MBA with a laptop. This is where I raise an eyebrow. If anything, the computer makes the market more efficient because it diffuses information faster and more accurately than any other mechanism. But what do I know?

Now, if hundreds of thousands of investors lose "big time" (to borrow a phrase from Veep Cheney), we do not need to worry if the market itself did not crash. So when exactly should we start worrying about the system? Or should we just concede that this is the only game in town — love it or leave it?

Matters, of course, run much deeper than what we see, hear or read in the mainstream media. I suspect that what we have is a manifestation of the moral breakdown of the system we cherish, and of which we are so proud. What we have, really, is cessation of proper mechanical function, which cannot be readily "fixed" with a pinch of legislation and a dash of regulatory remedies.

Before I go into the crux of my thesis, let me, as the song goes, accentuate the positive. It would appear that there is no longer such a thing as a complete loss or total disaster. If nothing else, at least the American language has been enriched by the Enron fiasco. Our vocabulary has been broadened by several variants of the word *Enron*, such as "enronization," "enroned me," "enronish," "enron-like" and more recently, "enronomics."

"'Enroned' a new verb of shame," tisk-tisked the headline of an article by the *New York Times* columnist William Safire.

This, of course, is Safire the etymologist speaking, not William the arch-conservative. In much the same way that holography uses laser light to produce images by splitting the laser beam into two and recording the interference pattern on a photographic plate, Safire/William produces holograms that, on the surface, reflect his brilliance as a linguist and, when tilted to the light, reveal the darker, underlying image of a single-minded zealot. It was the latter image that surfaced when William, a former speechwriter for Richard Nixon and Spiro Agnew (for whom he coined the unforgettable alliteration, "nattering nabobs of negativism"), attempted to deflect any possibility that the Enron fallout would damage the White House. He congratulated George W.'s cabinet members for not accepting SOS phone calls from Enron after it struck the iceberg of financial disaster and began its Titanic plunge. What the conservative William could not — or chose not to — see was evidence of George W.'s chumminess with the man he affectionately called "Kenny boy," with whom he has exchanged warm, personal correspondence since his gubernatorial campaign in Texas. Though George W. was widely photographed boarding an Enron jet that ferried him from one campaign stop to another on his way to getting appointed as a non-democratically elected president, the conservative William was apparently blinded to this reality and to the transparent (to everyone else, at least) transmogrification of "Kenny boy" to "Ken who?"

What we learn from Safire the linguist (the more brilliant half of the hologram) is that originally, the consultants Lippincott & Margulies suggested "Enteron" as the name of the firm that resulted from the merger of Houston Natural Gas and InterNorth. When the consultants learned that the medical meaning of the word was "intestines," the name was changed to Enron. Wouldn't you say that was an omen right there?

But, unless the GAO's lawsuit against Vice President Cheney is successful, we will never know the extent of Enron's influence on national energy policy, and how much of that acquiescence was a payback to Enron for helping put the Bush–Cheney ticket in the White House. Do not hold your breath for speedy disclosure. The Vice President has dug in his heels, combatively demanding what right the public has to know how a government official shapes public policy. Executive privilege, after all, is executive privilege.

So far, we know that the Enron executives enronized, and did so precisely when the whole nation was in shock and mourning in the wake of 9/11. During September and October 2001, the top brass cashed in their chips. But greed is good, as we learned from Gordon Gekko (Oliver Stone's paragon of unbridled rapacity in "Wall Street"), and as long as the house of cards did not collapse, both investors and executives did well. Some executives did exceedingly well even as the house of cards tumbled to shambles.

Sadly, if they want to get elected, politicians on both sides of the aisle need the help of corporate America. Enron was certainly helpful. Three out of five US senators, in fact, have received contributions from Enron over the years. Let us face it: this is the system we created, and it will not be easy, if at all possible, to undo. In fact, we are so proud of this system that we encourage the whole world to fashion their life according to American culture, both politically and otherwise. Why, just the other day, President Bush offered this advice to the Chinese, whose civilization, dating back 5,000 years, is among the earliest known advanced cultures, and whose art and system of writing are the oldest in the world, evolving in remote antiquity.

This kind of self-aggrandizement is not what disturbs me most about the Enron scandal. More shocking to me is a third cabal of beneficiaries who shamelessly accepted Enron money, not in order to be elected as a public servant or to maximize wealth for shareholders, but to line their own pockets. They call themselves consultants or analysts, but I call this camarilla — paid liars, or Enron encounters of the third kind. These confidential advisers are neither executives, however ruthless, who had to account to shareholders, nor accountants, who put their reputation and credibility on the line. No. These people were paid to make Enron look good.

We were told time and again, of course, that markets see through falsehood, nefarious deeds and tomfoolery. That is one good reason, we are reminded, to leave the markets alone. Go tell this to the multitudes that lost a bundle, their pension, or perhaps their life savings. Even George W.'s *schwieger* lost $8,000. Can you not feel the pain of the President, who now has to deal with an irate mother-in-law? Pleeeeease!

We were told that markets are omnipotent, that they know all and see all. (Now we learn that this was, in fact, the basic premise of Enron's corporate ethos.) Markets handsomely reward the *fidels* and punish the *infidels* (the manipulators and the cheaters). Markets must rule the world. Indeed, it is the new world order, globalization, the new age, the 21st century, the avatar of God. Springtime for Adam Smith and humanity!

Let us pause for a moment and talk about Adam Smith (1723–1790). Though his major work, *The Wealth of Nations*, earned him glory as a political economist, Smith was also a philosopher (perhaps before he was an economist), a moralist and a humanitarian of great sensitivity. Strangely, those who co-opted this Scotsman's work as the foundation for what we now call free-market economics picked one statement from Smith's great work:

> It is not from the benevolence of the butcher, the brewer, or the baker that we expect our dinner, but from their regard to their own interest (*Wealth of Nations*, Book I, Ch. II, p. 11).

True, Smith was a radical individualist who objected to the power of King and Church. Smith suggested leaving matters in the invisible hands of the market, where buyers and sellers find each other through a "just price." Both the Talmud and medieval Christian scholars had espoused this concept of just price. The meaning of "just price" was the agreement between a seller and buyer, under normal, perfectly competitive conditions, by which a good or service changed hands. Prices were considered unjust if:

(1)   There was price discrimination;
(2)   Cartels of either buyers and sellers were formed; and
(3)   The participants took advantage of emergency situations, i.e., what we now call price gouging.

Operation of the market, it was believed, could also be upset by nefarious or even dishonest activities on the part of either buyer or seller. Smith understood well the perils of such circumstances and was very clear about where a central government should stand:

> The government of an exclusive company of merchants is, perhaps, the worst of all governments for any country whatever (*Wealth of Nations*, Book IV, Ch. VII, Part III, p. 440).

He was also quite explicit about who should receive the lion's share of the economic activity:

> Our merchants frequently complain of the high wages of British labour as the cause of their manufactures being undersold in foreign markets; but they are silent about the high profits of stock. They complain of the extravagant gain of other people; but they say nothing of their own. The high profits of British stock, however, may contribute towards raising the price of British manufactures in many cases as much, and in some perhaps more, than the high wages of British labour (*Wealth of Nations*, Book IV, Ch. VII, Part III, p. 466).

I have never seen these two quotations in the playbook of today's free marketeers. On the contrary, it seems that most laws favor commerce and industry over the working man. Still, despite his economic insight and visionary talent, Smith, in the 18th century, could not possibly foresee the multinational corporation of the 21st century with its practically unlimited power and influence. Matters now are much worse than Smith could have ever envisioned.

Perhaps I am taxing your patience with this commentary on Adam to emphasize how the moral orgone was sucked from his ultimate premise. Unfortunately, without the moral foundations, Smith would have not known from Adam (no pun intended) what became of his theory of a new economic order.

Let us return now to the gallery of the paid liars who labored to turn the sow's ear that was Enron into a public relations silk purse, for no other purpose than to fatten their own wallets. These holier-than-thou types did not commit any crime for which they can be punished or even investigated by Congress. They are not the "corrupt" politicians we all love to loathe (so much so that we keep reelecting virtually all of them). They are not villainous executives. They are not even co-conspiratorial accountants whose "aggressive" practices helped cook the books. This cabal simply sold out without taking any real risks, something that is contrary to the previously mentioned concept of there-is-no-reward-without-risk-taking.

Foremost among the moral bankrupts is Ralph Reed, former director of the Christian Coalition and poster boy for Christian video-conservativism. Ralphie boy (borrowing the President's style) sold his soul to Enron for a mere $380,000. Considering Ralph's arrogance, it was one of Enron's better investments.

According to a *Washington Post* column, Reed proposed a broad political strategy to press Congress for legislation favorable to Enron. Reed suggested to the company that, because of his influence with the media and with conservative talk shows, he could promote the interests of Enron, flooding OP-Ed pages and generating articles in the print media which he would then "blast fax" to members of Congress.

Blast fax! I love this. Here is another example of how, in the hands of an opinion terrorist, a seemingly innocent device like a fax machine, much less sophisticated and far less costly than a jet airliner, can be used as a weapon of mass distraction (as in beguilement).

"In public policy it matters less who has the best arguments and more who gets heard — and by whom," Reed told Enron. And ain't that the truth! Although the memo was dated October 27, 2000, Karl Rove, George W.'s Svengali-er senior advisor, introduced Reed to Enron's top brass. *Judicial Watch*, a **conservative** watchdog group, asked for a federal investigation to determine whether the employment of Reed by Enron was a campaign finance violation.

But what about morality, supposedly the unshakable foundation of the moral majority that Reed so forcefully represented? How does selling himself for considerably less than 30 pieces of silver sit with the basic Judeo-Christian ethic upon which the whole idea of free markets rests?

How about indeed! According to the *Washington Post*, Reed wrote in the memo, "Elected officials and regulators will be predisposed to favor greater *market-oriented solutions* [my italics] if they hear from business, civic, and religious leaders in their communities." One must know not what the cookie is, but how it crumbles.

Next in line is Mrs. Phil Gramm. In 1993, for example, while working for an oversight commission, the wife of the senior senator from Texas helped exempt Enron from regulation. Five weeks later, she was named to Enron's board of directors. What an unexpected coincidence!!

The honor roll goes on and on, to wit: Professor Lawrence Lindsey, free market theorist extraordinaire, formerly with Columbia University, now chief economic adviser of the President; Bill Kristol, conservative extraordinaire, editor of the *Weekly Standard;* Paul Krugman, financial columnist and adviser; Larry Kudlow, another financial maven of the television persuasion; US trade representative Robert Zoellick; Marc Racicot, the incoming RNC chair; and the dozen or more financial analysts who still hand-picked Enron as a "strong buy" in the late fall of 2001.

These are only those we know about. Who knows how long the complete list is, how much these people were paid and for what purpose exactly? I would be interested to know. So would be those who were fleeced by Enron's demise. Wouldn't you be interested to know?

As I am writing this paper, I learn from my internet-streaming headline that Congressional investigators are requesting documents from ten Wall Street investment banking firms. They want to know what the connection was, if any, between these firms loaning money to an already failing Enron while their brokerage operations were pushing Enron stock to their clients. We do not even have to wait for the movie to come out. We already had "Wall Street" and "Boiler Room," two movies made for those who cannot read, so they also could enjoy moral decay.

And what do you know? Just now, Merrill Lynch agreed to pay a $100 million fine for this "conflict of interest" for the price of not admitting any wrongdoing and not having to face criminal charges. A guilty verdict of such a trial for sure would have produced a whole slew of civil suits by stockholders that would have cost billions to the Wall Street giant. Apparently there are still bargains "out there."

The most bizarre participant of the "Enron encounters of the third kind" is Alan Greenspan, icon of the *fin-de-siécle* bull market, who, only 19 days before Enron declared bankruptcy, received the "Enron Prize" from James Baker's public policy institute. This is the James Baker, by the way, who served as Secretary of State under George H.W. Bush, and who, only five months after George H.W. lost the 1992 election, began lobbying Kuwait on Enron's behalf — and the same James Baker who, when the junior George was desperately wrestling Gore for ballots in the Sunshine State, grabbed the nearest jet (Enron's, perhaps?) to the Land of Oz and took center stage as Dubya's mouthpiece to the national media.

But I digress. Greenspan received the Enron Prize, but for what, crying out loud? For forecasting erroneously the last 20 non-existent inflationary cycles and eventually putting the economy into a downward spiral? After the techies and the dot.coms wiped out not just the glory but also the daylight from the portfolios of yuppiedom, Greenspan was de-iconed. This was despite Greenspan's discouraging the movers and shakers from "irrational exuberance." Today, Greenspan is all "cautious optimism." But his luster has faded considerably. Perhaps people recall that Herbert Hoover was cautiously optimistic in 1932 when he declared that recovery is just around the corner.

So, what exactly was the Enron Prize? And how does the prize Greenspan got compare with the prize those who now use their Enron stock certificates to paper their bathrooms got?

As we arrive in this 21st century Oz, which we call free markets, we realize that, during the journey, Dorothy has been gang-raped. Alas, we are reduced to desperately seeking Toto, in need of someone to go behind the curtain and tell us that the wizard's name is enronomics.

Reference

Smith, Adam. 1776. *An Inquiry into the Nature and Causes of the Wealth of Nations (The Wealth of Nations)*. London and New York: George Routledge and Sons.

Chapter 10

And Now for Something Entirely Different[82]

Capitalism is the extraordinary belief that the nastiest of men, for the nastiest of reasons, will somehow work for the benefit of us all.

— John Maynard Keynes

On March 26, 2002, Joseph Berardino, Chief Executive Officer of Andersen LLP, fell on his sword on "Lou Dobbs Moneyline" on CNN in full view of millions of watchers. It was the final act of bemuscment for the man who has been fighting a muddled battle since January to save the beleaguered accounting giant.

Although he persisted in denying that he had done anything illegal or unethical during his 15-month tenure, Berardino said it was now necessary to distance himself from Andersen in order to save the company in the United States and perhaps worldwide as well. Removing himself from the scene, he said, would give Paul A. Volker, former Federal Reserve chairman, a much-needed chance to reorganize Andersen, and, with luck, foil efforts by the Justice Department to indict the accounting firm on criminal charges of obstruction of justice. Financial mavens agree that an indictment would almost certainly push Andersen into bankruptcy, regardless of the outcome of the ensuing trial. After all, who would be willing to entrust their cookie jar to someone accused not only of helping others make off with another firm's cookies, but also of conspiring to sweep up the crumbs and destroy other evidence of the raid?

Berardino's act, both in its deeper meaning and in its exogeneity, has something in parallel with the *auto-da-fé* (act of faith) of the Spanish Inquisition. The *auto-da-fé* was

> . . . a public ceremony during which the sentences upon those brought
> before the Spanish Inquisition were read and after which the sentences were

---

[82] Credits to Monty Python's Flying Circus.

executed by the secular authorities. The first auto-da-fé took place at Seville in 1481; the last, in Mexico in 1850. The ceremonies, which became increasingly elaborate and spectacular, were normally staged in the city plaza, often in the presence of royalty. They usually comprised a lengthy procession, a solemn mass, an oath of obedience to the Inquisition, a sermon, and the reading of the sentences.[83]

Berardino's resignation (in essence, his *felo-de-se*) was staged ceremoniously in that most public of all venues these days — a globally televised program set in today's electronic "city plaza," in the presence of all including, perhaps, royalty.[84]

Excited by my own courage to draw the parallel — and inspired by Robert H. Nelson's *Economics as Religion* (Nelson, 2001) — I began thinking that the Enron debacle, with its auditors' subplot, is more than just a scandal. It is quite possibly the harbinger of a new form of monotheism, i.e., the religion of free markets in which there is but one god and its name is Mammon. Mammon can afford to tolerate the other monotheistic religions because, bottom line, it knows that it rules the lives of most, if not all, of their believers and infidels. Like the world's other religions, the religion of free markets (subsequently, RFM) has its own hierarchy, sanctions and rituals.

Berardino is likely not as innocent as he made it appear during his public immolation. As I have argued elsewhere (Frankfurter, 2002), we have hardly scratched the surface of the Enron scandal. As more facts surface about the relation between the company and its auditors, it becomes clear that Andersen LLP knew about the troubles at the Houston-based energy giant much earlier than previously thought.

In a column in the *Washington Post* (March 29, 2002) titled "Auditor got early warning about Enron," writers Susan Schmidt and David S. Hilzenrath state:

> A top Enron Corp. executive told the chief executive of Arthur Andersen LLP a year ago that the energy company was doing a lot of complex financial transactions and needed more auditing expertise than it was getting, according to an Andersen spokesman.

---

[83] Excerpted from *The Encyclopedia Britannica*, 2001 PC Standard Edition.

[84] There are accounts that the royals of UK were involved with Enron, just like untold number of commoners.

This "top Enron executive" was none other than Richard Causey, Enron's Chief Accounting Officer. Causey's request for "more accounting expertise" was a cry for help. It was perfectly consistent with the responsibilities of a chief accounting officer who understood that something was not totally proper with Enron's books, yet had no other recourse than to ask for the help of an outside auditor. According to Schmidt and Hilzenrath,

> ... Richard Causey, met with Joseph Berardino along with the head of Andersen's Houston office and one of the firm's top audit executives in Houston on Feb. 21, 2001... The meeting occurred just over two weeks after Andersen executives, in a meeting Feb. 5, discussed whether the firm should resign as Enron's auditor because of the risks involved in Enron's off-the-books partnership dealings.

These facts make it clear that Berardino was far from the paragon of virtue he purported to be when he shifted the blame to a single senior partner, David Duncan,[85] in the Houston office and proceeded, in a public display of righteous indignation, to fire the man in late 2001. On top of this, it now appears that Berardino may have perjured himself during congressional testimony in early January 2002. Whether he is in fact a perjurer is a matter for Congress and the Justice Department to decide, and does not affect directly my view that his March 2002 resignation was tantamount to a religious act of faith.

More central to my theory on the emergence of a new religion is the role of Paul Volker in the campaign to save Andersen LLP from both criminal prosecution and ultimate ruin. The religious angle is not so far-fetched when one views Volker's dual role as both the savior of Andersen and an apostle of the free market system for which it stands.

If someone of Volker's stature is willing to intercede for a reprobate like Andersen, then the latter is certainly savable, is it not? This logic is consistent with the Judeo-Christian philosophy that a sinner who returns to the fold is more welcomed than a saint who spent an entire lifetime in the bosom of sanctity. The Talmud is clear about this:

מקום בו חוזרים בתשובה עומדים צדיקים גמורים אינם עומדים

---

[85] After months of haggling, on April 9, 2002, David Duncan copped a plea of one count of obstruction of justice to become a critical witness in the Justice Department's case against Andersen.

which can be loosely translated (my apologies) as: "The place [in front of God] where a repentant can stand even the righteous cannot stand." Volker thus exorcises Andersen — instant catharsis.

Taken out of religious context, however, Volker's involvement looks quite different. Andersen violated a trust for which it was handsomely compensated. Although generally accepted accounting principles (GAAP) give the firm some leeway in interpreting the rules and customs upon which it bases information for use by the public in making measured investment decisions, this flexibility does not include the willful destruction of documents and other evidence. The latter actions constitute a felony called obstruction of justice.

One thing is certain: Andersen LLP cannot plead ignorance of the law. The firm has a history of recidivism, having been warned and fined on a number of occasions for violating rules of reporting. Though the firm has, so far, escaped conviction for criminal activity, the prudent person would certainly consider the company's recidivist behavior and weigh such behavior against the accounting firm whenever new allegations of illegal activities are brought against Andersen. Thus, a criminal indictment is in order, regardless of the consequences.[86]

The question is: can Volker's involvement and the so-called Volker reorganization save Andersen LLP from its deserved fate?

This is a two-parter. The second part is easy. The Volker "plan" amounts to no more than the promise to adhere strictly, in the future, to GAAP, to divest Andersen's consulting services from Andersen's accounting practices, and to sell (possibly) the tax-advisory services of the firm. There is nothing new in this plan, which was bandied about even before Volker got involved.

With the plan, Andersen is saying, in effect, okay, we behaved rather badly in the past (as if violating GAAP can be dismissed as "rather bad"), but from now on, we promise to be exemplars of propriety, virtual choirboys with laptops (although many of these laptops' hard drives were wiped clean in the Houston office). To make sure that we keep our promise, we have on our side a man who, had he lived in biblical times, would have been among the righteous ten it would have taken to save Sodom and Gomorrah. The problem is that Volker, like the righteous who came later

---

[86] Indeed, on May 14, 2002, a Houston jury of 12 men and women returned a decision of guilty. Although a possible verdict cannot exceed $500,000 in fine and five years of probation, the judgment amounts to an almost certain demise of the firm.

to the twin cities of the desert, arrived too late to save the sinners: the damage, swift and irrevocable, had been done. Similarly, no promises of future sanctity can "save" Andersen from retribution for its long list of past sins, particularly now that it is already knee-deep in the ashes of its own ruin. The spectacle may — just may — serve as a deterrent to other like-minded accountants. When Lou Dobbs fronts a headline like "The Justice Department says 'Drop dead to Andersen'," it makes one wonder whether his services were recruited to help save the company.

The first part of my question is harder, if not impossible, to answer. It gives rise instead to other questions. What would motivate a retired chairman of the Federal Reserve — who is neither in his youth nor in need of funds to supplement a meager social security allowance — put his distinguished reputation on the line to save a firm involved in something that is both morally and legally wrong?

In 1987, when Volker accepted the Boyer Prize from the American Enterprise Institute (AEI), he made these comments during the Boyer Lecture:

> That something is what was termed at a conference jointly sponsored by AEI and Brookings last year as a quiet crisis. The reference is to the state of the public service in the United States, and especially to the state of the federal government bureaucracy down through the ranks.
>
> I am not thinking of the kind of thing that has captured so much of the attention of this town in recent months — the Irangate affair, the Bork hearings, or the intensity of the examination of the private foibles of those who aspire to national political leadership. Whether or not we think of those events as crises — and I am not at all sure we could hope for a consensus in this room on that point — they are certainly not quiet.
>
> Rather, what those attending the conference last year concluded was becoming a crisis was the unmistakable evidence that is accumulating that government in general, and the federal government in particular, is increasingly unable to attract, retain and motivate the kinds of people it will need to do the essential work of the republic in the years and decades ahead.
>
> It is a *quiet* crisis because not many people know about it or care very much about it. That has been true of many political candidates for some years, even though the plain danger is that any administration or Congress will be handicapped in carrying out its policies and programs by a weak civil service. But the situation is just too amorphous, too complicated, too distant for many to get excited about it — that is, until something happens.

And something — to wit, Enron cum Andersen — did happen! But 15 years after this address, Volker — the once and forever "Wall Street *liebling*," the ultra-conservative monetary economist and central banker — has taken an adversarial role against the very kind of public servants he championed back then as necessary to the "essential work of the republic," i.e., people who have the know-how and the courage to do their job (in this case, protect us from the likes of Andersen). Surely there is a moral issue here, one to which only Mr. Volker can speak.

At the core of every world religion is a deep, philosophical controversy. In the Judeo-Christian religions, it centers on the ways and means by which God rewards and punishes individuals and, perhaps, nations. How could God allow six million Jews to perish in the Holocaust? Why did He let 9/11 happen? Why do evildoers flourish? Many have attempted to answer these questions in their own fashion (some quite unfashionably, as did the Reverend Falwell with his explanation that it was our own fault for tolerating gays and lesbians), but the consensus remains that God's ways are mysterious and unknowable to humankind, or, more simply, one must not question God.

The RFM rests on the premise that nothing, especially not government, should interfere with the free exercise of the religion (i.e., unfettered operation of the market). Yet, when things go wrong in the religion, such as blasphemous acts by one or more of the higher echelon, the RFM perversely expects the government to intervene to protect the interests of the faithful. Woe unto the government should it fail to do so!

In the Enron case, the government — however late — is determined to bring criminal charges against the firm's auditors, more for the sake of deterrence than for actual punishment. Yet, the people who should be applauding the government for doing its job are throwing daggers instead, prostituting themselves to save those who should not be saved. Is this the case because the ultimate morality of the church of RFM has the metallic smell of mammon?

I cannot help but remember part of the panegyric delivered by the Reverend Dr. Duncan E. Littlefair at the memorial services for Mr. Arthur Andersen, the founder of what later became Andersen LLP:

> He believed in honesty of purpose and motive. He believed, of course, in truth; for him there was no alternative. He believed in being straightforward. From his mother he learned to "think straight, talk straight." This he practiced. He believed in the ultimate triumph of the right. All of these

virtues produced courage. Mr. Andersen had great courage. Few are the men who have as much faith in the right as he, and fewer still are those with the courage to live up to their faith as he did.

What is the meaning of these things we have been saying? For those of you who worked with him and carry on his company, the meaning is clear. Those principles upon which his business was built and with which it is synonymous must be preserved. His name must never be associated with any program or action that is not the highest and the best. I am sure he would rather the doors be closed than that it should continue to exist on principles other than those that he established. To you he has left a great name. Your opportunity is tremendous; your responsibility is great.

Perhaps closing the doors would be not just the right thing to do, but also would be honoring the memory and wishes of the founder of Andersen.

References

Frankfurter, George M. 2002. "The Socio-Economics of Scandals." *Homo Oeconomicus* 19: 257–267.

Nelson, Robert H. 2001. *Economics as Religion*, 1st ed. University Park: The Pennsylvania State University Press.

Chapter 11

After the Ball[*]

When he had explained these procedures, which had become common practice of American business, to his father, the great capo mafioso, Don Corrado Prizzi, the old man marveled with admiration. "You have *really* organized crime, my son," he said with awe. "Every year you skim off another two or three billion and the way you got it all figured out, nobody can call a cop."

"It is just the modern way, Poppa," Price had said. "There is no one to bother you. The Congress looks the other way, because there is also a big buck in it for them, and the Securities and Exchange Commission doesn't make any waves. There are private plaintiff suits, sure, but they all get settled using the stockholders' money — and we come away from every deal richer and cleaner."

"But you gotta tie up a lotta cash for that."

"No, Poppa. We borrow from the banks."

"But that's a lotta interest you gotta pay on loans like that."

"So sell off some of the companies and fire a few thousand people to pay the interest. The rest is not only clear to us, but we get it all free."

"Jesus," his father said, "and we used to have to use guns."

— *The Final Addiction*, 1991, Richard Condon

Only the history of free peoples merits our attention; that of men under despotism is simply a collection of anecdotes.

— Sébastian-Roch Nicolas Chamfort

A. More Enrons Than One Bargained for

Imagine, if you will, the grand ballroom of a luxury hotel where the big event of the season's opening just ended. The debutants and their escorts and chaperones are gone just as all the other guests dressed in evening gowns or black tie and tails are gone. The glitter of the chandeliers is

---

[*]An earlier version of this paper was published in *The Journal of Investing*, 2005, Volume 14 (Winter): 8–13.

turned into penumbra. The floor is littered with confetti and stamped-on streamers. A bumped-into waiter dropped a tray of canapés that was trampled on before there would have been a chance to clean up the mess. Evidence of other spills of the liquid kind is also all over. Broken glass, hastily swept aside, lines the walls. Soiled tablecloths are the only evidence of the once assembled Lucullous buffets and artfully carved ice sculptures. Garbage is strewn everywhere. The housekeeping crew of the establishment will have their work cut out when they arrive a few hours after the last of the celebrants left. This is my mental image of the Enron aftermath.

On June 14, 2002, a Houston jury of 12 men and women deliberating for a record length of time on the Andersen LLP's obstruction of justice case in federal court returned a verdict of guilty. Although Andersen faces no more than five years' probation and a $500,000 fine, with all practicality, the verdict was the kiss of death for the once giant CPA firm. The guilty verdict also opens the door for the Justice Department to go with full force after Enron and its merry band of executives and financial wizards.

This is about time, because not unlike the French Revolution, we love to see the heads of the ultra-rich and powerful roll. Yet, we are reluctant to make any serious effort to change the system. We are always looking for the single assassin, at the present Martha Stewart, the grandiose embezzler, and the super villain. And when we find those, we like to titivate them with flashy titles such as the Queen of Mean, the Emperor of Greed, the Sultan of Sleaze, etc. Having done that, we can turn around and say that the system is working, the market did not crash, investors' confidence returned; everything is perfect until the next scandal, and *moto perpetuo.*

Apparently, the Enron saga is just the tip of an iceberg that threatened to sink that Titanic that is the myth of free markets. We learn through view media reporting about rampant improprieties that touch many of the Fortune 500. The list includes, among many others:

- Adelphia
- GE
- Global Crossing
- Halliburton (under the CEO-ship of Vice President Cheney, reporting non-existent revenues of $100 million and perhaps even bribing foreign official)
- Microsoft
- Tyco International
- WorldCom

This last one turned into a bomb that exploded on June 26, 2002. The telecommunication giant acknowledged classifying $3.8 billion in expenses as capital investment. Mr. Scott Sullivan, the firm's CFO, was blamed for this "strain" of creative accounting. The CPA firm of WorldCom (you guessed it), Andersen LLP, commented that the accounting decision that grossly inflated the firm's earnings and thereby misled outsiders, investors, creditors and regulators regarding the true financial conditions of WorldCom was that of the CFO, and Andersen had nothing to do with it.

One must wonder two questions here, nevertheless. Every undergraduate student of business administration, from the Ivy League to the lowest of the low community colleges in the land, learns in Accounting 101 the difference between investment and expense, and how each is to be treated. Then, what has been Mr. Sullivan's background that made him the Chief Financial Officer of the firm without the knowledge of such an elementary thing?

The second question is perhaps even more important: why do we have a CPA firm to certify financial statements if the auditor, supposedly more knowledgeable in accounting matters than the client, cannot discover such an elementary ruse?

After the public revelations, the share price of WorldCom dropped in a single day by 73 percent. Experts commented that with all likelihood, bankruptcy seemed to be the only option for WorldCom.[87]

One hardly recovered from the developments at WorldCom before reading in the *New York Times* on June 29, 2002 that

> The Xerox Corporation, which conceded earlier that as part of a settlement with the Securities and Exchange Commission it would reclassify more than $2 billion of revenue from previous years, said yesterday that it was in fact restating a much larger amount, $6.4 billion.

> The result of the restatement will be to lower the company's revenues and profits in 1997, 1998 and 1999, and increase them in 2000 and 2001.

Although the knee-jerk reaction of the market was an immediate drop of the price by $1.90, Xerox's share recovered later, when word got out that the restatement was not the result of ". . . phantom sales or earnings that might lead to fresh accusations of accounting irregularities or additional

---

[87] On July 21, 2002, WorldCom filed for Chapter 11, the largest corporate failure in the history of America.

SEC action." Nevertheless, Xerox still dropped 12.9 percent for the day (this is just to "demonstrate" how informationally efficient the market is).

Xerox's Chairperson cum CEO, Ms. Anne M. Mulcahy, declared, "the firm's accounting issues with regulators 'have been resolved,' and Xerox will behave in the future, accountingwise, as a choirboy." This brought to conclusion Xerox's fight with the SEC that had been going on for over a year. At the end, Xerox agreed to restate its earnings, change its accounting methods of leases in foreign countries and pay a $10 million fine, the largest the SEC levied on a firm thus far.

Andersen LLP's involvement is but half of the problem. In the case of Enron at least, key political figures from both sides of the aisle are involved with the Enron scandal. People who are now shouting the loudest to investigate Enron's connection to the White House, in the past did everything they could to allay investigations of the SEC into Enron's off-books dealings. The names of Senators Lieberman and Dodd, and Congressman Billy Tauzin come up, repeatedly.

B. Other Strains of Enronomics

Then there is the Merrill Lynch case, perhaps the biggest sham in the meltdown of morality. The newspapers across the land reported in late May 2002 that New York State Attorney-General Eliot Spitzer settled with Merrill Lynch on a "modest" fine of $100 million, with a promise of separating Merrill Lynch research from brokerage, and a rather disingenuous expression of regret by Merrill Lynch for past practices, yet all the same admitting no guilt. This was after a year-long investigation by Eliot Spitzer who turned overnight to dragon-slayer[88] and now is viewed as a possible Democratic candidate for governor.

---

[88] Next to villains we love to hate and fear comes the dragon-slayer, the white knight who saves the public. The latest in this line of folk heroes is Rudolph Giuliani, whose tireless work on the wake of the 9/11 catastrophe earned him a knighthood (a real one), became a symbol of the American spirit and got surcease for being the most racially divisive mayor of New York City. Interestingly, Merrill Lynch is contemplating the enlisting of Rudi as a spokesperson of the firm to save its tarnished reputation. This is not unlike the enlisting of Paul Volker, discussed earlier, by Andersen LLP to save it from the ultimate demise. In 2007, Giuliani is contemplating a run for the presidency in 2008, and Eliot Spitzer was sworn in on January 2007 as the 54th Governor of New York State.

But, according to the *New York Times* on May 25, 2002;

As Merrill Lynch & Company prepares to defend itself in court against angry investors, the firm's 14,000 brokers are caught in the cross-fire. Despite agreeing this week to pay $100 million in penalties to New York and other states, Merrill still faces lawsuits from customers who contend that they lost money because they were misled by the recommendations of the firm's analysts. Estimates of Merrill's liability in those cases run as high as $5 billion and are weighing heavily on Merrill's stock price, which has dropped nearly 20 percent since April.

The $100 million fine for the investment banker/broker giant is, as someone remarked, akin to a traffic ticket for driving 40 miles/hour in a 35-mile zone for you and me. If Merrill would have been found guilty on charges of giving false advice to investors, and that in return opened the door for so cheated investors, court costs and damages could have totaled $5 billion, as quoted by the *Times*. The possibility alone is "weighing heavily on Merrill's stock price, which has dropped nearly 20 percent." Such a cash strain, if it became reality, could have meant closing time for the firm. Merrill Lynch had done the same thing before: recommending "buy" for a stock, therefore creating a run-up of the price, while all along planning to unload the holdings of Merrill in that particular security before the stock tanked.

The difference this time has been that Merrill's security analysts exchanged e-mails among themselves ridiculing the stock, all the while recommending it to Merrill's clients to buy it. And we thought that the computer cum internet would make us more productive!

The political ramifications and undertows of the Merrill Lynch case are perhaps as important and not less revealing as the Enron case. Perhaps there is an explanation why Merrill was let off the hook with a slap on the wrist, and a faint promise to be good citizens from now on.

The *New York Times* published a feature column with dragon-slayer Eliot L. Spitzer. The May 16, 2002 interview opens like so:

A few years ago, Eliot L. Spitzer, the Attorney-General of New York and a Democrat, was invited to speak before the Federalist Society, the legal group whose members abhor the use of courts to force political change — at least liberal political change — and have helped formulate the key conservative tenet that power should devolve from the central government, including the federal courts, to the states. "I told them that I had had an epiphany and I was now a fervent Federalist," Spitzer said. "Having won this job as attorney-general of a state, this devolution of power was a wonderful thing: they were limiting the feds, they were shifting to us, so we could go off and sue the tobacco companies." Spitzer claims that his audience was "ashen." This seems unlikely, but melodrama is so foreign to Spitzer's nature that perhaps he can be permitted this one moment of self-satisfied hyperbole.

We are, in fact, in the midst of an era of widespread state-level judicial activism, and Eliot Spitzer is the most active, or at least the most prominent, attorney-general around. Since being elected in 1998, at age 39, Spitzer has expanded the scope of the office by using novel approaches to the law in order to go after large-scale targets — including gun manufacturers, drug companies and mid-Western polluters — often in concert with other state attorneys-general. He has won some and lost some. But nothing Spitzer has done has remotely had the impact of the news conference he held April 8, at which he announced that research analysts at Merrill Lynch had published false and misleading stock recommendations, an act he characterized as "an outrageous betrayal of their trust and a shocking abuse of the system."

Merrill Lynch is not alone. On June 1, 2002, the media reported that the SEC opened ten inquiries over the last year into potential conflicts of interest by securities analysts. Five of these have been upgraded to formal investigations. Some of the investigations "involve potential conflicts arising from firms' investment banking activities," according to the SEC memo, which was released by Representative Edward J. Markey (Dem. Massachusetts). The memo added that a number of the inquiries might be expanded to include other possible violations of securities laws. Are deceit, fraud and casuistry endemic to Wall Street? To US capitalism? Richard Condon certainly thought so when, in his brilliant satire titled *The Final Addiction* (see opening quote to this paper), he compared American business to a criminal organization, a whole decade before Enron. He also made it clear that politics and business are inseparable. Perhaps there is a lesson there for us to learn before we build our models in a complete vacuum?

What is more alarming than the cases the SEC is working on is not the fact that gilt-edged investment houses perpetrate unscrupulous and perhaps illegal practices. The scary things are the immediate political ramifications Spitzer alluded to in the interview. Those that worked hard to shift regulatory power to the states (thereby weakening the better staffed and educated central government) made sure that the interests of the contributors to their campaigns would be protected. Less and less effective oversight has been the objective all along.

This was and still is the ultra-conservative agenda, the *New York Times* mentioned in the Spitzer interview. That is why Congress is still unwilling to go ahead with stiff legislation of the accounting industry, giving more power to the SEC,[89] or with regulating investment banking. What we hear again is the same old song: the industry will reorganize, learn from its mistakes and police itself. Ridiculous! Hell, even the caricature of a campaign finance reform bill, the McCain/Feingold Bill, is being watered down as we speak by the Election Commission before it could show any meaningful change of campaign finances.

Charles "Lucky" Luciano, the New York City mobster that organized crime into "families," when asked before his death if he could have lived his life again what would he have done differently, answered: "I would have done the same things, except I would have gotten a license."

Luciano might have been a hoodlum who had not just great organizational talents, but saw properly the ways and means of capitalism in America.. The inflection is in America, because capitalism need not either be or follow the American model anywhere else. Sure, there are political scandals involving business in other capitalist countries, most recently in France[90] and in Germany.[91] But nowhere in the industrialized world can one observe such connection between politics and business, between lobbying and business, as in the American strain of 21st century capitalism. I will come back to this point later.

C. Life on the Inside

There are other maladies, still, that make the expression "business ethics" (something which is widely taught in B-schools) an oxymoron. Let us turn to this variety of deceit and casuistry.

In a June 24, 2002 column of *Fortune Magazine*, titled "The Emperor of Greed" (how soon they forget Michael Milken, Rapacity Rex), Julie

---

[89] In fact, in spite of the gigantic expansion of the securities markets over the past ten years, the SEC's budget did not increase one red cent.

[90] Elf, and more recently, Vivendi.

[91] The Helmut Kohl affair.

Creswell and Nomi Prins provide the reader with a short biography of Gary Winnick, Global Crossing's CEO:

> Gary Winnick had never worked in the telecom industry before he founded Global Crossing in 1997. He had never run a public company before either. Yet in the late 1990s, Chairman Winnick was hailed as an industry giant, the creator of a telco that a year after going public in 1998 was valued at $38 billion — more than Ford. A little over two years later, Global Crossing is in bankruptcy and fighting to survive, part of an industry collapse that wiped out $2.5 trillion in market value. Investors and regulators are struggling to figure out what went so wrong so fast. But the real question is how such a company could survive — indeed prosper — for as long as it did.

So, what are we supposed to ponder here:

- What went so wrong so fast? Or
- The "real question": how could such a company survive — indeed prosper — for so long?

I think that what we academics should contemplate is the meaning of "market value." Specifically, how $2.5 trillion (I am shivering even as I am pecking out this astronomical sum on my keyboard) went puff when the so-called bubble burst. I will come back to the question of value a bit later, because that is where the gardener's dog is buried (I am borrowing the metaphor from Lope Felix De Vega Carpio's play, "The Dog in the Manger").

Here, I just want to mention Felix Rohatyn's remark about the superiority of American-style capitalism, when he compared the total equity market values of that of combined Europe and the US. Felix boasted that although the population of the two entities is roughly the same, the market values of the US is twice as much as that of Europe. One, of course, must ponder not just how fast "values" melt in our economy, something akin to an ice-cream cone left on the sands of the Sahara, but also three world wars (including that which was termed cold) that ravaged Europe and left America stronger each time. This is not to mention the fact that Europeans are not that used to investing in equity.

But back to the meltdown of Global Crossing. Although Creswell and Prins call Winnick "the emperor of greed," the subtitle of their column declares that Winnick treated Global Crossing as his personal cash cow "with the help of his bankers." Moreover, the two authors show a "report card" of who were "making out as bandits." Although Winnick pocketed a total of $750.8 million, other top executives and directors were not exactly standing in line at the Salvation Army's soup kitchen either. Their total stock sales brought in $582.3 million for their efforts of fleecing the market. Other financial institutions, which were part and parcel of the power play, such as CIBC World Markets, Loews/CNA Financial and Ullico also made $3.8 billion.

Creswell and Prins continue with their story:

> Global Crossing inflated its revenues by swapping capacity with other carriers, say analysts, and lured customers and investors by overstating the reach and capabilities of its network — a $12 billion "state-of-the-art" system that, several former employees told Fortune, simply doesn't work that well. It exploited its relationships with both Wall Street and its bankers on a scale unrivaled in the industry. "Winnick used to walk around the office saying he owned Jack Grubman and Jimmy Lee," says one former colleague, referring to fees paid to key underwriters at Citigroup's Salomon Smith Barney and J.P. Morgan Chase. A spokesperson for Winnick denies he made such statement.

In other words, Winnick, in an imaginary testimonial dinner, must use the cliché in his speech: "I couldn't have done that without you guys."

Although I remarked earlier, parenthetically, how fast they forget Michael Milken (because in my book no one else can vie for the title "the emperor of greed"), it seems that Winnick grew up on the master of public deception's knees:

> Given Winnick's prior experience, the incestuous relationship with Wall Street shouldn't come as too much of a surprise. A native of Long Island, Winnick had an unremarkable upbringing. His father ran a restaurant supply business, and after graduation from C.W. Post, a local college, Winnick worked as a furniture salesman. His life took a turn in the early 1970s when he joined Drexel Burnham Lambert. He developed a taste for the high life after he made his way to the Los Angeles office, where he worked on the bond sales desk alongside Michael Milken. While Milken ended up in jail for securities and reporting violations, Winnick escaped Drexel untarnished and founded Pacific Capital Group, an investment firm in Los Angeles (*ibid.*).

And then there is Tyco International. Although the last act of the Tyco tale of corporate larceny will play out in criminal court, it seems that L. Dennis Kozlowski, the Tyco's ex-CEO, and ex-CFO Mark H. Swartz are going to be indicted for tax fraud in New York State. Nevertheless, the two got away with $500 million and $100 million, respectively, before the firm's stock tanked. They carried out their version of corporate hold-up with a complicated scheme of selling the stock and returning it to Tyco, which concealed the sale for 12 months instead of the required reporting of ten days after the sale of the same month.

Tyco's shares suffered further decline when it was disclosed to the SEC that it paid outside director Frank E. Walsh, Jr., $10 million. Now, if this is not a way to keep board of directors' members looking the other way instead of watching stockholders' interests, I do not know what is.

Some more tales of the inside, if you have not caught my drift so far. On June 6, 2002, the papers reported about charging John M. Rusnak, a currency trader, with bank fraud and other crimes for allegedly hiding $691 million of losses at Allfirst Financial, an Allied Irish Banks unit, with fictitious trades and showing non-existent profits. All this, according to the indictment, with the help of Citibank, Bank of America and Merrill Lynch (hmm, again?).

On June 11, 2002, Adelphia Communications' Century Communications unit filed for bankruptcy protection, reported the *New York Times*. Newly appointed Adelphia directors Leonard Tow and Scott Schneider resigned, and Century Communications filed documents showing it overstated revenues and cash flows for the last two years. Bankruptcy filing by Century Communications is widely seen as a precursor to bankruptcy filing within days by Adelphia itself, the paper added.

And we must not overlook the ImClone story, as it is told in the June 22, 2002 issue of the *Times*:

Merrill Lynch and Co. Inc. on Wednesday rejected suggestions from congressional investigators that its biotechnology analyst received and disseminated inside information when he issued a report on ImClone Systems, Inc. a day before negative news sent the company's stock tumbling.

Investigators are examining a research note issued by the investment bank's analyst Eric Hecht on Dec. 27, which drew attention to market speculation that the US Food and Drug Administration might decline to review ImClone's experimental cancer drug, Erbitux. A day later the FDA did just that.

The House Energy and Commerce Committee, which is probing the ImClone case, is trying to determine "if there was any connection" between Hecht's speculation and Merrill Lynch stockbroker Peter Bacanovic, according to Ken Johnson, a spokesman for Rep. Billy Tauzin, a Louisiana Republican who chairs the panel.

Bacanovic's clients include ImClone's former chief executive Samuel Waksal and Martha Stewart, the lifestyle diva and friend of Waksal's who sold ImClone shares Dec. 27, Johnson said in an interview Wednesday.

Committee investigators already have interviewed Hecht and hope to interview Bacanovic next week, Johnson said.

Merrill Lynch (MER.N) said in a statement that Hecht's note "was based solely on publicly available information and his own research and views regarding the company."

Last week, Waksal was arrested and charged with attempting to sell ImClone stock based on non-public information, and on tipping family members to do the same. Investigators are examining whether Stewart also may have been tipped. She has said her trade was lawful.

In pointing out that investors were speculating approval of Erbitux might be delayed, Hecht was stating the obvious.

Investors had been discussing their concerns on internet chatboards as early as Dec. 18. They even speculated about possible insider trading as they watched the stock begin to slide two weeks ahead of the FDA's announcement on Dec. 28.

In the days leading up to the announcement, trading volume in ImClone's stock soared. On Dec. 27, more than 7.7 million shares changed hands, more than triple the average and the most in a single day since September 19, 2001, when Bristol-Myers Squibb Co. (BMY.N) agreed to pay up to $2 billion for US rights to Erbitux and a 20 percent stake in ImClone.

That level of trading activity and a sharp drop in ImClone's stock price prompted questions from Merrill Lynch's trading desk, Merrill Lynch said. Hecht's report came in response to these questions.

Perhaps the case of Martha Stewart, "the lifestyle diva," centi-millionairess who is on trial as we speak, is the true visage of free-marketism

(21st-century American capitalism). Some experts estimate her wealth to be close to $1 billion. But that is still not enough, even though not a single human being is capable of spending that much wealth in a lifetime. She must risk an insider's trading conviction to make perhaps, what? $200,000–$300,000? It is not about wealth anymore. It is about power, and the conviction that power puts one above the law.[92]

But the cake on the inside, without a doubt, goes to the President, George W. Bush. The President appeared before a Wall Street audience of 1,000 on July 9, 2002, just after the 4th of July 2002 national holiday. In this appearance, Mr. Bush vented his newfangled anger over corporate fraud. He promised stiffer jail sentences for corporate criminals, the establishment of a task force to ferret the criminals out. Yet, he made it crystal clear that there was nothing wrong with the system. One must remember that both the President and the Veep were members of the corporate establishment, just as four other members of the cabinet were. Moreover, the bulk of his campaign finances came from corporate America.

Although his speech did not calm Wall Street and the continuing slide of the major market indices, the news of the President's intention breathed fresh life into George W. Bush's own brush with suspected insider trading and other shenanigans — exactly the same activities of the top corporate brass the President condemned.

This story is worth discussing in some detail, not just because it sheds light on the character of the highest office holder in the land, on the interaction between politics and economics, and on the powerlessness of the market to discover the schemes of the rich and the connected, but also because it serves as a case study of how things are done "out there."

The tale begins with Mr. Bush, then the CEO of Spectrum 7,[93] a small, losing, debt-ridden Texas energy firm, being acquired by Harken Energy, another troubled Texas energy firm, for $2 million. George W. ended up with a hefty chunk of Harken's shares, a seat on its board of directors and a membership of its audit and restructuring committees (something that gave Mr. Bush immediate access to Harken's accounting information).

---

[92] Martha Stewart was found guilty on four counts, including obstruction of justice and lying to investigators, and on July 18, 2004 was sentenced to five months in prison, five months of house arrest and a $30,000 fine.

[93] Before Spectrum 7, Mr. Bush was associated with another losing oil venture, Arbusto (Spanish for bush, but I will translate it in his case as shrub to distinguish it from George the pére).

The *Washington Post* and the *New York Times* reported on July 10, 2002, that Harken was so interested in Mr. Bush joining its board of directors that it gave a low-interest loan to George W. Bush to buy shares of Harken, 80,000 in 1986 and 25,000 in 1988, respectively. At first, Mr. George W. was made liable for the loan with his personal assets, but that was waived later by Harken. The loan carried a 5 percent interest (when the prime rate was 7.5 percent), and the payments on the principal did not commence for eight years. Although there was nothing illegal with these loans, two nagging questions come to mind:

(1)   How can one look out for the interests of Harken shareholders when one is brought on board by the people who run the firm and whose activities the board member (an outside director) should be scrutinizing? And

(2)   How can Mr. Bush the President berate the practice when he was a beneficiary, albeit on a smaller scale, of the same treatment that the executives of Global Crossing or WorldCom enjoyed?

When the founder of Harken, one Mr. Phil Kendrik, was asked what was the deal, Kendrik responded, "His name was George Bush," as the legend goes by the *Times*' March 4, 2002 account.

What is in a name, one would ask? Well, George Herbert Walker Bush was the 41st President of the United States of America at that time. So, the story of George W. Bush is not exactly a rags-to-riches story we all love to hear because it gives us hope that everyone can make it. I am tempted to call this story "affirmative action for the connected and the privileged."

It just happened that Harken was a money-losing operation, too. Nevertheless, it successfully hid its losses by dealing with itself. It sold a subsidiary, Aloha Petroleum, for a substantial capital gain, which it reported as current revenues. Aloha Petroleum was bought by a group of Harken insiders who borrowed the money for the purchase, you guessed it, from Harken Energy itself. Have you seen a revolving door in a downtown hotel? That is the brilliant financial scheme where one gets in the door a pauper in one end and comes out a prince at the other end.

The scheme was so obvious that even a meek (as we know, they may inherit the world but not its mineral rights) SEC forced Harken to restate its 1989 earnings. Shortly before the bad news hit the streets, Mr. Bush sold a major portion of his interest in Harken for $800,000 plus. Mr. Bush promptly invested this money in a partial ownership of a major league baseball team, which netted him $16 million years later when he sold these shares. Mr. Bush is a Harvard MBA, and if nothing else, it shows what broad managerial talents one can acquire at that school and how successful one will be after that.

That was before the price of Harken started to tank. Divine wisdom? Perhaps yes, perhaps no. This is not the issue here, however. The concern is that Mr. Bush had to file a Form 4 with the SEC. The sale of his Harken shares took place on June 22, 1990 as a block trade, and the form had to be filed by July 10, 1990 (within 18 days after the sale) to disclose the unloading of his Harken shares. Brace here for the murky part.

Mr. Bush filed the form 269 (287–18) days too late, which made the SEC's Enforcement Division suspicious. From a letter of April 12, 1991 (dated just a week after the filing) addressed to Mr. Bush, one learns that an assistant director of the Division, Herbert F. Janick, informed the President that the SEC was conducting a preliminary inquiry in his trading of Harken shares (File No. MHO-3180). The letter demanded copies of all forms 3, 4 and 144, cover letters and attachments concerning his trade of Harken, and copies of all monthly brokerage statements in his name or under his control of Harken securities from September 1, 1986 to April 12, 1991.

The same Mr. Janick's June 21, 1991 fax to Joseph A. Cialone, Mr. Bush's lawyer, demanded additional, more extensive documentation, too specific to list here. Let us just state that the demand included every bit of piece of paper, electronic media or any other traceable form of conversation relating to Mr. Bush's dealings with the Harken shares. At first, the attorney declined to comply on the grounds of attorney-client privilege. Later, the SEC must have been satisfied, because the investigation was terminated.

The logic for terminating the investigation, as one can learn from an Action Memorandum dated March 18, 1992, was the following: Mr. Bush sold 212,140 of his Harken shares (in a block trade, not open market NYSE) for $848,560, or $4.00/share. On the morning of August 20, 1990, Harken reported a quarterly loss of $23.2 million for the quarter ending on June 30, 1990 (the action memorandum erroneously reports June 30, 1992). The loss was detailed as:

- Operating losses for the quarter $6.7 million
- Write-down for Aloha Petroleum $7.2 million
- Write-down for Harken Marketing $2.5 million, and
- Interest expenses of $3.9 million.

The SEC opened an inquiry into the Bush sale of June 22, 1990 because Bush filed Form 4, instead of July 10, 1990, on April 5, 1991. The memorandum then concludes that

> Based upon our investigation, it appears that Bush did not engage in illegal insider trading because it does not appear that he possessed material non-public information or that he acted scienter when he sold the Harken stock (pp. 2–3).

This conclusion is reached, mostly on the understanding of the staff at the SEC after consultation with the Office of Economic Analysis, that Bush did not have material knowledge of the extent of the loss for the quarter that ended on June 30, just eight days before his sale of the 200,000 plus shares.

The shares of Harken started to slide after the quarterly report became public information on August 20, 1990, and shortly after that were traded for $2.00/share (since March 18, 1991, the common of Harken has been trading on the AMEX).

Now, there are two critical issues involved with the Bush sale:

(1)   Why did Mr. Bush report the sale 269 days late? And

(2)   Did he possess material non-public knowledge of the 2nd quarter loss?

At first, George W. argued that it was his accountants' responsibility to file Form 4. Later, he contended that he filed it in time, but it was lost at the SEC. An internal memo of the SEC stated that Mr. Bush's failure was a violation of securities laws (indeed, that is why Bush was investigated by the SEC for insider trading).

The second issue is whether or not Mr. Bush had material knowledge. For if he had, and he did file late, then the late filing aggravates the criminal act of trading on insider information. This is so, because had he filed on time, it would have been a clear signal to the market that something was wrong with Harken's earnings, as it became public knowledge on August 20, 1990.

This aspect of compounding one violation with the other was never discussed in the SEC memorandum, because the SEC accepted the claim that Bush had no knowledge of the extent of the 2nd quarter loss. Being a member of the firm's audit and restructuring committees, and the fact that the bulk of the losses were timed losses (the two write-offs) or interest expenses that must have been known to the directors on the audit committee, it would not have been too difficult to interview company accountants and other board members to verify whether the claim of no knowledge was true. In fact, another member of both committees, one E. Stuart Watson, told reporters in 1994 that he and Bush had updated knowledge of the firm's finances.

The SEC opted not to file charges, however. Did the SEC negligence have anything to do with the fact that George W. was George H.W.'s son, who happened to be the President at the time? Perhaps no, perhaps yes.

The Harken issue was raised in the press several times when Mr. Bush was running for governor of Texas, and later during the 2000 presidential campaign. It surfaced again, now, amidst the aftermath of Enron and the President's claim that he is going to be tough with corporate criminals. His press secretary, Mr. Ari Fleischer, replied to the media questioning the President's action regarding the Harken affair that it is the usual Democrat partisanship, trying to beat a dead horse to weaken the President's hand when America is fighting a war. Besides, Mr. Fleischer continued, so many newspapers examined the case, and if they did not find anything incriminating, then there isn't anything incriminating. Perhaps yes, perhaps no.

The question that remains, however, is since when is the possibility of law-breaking in America, and by a no lesser person than the President, left to the media to decide? Better yet, when can the media subpoena witnesses who would testify under oath, risking stiff jail terms for perjury?

If the President has nothing to hide, he should be the first one to ask for an independent inquiry of the case. Instead, the President is preaching to other corporate moguls to mend their sinful ways, or else. One finds it as less than a miracle that securities markets do not respond positively to the President's posturing regarding the clean-up of American capitalism.

Oh, yes. A final question I almost forgot to ask: could you guess who was the outside auditor of Harken?

D. There is More

On the very same day (May 25, 2002) that Merrill Lynch agreed to pay into the coffers of New York State $100 million, another industrial giant, Schering Plough, agreed to fork over to the Federal Treasury $500 million, the largest fine ever levied on a US pharmaceutical firm. The fine was assessed on Schering Plough because of its failure to correct problems with several of its drugs, including its bestselling allergy drug, Claritin.

Another pharmaceutical giant, Bristol Myers, is being investigated by the SEC for its sales practices, newspapers reported on July 11, 2002. There must be some significance to this day, or else the SEC wants to show a "getting tough" stance on the heels of the President's speech earlier in the same week.

But there are more problems and accusations surfacing with pharmaceuticals, also called often, ethical drugs. Analysts argue that drug companies spend more on wining-and-dining physicians, ferrying them to conventions to exotic places, and on advertising than they spend on research. In many instances, they convince doctors to prescribe drugs that are very expensive when the over-the-counter and relatively cheap Tylenol would be just as effective. One must recall that pharmaceuticals charge an exorbitant price for medication on the grounds that they must recover their R&D expenditures, without which further R&D of more effective and better drugs would not be forthcoming. These medications are not even in the category of the super expensive drugs, such as drugs to help AIDS victims. These medications are prescribed routinely, especially for senior citizens, as their daily regimen. In some instances, the choice for these persons is between medication and food. Then, one must wonder where the adjective "ethical" comes to be attached to the name of the industry.

A new twist on the "drug crisis" comes from a rather unexpected angle. A study on hormone treatment sponsored by the government and published in early July 2002 shows that there are increased risks and little benefits from the use of the hormone progesterone. The study was conducted on 16,000 subjects over a ten-year period. The results showed such statistically significant increases in the risks of breast cancer and blood clotting that the 16,000 subjects in the study were informed to stop taking the drug progestine.

Six million women take the drug regularly on a daily basis and the drug manufacturers made $10 billion profit over time, yet did not contribute a cent in research for the benefits and hazards associated with the drug. Perhaps this is another good example that free markets are not the best vehicle for provision of certain public goods and services.

But there is still more: the phone companies. The deregulation craze of the telecommunication industry and the break-up of the Bell system brought about fierce competition among the baby Bells and other newly sprouting telecommunication firms. Because of the heavy investment in hardware and facilities, financed by excessive leverage, many either went bankrupt or are on the verge of bankruptcy. The situation of not being regulated as monopolists, and the fierce competition for revenues among the still surviving ones, brought about what *60 Minutes* calls "competing by cheating," the newest form of free marketism.[94]

One of the most common illegal practices of these firms is called slamming. Slamming means to produce a document, supposedly signed by the consumer, in which he/she expresses his/her desire to change long-distance carriers — the lucrative part of the business. The documents are forgeries. In fact, the consumer is not even aware of ever signing such document. To cover its tracks, the telecommunication firm employs a third party to do the slamming. In this way, it can deny any complicity in the act.

Another form of "competing by cheating" is placing all kinds of exotic charges on the phone bill the consumer does not have to pay, or else the extent of the charges are not explained.[95] They are just fancy names, and

---

[94] Apparently, these firms interpret free markets as the place where the supplier of goods or services is either free to cheat, or levy charges on the consumer that are patently illegal.

[95] Here is an example from my own monthly phone bill from Sprint:

- Interstate access surcharge $6.00
- Telecommunication relay surcharge $0.08
- Number portability surcharge $0.48
- Federal universal service fund $0.50

The sprint website has the following explanations for three of the four charges:

Interstate access surcharge ($4–$5, but I am charged $6): connection to local network to cover the cost of telephone wires, poles and other facilities. Although these were installed many years ago, there is no schedule provided on how the charge was calculated and over what time the costs are recovered.

Telecommunication surcharge: no explanation.

Number portability surcharge: this is for being able to retain my phone number when and if I move (almost everywhere) within my local service area. This is a FCC-approved surcharge, but it does not say how much it approved, nor does it say how it is calculated to recover the "cost" which most in the service area will never create.

Federal universal service fund: this is to "recover some of the costs Sprint incurs" in other areas. Again, no explanation is given why it is $0.50 each month and what the real costs of Sprint are.

For monthly service, excluding federal, state and local taxes and 911 surcharge, I am paying $11.12, which includes $1.01 for touch-tone service. Now, what does the monthly local service cover, if not also some of the investment of Sprint in exactly the same facilities and equipment for which it charges me again under clever exotic titles?

because they are relatively small, one is not necessarily paying attention to what one is being charged for. Several state attorney-generals are in the process of suing telecommunication firms for either illegal charges or connections to slamming. One company that was informed by the SEC on July 11, 2002 of being investigated already (for undisclosed reasons) is QWest, a still-surviving giant.

The point remains, however, that there is a new business ethics "out there." It hides under the surface of the concept of free markets, that in reality are only free for those who can control it. Freedom in this context means that they are free to do anything they can get away with. Given the politics, lax (*de facto*, non-existent) regulation and insufficient funds for enforcement by the regulatory agencies, it is quite a bit what the captains of industry, to borrow a title from Thorsten Velden, can get away with.

In the wake of the WorldCom scandal appearing before the House Financial Services Committee, ex-CEO Bernard J. Ebbers and ex-CFO Scott Sullivan joined the ranks of the Enron Fifth Amendment capitalists. Then, Bert Roberts, the chairman of the board, in his testimony before the committee, blamed the CPA firm Andersen, LLP. Melvin Dick, the senior partner of Andersen responsible for the audit of WorldCom, argued that they (the auditors) had no inkling of the accounting improprieties. This is strange, because for a small fee, a C-average undergraduate student majoring in accounting at Dumbfounded State Community College would have pointed out the difference between investment and expenses, and reporting the latter as the former showed profits to the tune of $3.8 billion that just were not there.

The President has promised jail sentences for CEOs caught signing off on false accounting statements. But that is about it. The Sarbanes bill intended to tighten up accounting practices of outside auditors is gutted out, in fact turned to token. Nothing will change until politics is taken out, to some degree at least, from corporate America. The first step in this direction must be stiff campaign finance reform and the abolition of the lobby system. Do not hold your breath!

So, perhaps this is not the end of the ball after all, but continuing with the cotillion in the gutters. In the meantime, the proponents of the status quo (guess who) are pointing to the recovery of the equity markets. The system is okay, they argue, it was just a few rotten apples in the bushel. Well, it is perhaps okay for those who pumped their windfall of the colossal tax cuts into the secondary and third markets. But what about the other 98 percent of us?

Chapter 12

Capitalism or Industrial Fiefdom[*]

As for freedom, it will soon cease to exist in any shape or form. Living will depend upon absolute obedience to a strict set of arrangements, which it will no longer be possible to transgress. The air traveler is not free. In the future, life's passengers will be even less so: they will travel through their lives fastened to their (corporate) seats.

— Jean Baudrillard *Cool Memories*[96]

A. Introduction

The two cardinally defining documents of the United States of America are the Declaration of Independence and the Constitution. In both documents, the synonym of freedom, "liberty," appears together with the words happiness and [unalienable] right to a decent life:

"We hold these truths to be self-evident, that all men are created equal, that they are endowed by their Creator with certain unalienable Rights, that among these are Life, Liberty and the pursuit of Happiness," and

"We the People of the United States, in Order to form a more perfect Union, establish Justice, insure domestic Tranquility, provide for the common defense, promote the general Welfare, and secure the Blessings of Liberty to ourselves and our Posterity, do ordain to establish this Constitution for the United States of America,"

respectively.

The first ten Amendments to the Constitution, called the Bill of Rights, and many of the following ones, together with the separation of

---

[*] The original version of this paper was published in *Homo Oeconomicus*, 2006, Volume 23(2): 239–254.

[96] *The Columbia Dictionary of Quotations* is licensed from Columbia University Press. Copyright © 1993, 1995, 1997, 1998 by Columbia University Press. All rights reserved.

powers and the checks and balances built into this separation, make the republic an exemplar of democracy. Although the founding fathers copied the ideas of the Baron de Montesquieu, as expressed in the *Parisian Letters* and *The Spirit of the Laws*, what evolved turned into a beacon of democracy to many nations during the 230 plus years of existence of the United States of America.

Thus, it is safe to say that democracy, freedom and the right to a decent life (whether we call it "the pursuit of happiness" or "the general Welfare") are part and parcel of the form of government under which we are supposed to live, and they are inseparable. Perhaps, albeit in a round-about way, Anatole France put it the best in *The Red Lilly*: "The law, in its majestic equality, forbids rich and poor alike to sleep under bridges, beg in the streets or steal bread."

There cannot be democracy or freedom, and very little "equality," if the commonality between the rich and the poor is that either one cannot sleep under bridges, beg in the streets and steal bread. That is to say, if some (or many) citizens of a country have neither the right nor the chance to a decent life, there cannot be either democracy or liberty.

It follows that without this comprehensive understanding of the word, freedom does not mean a thing. It is the same trigger mechanism as the bell to the sound of which Pavlov's dog learned to salivate. The word is just as valueless as calling French fries "freedom fries," or, as during WWI, renaming sauerkraut to "liberty cabbage."

B. Ideology

It is widely believed that politics and economics are separate and largely unconnected; that individual freedom is a political problem and material welfare an economic problem; and that any kind of political arrangements can be combined with any kind of economic arrangements (Friedman, 1962, 1982).

Capitalism and Freedom was the title of Milton Friedman's (1962) collection of essays/lecture notes in which the most significant Cold War warrior of neoclassical economics (*laissez faire*) turned his views on the connection between economics and politics into a treatise. Friedman also observed, and a Friedmanian opinion and observation turns very quickly into an axiom (which it later did), that capitalism is a necessary but not satisfactory condition for freedom. This is so, because, albeit some might argue that socialism and democracy can go hand-in-hand, "The thesis [of this chapter] is that such a view is a delusion, that there is an intimate connection between economics and politics, that only certain combinations of political and economic arrangements are possible, and that in particular, a society which is socialist cannot also be democratic, in the sense of guaranteeing individual freedom" (*ibid.*, p. 8).

Friedman then devotes a whole book, an anthology of 11 essays and a concluding part, to show that only capitalism can go together with freedom, and only the total freedom of the individual, where the government's sole role is to guarantee such freedom, can be consistent with the total welfare of society.

Friedman's contentions and arguments have no historical precedence. Quite the contrary, it would take a volume to cite all the examples which show how his theory does not work. I, however, cannot help but remind the reader of Katrina's disaster to have a perfect illustration of how a purposefully ineffectual government, seized by ideologues who carried some of Friedman's ideas into stark reality, can cause irreparable damage to hundreds of thousands of citizens, indeed, to an historical landmark treasured by a whole nation.

There is one part of the Friedmanian thesis I cited earlier with which I totally agree. In fact, the idea of the one-on-one connection between economics and politics is the starting point of my essay titled "The Theory of Fair Markets"(Frankfurter, 2006). With all fairness to Friedman, however, perhaps the kind of capitalism we have is not the strain Friedman's utopia is all about. But, to paraphrase a past German Chancellor, "this is all the capitalism we have." And, as far as the weakening of government with respect to economic security and cushion to its citizens goes, it is a government that does everything to rob us of our civil rights and freedoms to which we were accustomed through more than two centuries of evolution.

Strangely, however, this early thesis of Friedman, the connection of politics and economics, has never found its place in the theories that financial economics promoted and, later, were called modern finance. To underscore my point, a fairly detailed laundry list is the following:

(1) Markowitz's Portfolio Selection Model (Markowitz, 1952; Markowitz, 1959);
(2) The Modigliani–Miller (Modigliani and Miller, 1958) and Miller–Modigliani (Miller and Modigliani, 1961) indifference theory;

(3)   The Capital Asset Pricing Model (Sharpe, 1964; Lintner, 1965; Black, 1972; Black, Jensen *et al.*, 1972) and others;

(4)   The Efficient Markets Hypothesis (EMH) of Fama (Fama, 1965; Fama, 1970);

(5)   Arbitrage Pricing Theory (APT) of Ross (Ross, 1976);

(6)   Option pricing and contingent claims models (Black and Scholes, 1973; Merton, 1973);

(7)   Agency Theory (Jensen and Meckling, 1976); and perhaps

(8)   Signaling (Bhattacharya, 1979; Bhattacharya, 1980).[97]

Not a single one of these models/theories conjures up any connection whatsoever between their economic rationality and politics. Neither has modern finance any models that would take into account, much less predict, nefarious activities by any market participant. On the contrary, the market is supposed to be the avatar of god, that with the greatest justice bestowed on earth to any entity, whether real or imaginary, fixes things in a Pareto optimal way, if one just has the patience to wait for it or perhaps survive the material loss one has to incur until and when the market finally fixes things.

In the following, I will argue that the loss of personal freedoms of choice and the concentration of power in the hands of the executive branch of government under the capitalism we know is a logical and perfectly consistent development of the allocation of wealth, both private and corporate. This has strong consequences for us, as well as for other generations to come. I will hazard, also, some predictions on how this process, if not curtailed or aborted, will affect individual and institutional investors, and what would be the reasonable course such investors should follow.

C. Allocation of Wealth

Propaganda, defined as that branch of the art of lying which consists in very nearly deceiving your friends without quite deceiving your enemies.

— F.M. Cornford *Microcosmographia Academica*

---

[97] I say perhaps, because signaling was more a fashionable way to call certain things management does or does not do than a realistic theory that would stand up to empirical testing.

Economics, at the end of the day, is about the allocation of wealth. Politics is nothing more or less, but to put a socially acceptable face to the way wealth is allocated. Perhaps better put the other way around: politics is about the allocation of wealth, and economics is the gauge by which this allocation can be measured.

If one accepts either one of the two formulations, then one cannot take issue with the following:

- Taxation cannot be looked at independently. Taxation goes hand-in-hand with fiscal policy.
- If one says that taxes are too high, then one means to say that one does not get back enough in return. That is, the objection is not the tax per se, but who gets what back from the taxes paid.
- The richer one is, the less one gets back of taxes paid. This would be true, even if taxation were not progressive.
- The less even is the allocation process, the more wealth is accumulated at the hands of the very rich, which is then translated to political power.
- The process is never at a final or steady state. The more wealth is accumulated in the hands of a few, the more will accrue to these few in the future. Consequently, the same goes for power.
- Taxes can be of three types: progressive, neutral or regressive. Which one of the three types a particular tax is depends on how it affects one's income.
- Although some regressive taxes are negligible,[98] only an income tax and some wealth taxes can be truly progressive.
- A sales tax or an excise tax can never be progressive. When one looks at the effect of these taxes on free income (income that is left after paying all obligation and numeraire needs for civilized living, also called the poverty line), a sales tax is a regressive tax, just as any other flat rate tax.

There are, however, other factors and trends in play that make concentration of wealth in the hands of a few faster and more pronounced.

Fiscal policy. That is, how the government spends the taxes it collects, and whether it borrows or lends funds (deficit or surplus budget, respectively) to meet its budgetary targets, roles and obligations.

The defining character of US fiscal policy, starting with the Vietnam War through Carter and Reagan/Bush, was deficit spending, where the

---

[98] For instance, an entrance fee to a state park, or a toll.

bulk of the deficit went toward defense. The logic for this was twofold: (1) to goad the Soviets into an economic race (mislabeled "arms race") to drive them into bankruptcy as the key strategy of the Cold War (which Baudrillard calls WWIII); and (2) during the 12 years of Reagan/Bush, to cut social spending to the bare bone and below.

Deficit budgets are not necessarily a bad thing. In the words of George Washington, "A national debt, if it is not excessive, will be a national blessing."[99] In order to be a national blessing, however, it must be spent on real investment in goods and services. The nature of the deficit during the Vietnam War and during Reagan/Bush was totally different.

It was invested in military goods, which at the best are stockpiled and never used (like the insane number of nuclear warheads with which we must contend sooner or later, to avoid a nuclear disaster at home), and at the worst, used, which creates even more spending on weaponry to replenish the stockpiles and to deal with our own war casualties.

The insanity of piling up national debt was abated for a short while under the Clinton Administration, only to start up again with greater fervor than ever before during the first six years of George W. Bush. The Bush Administration mastered an economic policy of gross tax cuts, chiefly to the very rich, with the astronomical and still mounting costs of the war in Afghanistan and Iraq. This practice of being in a costly war and coincidentally cutting taxes is unprecedented in the brief history of this country.

As a consequence, just recently, the ceiling on the national debt was increased by Congress to $9 trillion. This is a sum compared to which everything else pales. 9,000,000,000,000. Most computers can express this figure only in scientific notation: $9.00E + 12$. If a dollar bill's thickness was 0.5 mm, then a stack of $9 trillion would be 28,125 miles. My imagination stops right here, because I cannot fathom what one can buy for this kind of money.

To make matters worse, and to finance war necessities on one hand and to fuel the conspicuous consumption[100] of the general public on the other, we are in hock to the Chinese (the next superpower to come) up to our ears.

The systematic weakening of labor unions. This was a declared policy of the Reagan Administration that manifested itself first in the merciless crushing of the PATCO strike, early, at the time the Reagan revolution

---

[99] Letters to Robert Morris, April 1781.

[100] A phrase coined at the first quarter of the 20th century by Thorstein Veblen.

was unfolding. Ronald Reagan had a great deal of experience in the matter, even before he became the Governor of California, when he was a union buster spoke-person of GE as a side occupation to making movies of the genre of *Bedtime for Bonzo.*

But this was not the end. NAFTA and globalization, which brought us outsourcing as a noble and American thing to do, contributed to the weakening of labor and to the replacement of high-paying industrial jobs with low-pay service jobs of teaching, pumping gas, flipping hamburgers and answering inquiries. To put the blame solely on Republican administrations would be hypocritical. The Clinton presidency contributed more to this process than anyone both before and after. Clinton not just pushed through NAFTA, which could not have ever happened under Bush the elder, but also made globalization both incontrovertible and irreversible. Let us also not forget that the arms race got its start under the Carter presidency.

The results are irrefutable. Today, only 15 percent of the total labor force is unionized, and the mega-corporations usually have the upper hand in any and all labor disputes and strikes. The Delta pilot strike serves well as a demonstrative example. This recent strike left the Delta pilots with another salary cut as a means of avoiding large-scale job reductions. And the government bailout of American Airlines went more toward stockholders' bailout than to the workforce of the carrier.

The turning of the Supreme Court toward a Conservative agenda. The last two appointments to the Court, Justices Roberts and Alito, are clear signals that the hard-fought battle over Roe vs. Wade is to be won by those who want to make abortion, especially for poor women, not just practically impossible, but also a crime for a physician to perform. This is the smoke-screen the mass media manipulators put on a moral issue to make it political. The economic reality, however, is that both justices (one of whom is Chief) in the past either represented large corporations, or ruled consistently in favor of capital over labor. One can surely expect that in the future, this stance to favor capital is not going to change, adding to the slant of wealth allocation to the richest and further weakening labor.

The burst of the real estate bubble. In a gloom-and-doom article, Hudson (2006) foresees a terrible future for those who were foolish enough to follow the Sirens' song of mortgage bankers, and the sudden and dazzling appreciation of real estate values in many areas of the country. The combination of these two with low interest rates and a Federal Reserve policy to supply the money to sate the demand for mortgages, according to Hudson, will make a great number of the population practically debt serfs to banks.

If one accepts Hudson's reasoning, then it is clear that when the bubble bursts, and all bubbles eventually will, the ones left holding the proverbial bag will be those who expected the rise of real estate values to continue indefinitely. The many bankruptcies that will follow and the further dwindling of disposable income will push the already skewed wealth allocation further and faster from the poor toward the rich.

I am not a great propagator of bubbles. In my opinion, bubbles are an invention of economists who cannot squeeze an observable phenomenon into the confines of their cherished models. Bubbles happen, so we can still believe in the predictions of models which clearly failed to anticipate reality. But fear not, because the bubble will eventually burst.

I find Hudson's analysis both too simplistic and too generalized. The golden rule of the real estate business is that there are three determining factors of real estate value: location, location, location. That is, although in some parts of the country real estate prices clearly slowed down, in some other parts they not only did not fall but in fact increased. We have been waiting for the "bubble burst" since September 2005, and it has yet to come.

Another important differentiation is whether the real estate purchase was for the purpose of investment (speculation, one may say), or for the purpose of one's domicile.[101] In the former case, although down payment in many areas went below 10 percent of appraised value, it was usually the well-to-do who exploited the boon in prices. If indeed the bubble will burst, these people would be the most affected.

Perhaps many will turn into serfs of mortgage banks, or worse case scenario, will go bankrupt (something this administration made very difficult, favoring lenders). Yet, the deciding issue will be their future cash flow expectations from other sources of their wealth, and from their anticipated personal earning power. Also, their capital losses will be mitigated by the write-offs they can use to reduce their tax liabilities.

For those who purchased real estate for the purpose of domicile, whatever happens to real estate values will not affect them unless they cannot keep up with their mortgage payments given their future earning potential.

---

[101] Hudson considers the idea of "investing" with incurring debt an absurdity. If that were the case, we can throw out the window 50 years of financial theory-making and the obvious relation between leverage and return, and financial risk and business risk.

Because of periods of low interest rates and easy mortgage money, and because of government subsidies of mortgage borrowing for individuals, it would be foolish not to take advantage of opportunities that promise also a sizeable appreciation of value, *vis-à-vis* rent that gives none of these.

If real estate prices will decline, but wages and salaries will not, then the value of one's home is important only in the case one has to sell. This happens, usually, when one changes jobs for higher future income. Even if one created "negative equity" (Hudson, 2006), where the sale price of one's home is less than what one owes, the purchase price of a home at the new domicile will be lower as well, and the realized capital loss is, again, tax deductible.

Whether the gloom of Hudson or my more optimistic view will come to pass, the fact remains that if there is a bust of the real estate market, wealth distribution will be further distorted toward the rich.

Environmental effects. The recent catastrophic consequences of hurricanes, mudslides, tornados and flooding brought into focus how vulnerable the poor are and how ineffectual our government is to protect those who do not have substantial reserves to rely on in case of a natural disaster. Global warming that supposedly triggers many of these natural disasters, if not abated, will bring in the future more Katrinas. The current regime, which refuses to accept the consensus of the overwhelming majority of scientists, is not going to do a thing to move toward a change that perhaps can alter the disastrous course set for our future.

If indeed we have to face more and more intense occurrences of environmental emergencies, the poor will get poorer, the middle-class will get poor and the rich will be only marginally affected, if at all.

Then, there is the gasoline crisis rearing up its ugly head yet again, just the same as it did twice during the 1970s. As Yogi Berra would quip: "It's *déjà vu* all over again." The price hikes found us just as ill-prepared as the gasoline shortages found us then. Perhaps the situation today is worse. Although we do not yet have shortages to the extent that people will kill each other at the pump or get gas on either odd or even days depending on their license plate number, prices of a regular gallon went over $4.00 in several places in the country.

The price of a barrel of oil is over $70 and, given the situation in both Iraq and Iran, the market is hinky, which pushes future and spot prices up. Again, the most affected are the middle-class that has to cut on other budget items, because getting to work with their recently acquired Hummers, Excursions, Yukons and Suburbans is a must. Therefore, their demand for gas is extremely price-inelastic and impacts on disposable income.

The poor, at the bottom of the wage scale, are reaching the point where it makes more sense to go on welfare than go to work.[102]

The President in his 2006 State of The Union address contended, correctly, that we are, as a nation, addicted to oil. Yet, his tax program promoted the behemoths of the road. The average fleet mileage of new cars produced has not changed from 27.5 gallon a mile for the last 20 years.

Concurrently, we do not have an aggressive fuel conservation program, and substitutes for gasoline (wood chips, ethanol and switch grass?) are but a pipe dream.

Although we do not have shortages, oil companies are making record profits, company executives' compensation are beyond imagination and we still do not have a transcript of VP Cheney's meeting with these executives while developing an energy plan for the country.

China's exponentially-increasing demand for oil must be considered as well. It is a market that is beyond any reasonable imagination as far is its future hunger for oil will go. All these point to a conclusion that things at home are not going to get better before they get worse.

Demographic effects. We are facing an aging population, constituting a demographic shift that makes elderly and retired-from-the-workforce people proportionally much larger than the in-the-labor force would be able to sustain.

Although some of the retiring are the "baby-boomers" whose emergence in the late 1940s and early 1950s is partially responsible for this demographic skew, they are generally well-to-do, with investment portfolios and retirement packages sufficiently secure. Many others are not in this enviable category. Further, because of the reduction of fertility rates that followed later, family members who should take care of their aging parents are fewer than before. This will add to the already mounting social welfare burden, with grave consequences.

The demand for unskilled labor, therefore, will rise even further. This will draw in more illegal aliens from Mexico and other Central American countries to fill the void, because Americans are not used to and cannot survive on the wages these jobs pay. Thus, no matter how much Lou Dobbs excites his viewers with anti-immigration propaganda to increase

---

[102] Did Friedman not opine once that the Great Depression was caused by the laziness of labor that refused to work for starving wages?

his ratings, the "push-pull" of illegal immigration will not stop. This work-force will have no political power and will be easy prey for employers who will surely turn them into obedient serfs.

All the factors I discuss here contributed to a wealth allocation reality in which the top 2 percent of the population controls 85 percent of the total wealth. What is even more frightening is that, if this process continues unabated, 1 percent of the richest individuals will control 53 percent of the corporate wealth. Thus, it is a situation where "maximizing shareholders' wealth," a mantra we put in the heads of business school graduates, will be tantamount to shifting even more of the wealth of the nation to the top 1 percent.

This is something which will have further consequences not just in pushing more and more people to the bottom of the income class, but will curtail even more our personal as well as our economic freedoms, because most business organizations operate in an authoritative manner. Read on!

D. EASE

> Panics do not destroy capital; they merely reveal the extent to which it has been previously destroyed by its betrayal into hopelessly unproductive works.
>
> — John Stuart Mill

Extreme Authoritative Structured Enterprises (EASE) is the name I use to categorize organizations like the police, paramilitary, military, penitentiary, DOD, NASA, the many Intelligence Agencies, Homeland Security, etc. These organizations adhere to a strict chain of command and immunize themselves from internal dissent, sometimes even to the point where such dissent is punishable by law.

At the same time, they are more than likely to operate outside of the Constitution and to prefer an executive branch capable of supporting their activities, more often then not outside constitutional boundaries or beyond the control of the legislative branch.

But this organizational structure is not unique to EASE, which operate the way they operate under the excuse of both efficiency and the obvious need for secrecy. Many corporations that are School X, function the same way. Drug testing, spying on e-mail and rest rooms, making demands on the private lives of their employees and their immediate families are common practices in tens of thousands of American corporations. The leverage is always the job, or health insurance, or both. Tens, perhaps hundreds of thousands of employees are willing to sometimes accept ridiculous rules of the workplace, all limiting their personal freedom, which Friedman was designating as the ultimate requisite of a happy society, for the sake of keeping their and their families' health insurance that would be lost if they changed jobs.

The transformation to a tightly controlled society was further exacerbated during the new millennium by two factors:

(1)   The so-called "War on Terror" which brought us the two PATRIOT Acts, and
(2)   The outsourcing of production jobs and the shifting of employment of service and usually menial jobs to immigrants, both legal and illegal.

The former seriously hindered civil rights of American citizens by allowing arrests and detentions for indeterminate periods without a formal charge and without the right to a lawyer, based on unsubstantiated suspicions. The latter absorbed into the labor force more than 11 million who are too scared to complain or organize for fear of being deported back to their country of origin.

An unhealthy symbiosis came into effect: an executive branch that is thriving for more control and more secrecy; a corporatocracy that favors a most powerful executive branch "to get things done"; and an election system where money, controlled by the richest two percent of the population, decides the outcome.

This symbiosis is not stagnant, however. The more it exists, the more it will shift power, i.e., the more it will reduce the separation of powers and the control mechanism of "checks and balances."

Are we being transformed to space-age sharecroppers as Hudson claims (*ibid.*)? Are we going back to the future, to borrow a popular movie title, to turn the country into "industrial" feudalism? Hard to tell. The prospects are not too good, though.

E. The Relevance to the Investor

Probable impossibilities are to be preferred to improbable possibilities.

— Aristotle *Poetics*

What can the investor do about all this? There is an activist solution and there is a "going-with-the-flow solution."

The activist's solution is the changing of the political process to reverse, turning the US into an industrial fiefdom. The first two immediate things that must happen in order to accomplish this are the neutralization of the influence of money in the election process, and the elimination of the lobby system.

Both are very simple to model. The first involves a strict campaign financing reform instead of the token McCain–Feingold bill which has already been gutted of the hen's teeth it originally had, to use a mixed metaphor. The UK model would do the job efficiently, including free access to TV media for political candidates running for office.

The second is also very simple: make lobbying politicians illegal (in fact, it is no less now than legalized bribery). Perhaps if a strict campaign financing law is put into effect, lobbying will almost disappear naturally.

Although I am neither a swami nor a soothsayer, I am quite confident in foretelling that neither one of these two requisites will happen. This is so, because both parties are happy with the existing situation, feeding at the trough of big money, whether corporate or in the hands of a few hundred.[103]

We do not have an opposition party per se. We do have sporadic fragments of flurry against policies, dictums and orders that the administration tries to put in effect. And this is only when and where the constituents of elected officials are so badly hurt that their displeasure may jeopardize the reelection of their representative.

The media, radio, TV and print are owned by big money: 85 percent is owned by 15 companies or individuals. Their focus is on issues which are marginal to our real problems: same-sex marriage, prayer in schools, the showing of the Ten Commandments in public places, pro-life or freedom of choice — OxyContine-induced propaganda, or where the truth lies.

Or else they spend untold weeks on the disappearance of Natalee Holloway in Aruba, who vanished without a trace while on a high school binge of alcohol and drugs, or with whom did Michael Jackson share his bed. Although enough information is available on the internet for those who care to seek it out, for most low-income people it is, just as cable TV, practically, inaccessible because of high costs.

---

[103] The 600–800 families George Carlin calls the "ownership class," a rather appropriate name as it not only conjures up the images of fiefdom, but is also a true label for the reality of the concentration of capital.

Thus, in the words of Don Corleone: "*Fowgdabodit.*"

The passive reaction is whether the political–economic process, if it continues, will change the way the risk-averse investor should secure his future, and what are the consequences one should be aware of.

One of my statistics professors of the very distant past used to say that although the law of large numbers will not always take precedence, nevertheless, the way to bet is on the powerful. This seems to me still the perspicacious advice.

That would mean the mixing of a conservative and a defensive investment portfolio. Because inflation will surely increase as a result of the breakneck deficit spending[104] and because of rising energy cost that will affect all sectors of the economy, I would still recommend a carefully selected real estate portfolio,[105] the reduction of debt servicing costs, and substantial near cash holdings.

Stocks, perhaps, would be suitable for those who would tolerate higher risk for the promise of more return. But even for those I would stick with my ex-professor's wisdom and diversify into blue chips. None of the high-tech, garage-industry stuff, you hear!

But do not listen to me. As the Brits say: the value of what you get for nothing is what it costs. Make your own analysis and choice.

F. Final Cogitations

In order to arrive at what you do not know
You must go by a way which is the way of ignorance.
In order to possess what you do not possess
You must go by the way of dispossession.
In order to arrive at what you are not
You must go through the way which you are not.

— T.S. Eliot

---

[104] In a recent speech, Senator John McCain of Arizona remarked that the government is spending money "like a drunken sailor." The good Senator forgot to mention in the same breath that he has been a staunch supporter of the war in Iraq, the biggest ticket item in spending, and that the "drunken sailor" is giving huge tax cuts to that segment of the population who will be less likely to spend it in a way that it will trickle down, a policy he also supports.

[105] Watch where the retiring baby-boomers are heading.

Perhaps Friedman would not call today's American capitalism that capitalism he wrote about the first time in 1962. Yet, his attacks on government that supposedly should be there to help people but instead is curtailing their freedoms, helped to usher in the political and economic realities facing us today and for some time to come.

The fact remains that a government which is systematically weakened in favor of private enterprise is going to perform under par during conditions of emergency, with devastating consequences. That this weakening of government was not a natural evolution, but created on purpose just to prove the point of ineffective government, notwithstanding, we have to live with this, or repair it. The upshot, however, remains that all the good things Friedman foretold his disciples is not reality and can never come to pass.

Quite the contrary. The more we privatize, the more government and business will curtail our freedoms as citizens and our freedoms of economic choice, and the more the activities of our government will be cloaked in secrecy.

The more loss of freedom, the more improbable democracy is. Without democracy, ultimately, we will have very little freedom, if at all. Not surprisingly, the PATRIOT Acts are already sarcastically called 1984. I, who had the dubious pleasure to live under fascist and communist rule, feel that we are getting very close to the invisible hand controlling our lives.

But there are still differences. For one, we still have freedom of speech, and we still do not have a Dachau-style experimental concentration camp to put away Moslems, Gypsies, homosexuals, and anyone who openly criticizes the administration.[106] Nevertheless, similarities are abound with the inexplicable fact that people are willing to accept the propaganda funneled into their homes, courtesy of the media, owned by those who sponsored the evolution of this system.

Under the two dictatorial regimes I mentioned and experienced personally, people knew that the official line was a lie. Moreover, listening to other sources such as the BBC or Voice of America was treasonous, punishable by prison or concentration camp. Yet, they did everything to seek out the truth, because that was the glimmer of hope that showed a different future. Today, Fox News is the leading source of information to millions who cannot accept facts which are inconsistent with their beliefs. The flag and the word "freedom" cover everything they do not want to hear or see.

---

[106] Just do not name your son Aziz, Abdul or Mohammed. If you are Aziz, Abdul or Mohammed, and an American citizen, change it, legally, to Fitzgerald.

Capitalism and Freedom sold 400,000 copies by the time the second edition in 1982 went to print. It is still going strong, because Friedman's contentions regarding freedom and capitalism provided the ideological bricks and mortar for where we got at the start of the 21st century. Friedman's book was just carefully selected conjectures displayed with great ideological bias. One cannot miss this if one is willing to admit that it achieved exactly the opposite of what its author propagated and foretold.

Yet, one has to remember that economics is more art than science (Szostak, 1992), and that Friedman is a Nobel Laureate practitioner of the genre. Just as Jackson Pollock is considered by some as one of the greatest painters of the 20th century, yet, for many others, Pollock's works are the random splattering of paint on large canvases by a dipsomaniac, referring to Pollock as "Jack the Dripper." What should be Friedman's sobriquet?

References

Bhattacharya, S. 1979. "Imperfect Information, Dividend Policy, and 'the Bird in the Hand' Fallacy." *Bell Journal of Economics* 10: 259–270.

———. 1980. "Nondissipative Signaling Structures and Dividend Policy." *The Quarterly Journal of Economics* 95: 1–24.

Black, F. 1972. "Capital Market Equilibrium with Restricted Borrowing." *Journal of Business* 45: 444–455.

Black, F., M.C. Jensen *et al.* 1972. "The Capital Asset Pricing Model: Some Empirical Tests." In *Studies in the Theory of Capital Markets*, edited by M.C. Jensen. New York: Praeger.

Black, F. and M. Scholes. 1973. "The Pricing of Options and Corporate Liabilities." *Journal of Political Economy* 81: 637–654.

Fama, E.F. 1965. "The Behavior of Stock Market Prices." *Journal of Business* 38: 34–105.

———. 1970. "Efficient Capital Markets: A Review of Theory and Empirical Work." *Journal of Finance* 25: 383–417.

Frankfurter, G.M. 2006. "The Theory of Fair Markets: Toward a New Finance Paradigm." *International Review of Financial Analysis* 15(1): 130–144.

Friedman, M.M. 1962, 1982. *Capitalism and Freedom*. Chicago: The University of Chicago Press.

Hudson, M. 2006. "The Road to Serfdom." *Harper's* 132(1872): 39–46.

Jensen, M.C. and W.H. Meckling. 1976. "Theory of the Firm: Managerial Behavior, Agency Costs and Ownership Structure." *Journal of Financial Economics* 3: 305–360.

Lintner, J. 1965. "Security Prices, Risk, and Maximal Gains from Diversification." *Journal of Finance* 10: 587–615.

Markowitz, H.M. 1952. "Portfolio Selection." *Journal of Finance* 7: 77–91.

———. 1959. *Portfolio Selection.* New Haven: Yale University Press.

Merton, R.C. 1973. "Theory of Rational Option Pricing." *Bell Journal of Economics and Management* 28: 183–184.

Miller, M.H. and F. Modigliani. 1961. "Dividend Policy, Growth and the Valuation of Shares." *Journal of Business* 34: 411–433.

Modigliani, F. and M.H. Miller. 1958. "The Cost of Capital, Corporation Finance, and the Theory of Investment." *American Economic Review* 48: 261–297.

Ross, S. 1976. "The Arbitrage Theory of Capital Asset Pricing." *Journal of Financial Economics* 4: 129–176.

Sharpe, W.F. 1964. "Capital Market Prices: A Theory of Market Equilibrium under Conditions of Risk." *Journal of Finance* 14: 425–442.

Szostak, R. 1992. "The History of Art and the Art in Economics." *History of Economics Review* 70: 70–107.

Chapter 13

The Theory of Fair Markets (TFM): Toward a New Finance Paradigm[*]

All new and truly important ideas must pass through three stages: first dismissed as nonsense, then rejected as against religion, and finally acknowledged as true, with the proviso from initial opponents that they knew it all along.

— Karl Ernst von Baer

Foreword

The last 50 years of academic work in finance has been dominated and overshadowed by a single paradigm. At the foundation of this model one finds the ideology of *laissez faire* and the methodology of positive economics as postulated by Friedman (1953) in his now classical essay of the same title. During the financial paradigm's early evolution, this combination of ideology and methodology served as the basis to the capital asset pricing model (CAPM, subsequently) of Sharpe (1964), Lintner (1965), Black (1972) and others. Later, the finance paradigm was further modified by the hypothesis of efficient markets (EMH, subsequently) of Fama (1970, 1965), after which it was renamed to be known as financial economics.

My financial education got its start in the late 1960s. This was the era that celebrated the newly found paradigm (where there was none before) and let it totally overwhelm the research agenda. Yet, I, instead of following the equilibrium-based positive model, "fell in love" with Markowitz's (1959) normative model of portfolio selection. Although I had an interest in accounting and applications of operation research to financial

[*] The original version of this article was published in the *International Review of Financial Analysis*, 2006, Volume 15: 130–144, and is reprinted here with the permission of the publisher, Elsevier.

and other modeling, the bulk of my academic work, for quite a while, was normative portfolio theory.

Through my work with the Markowitz model and even more so with its "simplification" by Sharpe (1963) (the work that, incidentally, sired the CAPM), using large stock universes for empirical testing I quickly learned that something was profoundly amiss with the CAPM. This was so, because I found that only a small subset of a stock universe[107] was included in what Markowitz termed the "E-V efficient set," and that over repeated time periods, many stocks were never included in the efficient set. By that time, the EMH/CAPM became a religion and I became an agnostic.

My professional thinking turned 180° from the ruling dogma when I was first exposed, completely by coincidence, to philosophers of science the ilk of Popper, Kuhn and Lakatos. Although my ultimate academic degree declared that I was a Doctor of Philosophy (meaning a research degree), I have never, during some eight years of university education, had a course in philosophy. Reading some of the works of these philosophers, I realized that my research has been an imitation of others without understanding what lies beneath the surface and without contributing much to the process of discovery: the search for truth, that must be the ultimate, all-dominant and most noble objective of science.

This new way of thinking transformed me from an agnostic to a heretic. My conversion was complete when I realized how much the finance paradigm was ideology-dependent and how much the professional elite denied this fact and at the same time forced everyone to accept its ideological base.

Parallel to this discovery, I also happened to find, again by complete "accident," a fellow traveler, Elton "Skip" McGoun, a discovery that resulted not just in a decade of cooperation producing two books and a dozen papers, but also in a monumental intellectual enrichment. I must emphasize Skip's contribution to our joint work, because although this paper is my own, nevertheless, I have to repeat in the following some of our joint efforts in order to clarify my thesis. In these works, especially regarding the ideology of the field and the effect of the methodology of positive economics on finance, his contribution is equal to if not greater than mine.

It has been argued that criticism is the manure in which academic knowledge grows. Karl Popper also said that the beginnings of all science

---

[107] Indeed, the larger was the stock universe, other things being equal, proportionally fewer stocks were included in the efficient set.

are myths and the criticism of myths. Yet, finance does not allow, on philosophical grounds, the criticism of the paradigm. One of our joint papers we tried to publish in the *Journal of Finance* came back, among other comments with this paraphrasing of Socrates: "The unexamined academic discipline is not worth practicing." Yet, in spite of the fact that the editor promised to publish it together with the reviewer's criticism and our rejoinder, the paper, eventually, was rejected.[108]

But there is that much room for criticism, published or muttered in corridors of professional meetings, without offering a way for an alternative. Although I have been thinking about an alternative paradigm for some time, the crash and burn of the dotcoms and the close to $10 trillion loss of value of the ever so "efficient" markets within less than a year gave me the final thrust to organize my thinking and put to paper my theory of fair markets (TFM, subsequently) as an alternative way of thinking, and as a springboard for a new research agenda. The astute reader will notice that this acronym is the reverse of the ubiquitous acronym: MFT, modern financial theory, aka financial economics, aka modern finance, aka the ruling paradigm. (Perhaps the evil twin brother?) This by no means is a coincidence.

Miramar Beach, FL
2004

A. Introduction

In order to develop the TFM, it is necessary to look at the evolution of finance both as a way of thinking and as a research agenda. This examination necessarily involves some basic definitions that later will serve also for the understanding of the theory I am proposing. This I do in the next section, titled "The Old Paradigm." Following Section B, I develop the social policy implications of fair markets and plead my case for what I call a leveled playing field. In the last section of the paper, I offer an alternative research agenda to replace the never-ending desire to prove or disprove market efficiency with yet another empirical study, slicing and dicing data as they become available.

---

[108] The paper, its two reviews and all the correspondence appears in Frankfurter and McGoun (2002).

Before I get to Section B, it would be useful to discuss certain concepts that may bear on the meaning of arguments to come later in the paper. One such concept is postmodernity. I was impressed, albeit not convinced, with the ideas developed in two papers by two eminent scholars, one published and one unpublished as yet. I am referring to McGoun (1997) and Mcintosh (2002). Both papers are directed toward the academic accounting readers, albeit the McGoun paper is about finance as we should know it, while the Mcintosh paper ties the connection between accounting and financial markets as we should know those. This latter paper is especially useful to understand the connections between accounting, the problems accountants are facing, and the collapse of the dotcoms and the telecoms, resulting in the evaporation of confidence in financial markets that at its crescendo looked like a mini-crash.

The similarities between the two papers do not stop here, however. First, and perhaps foremost, there is an intellectual superiority in these works that, unfortunately, one cannot find in the mainstream finance journals. Second, both papers are influenced to a great extent by the ideas of the most highly respected philosopher and semiotist of our times, Jean Baudrillard, especially by his work, *Simulacra* [plural of simulacrum = image, my comment] *and Simulation* (Baudrillard, 1994). Thirdly, they both look at the problems facing finance and accounting from a postmodernist view. Finally, both rely, extensively, on semiotics[109] of de Saussure (1959) and Peirce (1991).

What we learn from these works is that there is a hyperreality[110] out there for both finance and accounting — something *above* reality that evolved through time with the changes of regimes from feudalism to the emergence of the bourgeoisie to the industrial revolution to our times, such that things mean more than to what signifiers pointed in the not-so-distant past. This is what de Saussure called *la Langue*, which is a result of sociological evolution, as opposed to *la Parole*, the spoken language. In other words, the signified is different than what the signifier used to mean. Therefore, earnings and earnings estimates mean something else than the

---

[109] The Swiss linguist Ferdinand de Saussure created *semiology* around the turn of the century. The American philosopher C.S. Peirce independently developed his own science of signs under the name *semiotics*. Consequently, this term is more common in the United States than Saussure's *semiology*.

[110] Baudrillard coined the term to mean that there is a super reality, or that things are more real than they look.

measurement of income in simple reality, and so do the value of stocks, and for that matter, the markets for stocks.

The Mcintosh paper is especially clear about this. The author argues that earnings reported by the firm and earnings estimates by financial analysts make people trade in the markets, where in fact these figures have nothing to do with some real "reality" (for a better term), connected to the "value" of earnings. This, although agreeing with Mcintosh's assessment, I find baffling, because modern finance from its early going made it clear that what counts is not earnings, but the maximization of wealth. For four decades we preached in B-Schools that maximizing profits has no meaning, because it is an accounting illusion, among many other problems.[111] Maximizing earnings can also be out-and-out detrimental to value, because management will make myopic, short-term decisions.[112]

Because of this evolution of meaning, what Baudrillard called the *implosion*, we cannot study both finance and accounting phenomena the way we were trained to study them in the confines of neoclassicism. Regretfully, neither one of these two authors tells us exactly what to do, except that perhaps linguistics and semiotics would be a good starting point to revise the methodology (the ontology and epistemology) of the research program of both academic disciplines.[113] Mcintosh even suggests that this "wild card possibility," the subtitle of his piece, would reverse the trend of "diminishing joy" in accounting research.[114]

---

[111] For instance, error in measurement, converting flow to stock, expressing everything in terms of dollars and cents, timing of accruals, etc.

[112] An interesting and revealing anecdote of this hyperreality is the case of WorldCom. Shortly after it was disclosed in late spring, early summer of 2002 that WorldCom "capitalized current expenses" in order to inflate income to the tune of $3.8 billion, the firm declared bankruptcy. Some WorldCom executives were paraded in handcuffs before the television cameras of the news media to show that the Justice Department was out to punish the evildoers. At the beginning of August, investigators and auditors found an additional $3.3 billion of ill-reported income, bringing the total to a staggering $7.1 billion. The day following the additional disclosure, the stock market dropped another 100 plus points. Financial analysts and news media interpreters explained the drop by the additional sums discovered. Just how this could affect the market as a whole when the single firm to which the news pertained was already in bankruptcy no one is to know. Yet, this is how pundits manufacture new meanings to old concepts.

[113] Mcintosh (2002) argues that the two are mutually feeding one on the other.

[114] If I ever heard an oxymoron and irrationality, it is "diminishing joy in accounting research." The oxymoron part should be self-explanatory. The irrationality is "diminishing," for how can something that never existed diminish? It is not unlike the declaration of has-been university administrators that after relinquishing their positions they "return to research," something they have never done.

With all the fascinating ideas developed and proposed in these two papers, unfortunately, I find them unfit for becoming a pragmatic vehicle by which a new research agenda can be forged that, hopefully and eventually, will have a chance to lead to a new paradigm, replacing the only one we knew thus far. This is so, not just because the old guard of finance academia is not trained in the subjects of semiotics and linguistics (and thus it looks at this proposal not just with suspicion but also as threatening), but also because the education process of new Ph.D.'s gives a wide berth around any supporting discipline that is not economics, to avoid preparation in these subjects.

Another consideration that influenced me to steer away from the linguistics cum semiotics route was my conviction that there is a close connection between politics and finance, and politics and financial economics. This frieze was especially reinforced during the last meltdown of financial markets across the world. That is, the one-to-one relevance of the new world order, market economy, globalization, or any other euphemism we wish to call American-style 21st-century capitalism, and the politics behind it all. One then must reach the conclusion, as many others and I already do, that what we see is the emergence of a religion in which markets are the political frameworks, practitioners are the laymen, and academics are the church's theologians. Thus, my conclusion is to grope with a theory using tools of analysis most of us readily understand, rather than wrestle with a new terminology and conceptualization that very few feel comfortable with, whereby judging the resulting theses as stillborn.

It is necessary to summarize the salient features of the existing paradigm and its ideological base in order to present a new theory, part of which is a takeoff from the new paradigm. This I do in the next section.

B. The Old Paradigm

When a well-packed web of lies has been sold gradually to the masses over generations, the truth will seem utterly preposterous and its speaker a raving lunatic.

— Dresden James

The methodological foundation of the established finance paradigm, which for simplicity I will call the EMH, is without a doubt the methodology of positive economics as set out by Friedman's (1953) classic essay. In Frankfurter and McGoun (2002), we portray the parameters of this methodology:

> Good predictions equal good economic modeling,[115] and that the best models are those that are simple and fruitful. Simple models have fewer variables, and fruitful models, in addition to making good predictions, have broad applicability and suggest new lines of research (p. 35).[116]

Combined with these requirements, Friedman's proposition that

> Truly important and significant hypotheses will be found to have "assumptions" that are wildly inaccurate descriptive representations of reality, and, in general, the more significant the theory, the more unrealistic the assumptions (Friedman, 1953, p. 14)

completes the boundaries of the world we know as positive economics, and which serves as the realm of financial economics/modern finance in academic research.

Particularly circumscribing is the last part of this quote. According to this Friedman doctrine, *de facto* an arbitrary assertion, there is a strong positive connection between the *unreality*[117] of the assumptions and the *significance* of the paradigm. Friedman never explains why this is so, making the statement unquestionable as if it is a monarch's ukase. Friedman makes it also clear that there is a multitude of theories out there, and that one never can prove that a theory is *true*. One can only show that a

---

[115] "Its [positive economics'] task is to provide a system of generalizations that can be used to make correct predictions about the consequences of any change in circumstances" (Friedman, 1953, p. 4).

[116] "A theory is 'simpler' the less the initial knowledge needed to make a prediction within a given field of phenomena; it is more 'fruitful' the more precise the resulting prediction, the wider the area within which the theory yields predictions, and the more additional lines for further research it suggests" (Friedman, 1953, p. 10).

[117] Perhaps hyperreality?

theory cannot be rejected as *untrue*. Then, when the theory cannot be rejected as untrue, the paradigm should be used to formulate social policy, until or unless another model is found that seems to have more predictive power.

This, indeed, is a very clever way to perpetuate a paradigm. First, because of its subjective requirements, and second, because of the working of the academic publication and promotion and tenure processes. Once a model, a way of thinking and a method of analysis take hold of the research program, it is almost next to impossible to bring about the scientific revolution Kuhn (1970) had foreseen. If all this is strongly tied to an ideology that is the underlying philosophy of those that finance the education process, the "almost next to impossible" becomes unfeasible.

What we had shown in Frankfurter and McGoun (1999) was that financial economics is ideology-based. Finance's entire methodological structure is built on the idea of *laissez faire*, i.e., let the market alone, because this is what is Pareto optimal, and therefore moving away from this optimality will result in suboptimality at best, and total waste, as far as society is concerned, at the worst.

As modern finance emerged, to be respectable it had to be "scientisized." If finance were not scientific, then it could not have been modern. More importantly, finance could not have been credible if it were not modern. The scientification of finance started earlier already with the importation of methods of operation research, most notably, mathematical programming. Mathematical programming found its perfect application in finance with Markowitz's (1952, 1959) formulation of a normative portfolio selection algorithm, a combination of statistics with quadratic programming. Thus, I see Harry's seminal paper of 1952 as the introduction of modernity to finance.[118] By no means, however, was the Markowitz algorithm a positive model.

Later, a whole host of mathematical and statistical models found their way to modern finance, more often than not because of their

---

[118] The other such path-breaking works were Modigliani and Miller (1958) and Miller and Modigliani (1961).

abstruse nature, rather than their ability to explain complex social phenomena.[119,120]

Thus, there was a dire need for a paradigm that was both statistically testable, and provided a theoretical umbrella for statistics that were already in use. Enter Sharpe's (1964) CAPM that reduced a complex mechanism, with the help of "wild" assumption, to a simple regression model. This was not without a "price," however. Sharpe had to find a way out of Friedman's rather restrictive requirement of "good" predictions. Sharpe could not risk the disapproval of his newly found machine by the simple fact of being a poor predictor (as it often appeared to be). Therefore, Sharpe found surcease for predictive ability by stating that his model should be accepted because it was internally consistent with prevailing economic tenets:

> ... since the proper test of a theory is not the realism of its assumption but the acceptability of its implications, and since these assumptions imply equilibrium conditions which form a major part of classical financial doctrine, it is far from clear that this formulation should be rejected (Sharpe, 1964).

The final cosmetic surgery to the paradigm came with Fama's *invention* of the EMH (Fama, 1965; Fama, 1970). Before I proceed with the

---

[119] For an interesting discussion on whether economics, financial or otherwise, should be scientific, and whether mathematics makes economics scientific, I refer the reader to Lawson (1997). The author argues that correlating surface observations is one thing, but the role of science is to find the mechanisms below the surface reality, even when observable correlations, for one reason or another, are not to be (immediately) present.

[120] The best and most compact description of the scientific method I found on the internet (author unknown) goes as follows:

> The scientific method is the process by which scientists, collectively and over time, endeavor to construct an accurate (that is, reliable, consistent and non-arbitrary) representation of the world. Recognizing that personal and cultural beliefs influence both our perceptions and our interpretations of natural phenomena, we aim through the use of standard procedures and criteria to minimize those influences when developing a theory. As a famous scientist once said, "Smart people (like smart lawyers) can come up with very good explanations for mistaken points of view." In summary, the scientific method attempts to minimize the influence of bias or prejudice in the experimenter when testing an hypothesis or a theory.

Accordingly, one cannot find in the definition even a single hint that mathematics is a *sine qua non* of the scientific method, but rather that it has to be "collectively and over time" a "consistent and non-arbitrary representation of the world."

hypothesis itself, I would like to draw the readers' attention to the power of language, and the connection between language and ideology (the difference between *parole* and *langue*).

Markowitz, who called the optimal mean–variance combinations of stock portfolios E-V efficient, first used the adjective "efficient" in finance. In a private correspondence, Markowitz explained the origins of and the reason for the adjective:

> I was taking Tjalling Koopmans' course on "Activity Analysis," a.k.a. linear programming. Koopmans spoke of efficient (i.e., undominated) and inefficient (i.e., dominated) allocations of resources. Having this terminology in my head, I distinguished efficient versus inefficient portfolios and EV combinations.

At Koopmans' advice, Markowitz, from a term paper, developed his normative algorithm of portfolio selection that finally earned him a Nobel Prize. In the mechanical context of mathematical programming, the adjective signified no quadratic dominance. It had no moral, ideological or other hidden meaning. Of course, Markowitz could have used any other name, perhaps some, such as, say, the wisdom-of-the-quadratic-man, that would have been more evocative. It is important to remember, however, that the term *efficient* in the context of the normative model was just *parole*.

Fama's invention of the EMH gave a religious meaning to efficiency. A philosopher of science I asked to explain the meaning of efficiency replied that he did not know what efficiency was. He did know, however, what inefficiency was, and efficiency must be the direct opposite of inefficiency. Because inefficiency means wastefulness — something unforgiven, especially in the Protestant religious philosophy — efficiency must be very good, something we all should make every effort to achieve. Efficiency, therefore, takes on a religious meaning that was not there before. That is de Saussure's *langue*.

At the daybreak of modernity in finance there was random walk. Then, markets were considered a fair game of "chance." Later, markets became a fair game of "skills" (a term that made the practitioners of the investment industry respectable). Lastly, markets became efficient. As we note in Frankfurter and McGoun (1999):

> In a sense, we have come full circle, ideologically and metaphorically, with the term "efficiency." Although we have negated the image of "game" (which

is incompatible with practitioner professionalism, academic scholarly respectability and religious beliefs), we have enhanced the image of "fair." Now, markets are not only value-free ("fair"), but also exceedingly good at doing whatever it is they do at the least social cost ("efficient"). They are the same markets, but they look a lot better after the terminology makeover (p. 169).

Still later, Fama (1998) rejected what he called the anomalies literature, *de facto* behavioral finance's challenge to the EMH, and by association to the CAPM, tying the latter to the former and making it practically irrefutable. Consequently, the *pas de trois* of Friedman, Sharpe and Fama not just confined financial economics in the most orthodox boundaries and immunized it from attacks of opposing *mimes* from the outside, but also directed its research program toward proving or rejecting market efficiency. This program, because of the availability of ever-increasing volumes of data and invention of new methods of econometrics that together make it possible to examine, reexamine and overexamine the same hypotheses, can never reach a definite conclusion.[121]

In the next section I will argue that this program is not just futile, but it is also a clever ruse to concentrate on something well-established forever, instead of redirecting research resources toward discovery.

---

[121] Lately, I condemned myself to the interminably boring task of reading Leo Strauss, the supposed ideologue of the neocons' book, titled *Persecution and the Art of Writing*, an anthology of five essays and an introduction (Strauss, 1988). In the treatise titled "The Literary Character of the *Guide to the Perplexed*," the seminal work of Moses Maimonides (1135–1204), one of the greatest philosophers of the Middle Ages, Strauss contends that mistakes and inaccuracies that appear in the works of great scholars are there for the purpose of hiding their true beliefs and ideological convictions from the superficial and careless reader, about whom the author does not care. The right message and the intention of the author, nevertheless, would be clearly revealed to the anointed and to those young scholars whose minds the writer set out to steer in the right direction. As I find more often than not this strategy adopted in the current political scene by not the oppressed but precisely the oppressors, I cannot help but interpret Fama's (1998) constant reference to the "event study methodology" instead of classifying it where it surely belongs: a method, not coincidental. Fama, one of the most eloquent and precise writers and respected scholars, perhaps the physical embodiment of financial economics, surely must know the difference between method and methodology. It is, therefore, a clever ruse to elevate a simple regression method to the philosophical underpinning of a discipline, which makes it possible for Fama to call anything that does not confirm the EMH a mere anomaly.

C. The TFM

1. *Post-autistic economics*

Perhaps the only real challenge to the hegemony of neoclassicism in economics, especially in that subset of economics that is called financial, came with the movement that called itself Post-Autistic Economics, or PAE for short. Although I have written elsewhere at length about PAE (Frankfurter, 2001), for the sake of continuity it would be useful to recapture the brief history of PAE and the manifesto called the Kansas City Proposal (KCP, subsequently).

In June 2000, a group of French economics students published a petition on the web protesting the teaching of economics in institutions of higher learning because of:

- Economics' "uncontrolled use" and treatment of mathematics as "an end in itself," and the resulting "autistic science,"
- The repressive domination of neoclassical theory and derivative approaches in the curriculum, and
- The dogmatic teaching style, which leaves no place for critical and reflective thought.[122]

The students' manifesto demanded that the economics curriculum be changed with regard to:

- Engagement with empirical and concrete economic realities,
- Prioritizing science over scientism, and
- A pluralism of approaches adapted to the complexity of economic objects and to the uncertainty surrounding most of the big economics questions.

They also demanded that their professors ". . . initiate reforms to rescue economics from its autistic and socially irresponsible state."[123] The French students called their movement *Le Movement Autisme Économie* that turned to be referred to later as PAE.

---

[122] From http://www.paecon.net
[123] *Ibid.*

As chronicled on the PAE's website, there was a positive reaction to the students' manifesto by many French professors of economics:

> Almost immediately, a group of French economics teachers responded with a petition of their own, supporting the students' demands, adding to their analysis, and lamenting the cult of scientism into which economics has in the main descended. The professors' petition also called for the opening of a public debate (http://www.paecon.net).

This started a debate on the pages of French dailies that spread to other media, and eventually led to the appointment of a commission to study the demands of the students and professors:

> That debate began on the 21st of June, when the French national newspaper, *Le Monde*, reported on the students' petition and interviewed several prominent economists who voiced sympathy for the students' cause. Other newspapers followed. As the French media, including radio and television, expanded the public debate, fears among students and teachers of persecution diminished and the number of signatories to their petitions increased. This fueled further media interest. Jack Lang, the French minister of education, announced that he regarded the complaints with great seriousness and was setting up a commission to investigate (*ibid.*).

Four months later, the original signatories of the June 2000 petition and their supporters met at the Sorbonne. Soon, other universities throughout France joined the fray. The movement became a groundswell, prompting widespread discussion of the reform of economics teaching and the direction of economics, and economic research as a science.

The movement did not stop in France, but crossed the channel.[124] In June 2001, a group of 27 doctoral students at Cambridge published a proposal on their website, asking economics students and economists everywhere who were sympathetic to their cause to endorse their plan by corresponding to cesp@econ.cam.ac.uk. The Cambridge proposal raised the same points as the French initiative, and added other criticisms (all supporting the argument that contemporary economics is monopolized by a single approach which is formalistic, and that this approach cannot be

---

[124] I am quite sure that the "crossing" was by way of the internet and not by way of the channel.

conducive to understanding economic phenomena, etc.). The Cambridge students were keen on stating, however, that all they asked for was a debate, not the total abandonment of neoclassical economics. For the convenience of the reader, I reproduce the Cambridge Proposal in its entirety in the Appendix to this paper.[125]

The "Cambridge Letter" appeared on the students' website on June 14, 2001. Not to be undone by the French and the British, in August 13, 2001, the Kansas City Proposal (KCP, subsequently) was penned and published in America. The KCP was the work

> . . . of 75 students, researchers and professors from twenty-two nations who gathered for a week of discussion on the state of economics and the economy at the University of Missouri–Kansas City (UMKC) this June 2001. The discussion took place at the Second Biennial Summer School of the Association for Evolutionary Economics (AFEE), jointly sponsored by UMKC, AFEE and the Center for Full Employment and Price Stability (see http://www.paecon.net).

This manifesto incorporates many of the points of the French and the Cambridge ideas (an explicit purpose of the creators of the KCP), and it is *de facto* an outline for a new paradigm for economics that, among other things, must include the following ideas (when compared to the neoclassical paradigm):

- A broader conception of human behavior
- Recognition of culture
- Recognition of evolution
- Empirical grounding
- Expanded methods
- Interdisciplinary dialog.

The KCP ideas serve both as a starting point and as a basis for a new methodology on which the paradigm of TFM can build. For the sake of

---

[125] David Power of the University of Dundee makes the following comment regarding The Cambridge Letter:

> I was struck by the absence of any acknowledgment in the Cambridge letter to the French initiative and influence — seemed a bit shabby of them to me. (Maybe they did that elsewhere.)

Not that I know of (GMF).

convenience, I am following the methodological structure I discussed in Frankfurter (2002). Other lines of development may serve the purpose just as well. I am selecting this particular one for the obvious reason of familiarity.

2. Ideology, axioms and assumptions

> Labor is prior to, and independent of, capital. Capital is only the fruit of labor, and could never have existed if labor had not first existed. Labor is the superior of capital, and deserves much the higher consideration.
>
> — Abraham Lincoln. Message to Congress, December 3, 1861.

Ideology

The ideological basis for the TFM is capitalism of the welfare state. As noted in Collison and Frankfurter (2000), there are several forms of capitalism, out of which the American–UK type is the one most resembling *laissez faire*. Other types, particularly the Scandinavian type of market system, are concerned with the well-being of those who, for reasons out of their control, are less fortunate than those who accumulated the wealth of Croesus[126] by hook or by crook. Because wealth equals power in every society, therefore the have-nots must be protected by the state from exploitation.

The total elimination of exploitation is utopia. Nevertheless, the welfare state can and should mitigate its extent by providing healthcare, catastrophic health insurance, pre- and post-natal care, family leave, job security, daycare for those who otherwise could not afford it. This necessarily means that markets are not free, nor are they global. The former is so, because the powerful must be regulated to insure a level playing field. The latter is true, because globalization is possible when and where the same market, political, judicial, and social structures and laws exist. The Scandinavian economies came, and perhaps after a while the European Union will come the closest in reality to this ideology and the resulting system.

---

[126] The last king of Lydia (reigned 560–546 BC), known for his great wealth.

Axioms

(i) Human nature:

   (1) Individuals are greedy by nature.

   (2) In certain circumstances, such as emergencies, natural disasters, wars, etc., greed is subordinated to the needs of the collective. This is, however, not a universal occurrence, because for some individuals greed is always the only dominating factor.

   (3) In every relationship that involves humans, there is always a domineering presence. In many instances domination is used not for the good of a collective/society, but only for the enhancement of personal wealth. I call this circumstance exploitation.

   (4) Humans like to work, and receive a reward that is concomitant with the perceived effort they put in their work. This is also not universally true, because some humans are lazy and they prefer compensation for no work, however little. Some are lazy, but they are exploitative and get compensation that outdoes the compensation of those who work (in similar activities). Most humans do not like other humans who are lazy or live on the dole.

   (5) For many humans, a peer group's (such as family, clan, collective, religious organization, military unit, etc.) objectives come before their own well-being (welfare).

(ii) Markets:

   (1) The evolution of market economies is from Judeo-Christian ethics.

   (2) The pricing of goods in these markets must be just, i.e., unjust pricing (differential pricing, price collusion, price gouging) has no place in these markets and must be prevented by law.

   (3) Value is subjective, yet all efforts must be made to disclose all relevant information to assist individuals in deciding on value. This is akin to the full disclosure principle of accounting.

   (4) Opportunistic sellers and buyers should be eliminated as much as legally possible. This is more evident on the buyers' side than on the sellers' side because unjust pricing is a protection already for the buyer. However, a small seller can be driven out of the market if a giant can undercut prices temporarily until the small business defaults, for the sake of raising prices after such default.

(5) The market should be freed from nefarious conduct by severely and timely punishing those who are found in violation of securities' and other laws.

(6) There are market goods and social goods (social goods: health, education, public interests, the right of the public to know, campaign financing). Although the market is the best known vehicle for the pricing of market goods, granted that there is fair and unimpeded competition, it is a miserable instrument of allocation for social goods. The notions of "let the market alone" and "markets know best" is a myth, created and nurtured by those who want to take advantage of their political power to keep any regulating body off their hands.

(7) The for-profit firm must have a finite lifetime, just as much as humans have a final lifetime. At the conclusion of the firm's lifespan, public hearings must be held to verify whether or not the conduct of the firm was consistent with the concept of market fairness. Only if the conclusion of the hearing is positive should the firm be granted a successive life term.

(8) Efficiency is a myth, invented and promoted by those who want capital, and capital alone rule their society and eventually the whole world. In economic terms it means that Pareto optimality can never be proven. It is only a belief rooted in ideology. When unchecked and unperturbed, markets are manipulable[127] by those who control capital and, *de facto*, the political process (see also below).

(iii) Government:

(1) Politics and economics are intertwined. In fact, politics is nothing else but the socially supported system that allocates wealth and scarce resources. Therefore, if left to its own devices, any grossly exploitative system such as American-type capitalism can and will put up a façade of democracy, whereas in fact the few powerful and influential get an unjust share of the wealth on the account of the rest of society. The role of the government, therefore, is to counterbalance the power of the powers that be.

---

[127] Elton McGoun coined the term "manipulable markets."

(2)   Counterbalancing the powers that be is through labor and social laws that will ensure a fairer allocation of the national wealth. A key concept of such laws is that the employee/laborer is assuming a risk when he commits himself to work for an entrepreneur, and thus he cannot be thrown out on the street whenever the entrepreneur can find a better "deal," such as in case of moving to another country or downsizing for the sake of increasing the market price of the share to take advantage of stock options and SARs.[128]

(3)   The nimbus that business knows best, and the deference to the needs of business because business creates jobs, must be abandoned. In fact, historically, governments create jobs, especially in times when the business cycle turns from bad to worse, and from worse to depression.

(4)   The government must make all efforts possible to both ensure truthful accounting reporting, and educate the public with regards to the investment opportunities and their synchronous risks. Truthful accounting reporting means verification that the financial statements of the firm released to the public are reflecting to the best of the accountant's knowledge the true picture of the firm, not liberal interpretations of existing reporting laws and accounting principles.

(iv) Infrastructures:

(1)   The necessary legal, social and economic laws must be in place in order to ensure the operation of the government is consistent with the notion of fair markets.

(2)   The conditions for the infrastructure must be spelled out in terms similar to the terms of "contract with America" that brought the Republican Party into a majority of the House during the first term of the Clinton presidency.

Assumptions

(i)   Most individuals are honest and fair regarding their relative standing in society and in their peer group.

---

[128] Stock Appreciation Right.

(ii) Most will support a system that truly portrays the process by which resources are more evenly allocated, something that is captured by the maxim: *laben and laben lassen* (live and let live).

(iii) The implementation of the axioms is politically feasible.

(iv) The implementation of the axioms is not revolutionary, but rather evolutionary. This is so, because history shows that revolutions do not solve a societal wrong: they create from one wrong an even worse one.

3. *Theory*

The central idea behind the theory of fair markets is that society is better off when markets are fair rather than efficient. This is so, because efficiency is neither a necessary nor is it a satisfactory condition of social welfare. The fact that totalitarian political systems, usually, but not exclusively, result in economies that are not for the benefit of their majorities notwithstanding, *laissez faire* is not the antidote for such political ills. What we observe is that although totalitarian regimes may opt for a free market-type economy (or something nearly so, such as China at the present), if markets are let alone they end up not free, but controlled by the gross concentration of capital.

Accordingly, and because a theory needs time to evolve and crystallize, economic research, financial or otherwise, must concentrate around two separate, yet intertwined themes:

- The criticism of the idea of market efficiency, and
- Measuring the marginal effects of social legislation, whether they contribute to or subtract from market fairness.

The former is easy to accomplish. Instead of discouraging the criticism of market efficiency to the point of non-existence (i.e., not publishing papers that refute market efficiency, either empirically or theoretically), research in that direction should be encouraged or even solicited. The difficulty is with the latter theme, because very little has been done in this direction. Nevertheless, this is not an impossible task, because several topics are well-suited for this kind of research. For instance, the real social costs of downsizing, NAFTA, the WTO, charity vs. taxation to take care of social problems, the real costs of national, single payer health insurance, mergers and acquisitions, environmental clean-up and hazards, just to mention a few.

Whether such research is going to be forthcoming is a matter of monetary incentives. When funding for such research is available, there would be plenty of academics who will apply for these funds and do research with market fairness in mind. To make such funds available is a matter of legislative pressure.

The blueprint I am offering here is, admittedly, just a start.

Acknowledgments

I gratefully acknowledge the comments and suggestions of David Collison and David Power, both of the University of Dundee, who were kind enough to read an earlier draft of this paper. In no way are they responsible, however, for the content of this article, a liability that I must shoulder alone.

Appendix

Released June 14, 2001

**27 Ph.D. students at Cambridge University support
the following open letter:**

Opening Up Economics: A Proposal By Cambridge Students

As students at Cambridge University, we wish to encourage a debate on contemporary economics. We set out below what we take to be characteristic of today's economics, what we feel needs to be debated and why:

As defined by its teaching and research practices, we believe that economics is monopolised by a single approach to the explanation and analysis of economic phenomena. At the heart of this approach lies a commitment to formal modes of reasoning that must be employed for research to be considered valid. The evidence for this is not hard to come by. The contents of the discipline's major journals, of its faculties and its courses all point in this direction.

In our opinion, the general applicability of this formal approach to understanding economic phenomenon is disputable. This is the debate that needs to take place. When are these formal methods the best route to generating good explanations? What makes these methods useful and consequently, what are their limitations? What other methods could be used in economics? This debate needs to take place within economics and between economists, rather than on the fringe of the subject or outside of it altogether.

In particular we propose the following:

(1) That the foundations of the mainstream approach be openly debated. This requires that the bad criticisms be rejected just as firmly as the bad defences. Students, teachers and researchers need to know and acknowledge the strengths and weaknesses of the mainstream approach to economics.

(2) That competing approaches to understanding economic phenomena be subjected to the same degree of critical debate. Where these approaches provide significant insights into economic life, they should be taught and their research encouraged within economics. At the moment this is not happening. Competing approaches have little role in economics as it stands simply because they do not conform to the mainstream's view of what constitutes economics. It should be clear that such a situation is self-enforcing. This debate is important because in our view the status quo is harmful in at least four respects.

(a) Firstly, it is harmful to students who are taught the "tools" of mainstream economics without learning their domain of applicability. The source and evolution of these ideas is ignored, as is the existence and status of competing theories.

(b) Secondly, it disadvantages a society that ought to be benefiting from what economists can tell us about the world. Economics is a social science with enormous potential for making a difference through its impact on policy debates. In its present form its effectiveness in this arena is limited by the uncritical application of mainstream methods.

(c) Thirdly, progress towards a deeper understanding of many important aspects of economic life is being held back. By restricting research done in economics to that based on one approach only, the development of competing research programs is seriously hampered or prevented altogether.

(d) Fourth and finally, in the current situation an economist who does not do economics in the prescribed way finds it very difficult to get recognition for her research. The dominance of the mainstream approach creates a social convention in the profession that only economic knowledge production that fits the mainstream approach can be good research, and therefore other modes of economic knowledge are all too easily dismissed as simply being poor, or as not being economics.

(3)   Many economists therefore face a choice between using what they consider inappropriate methods to answer economic questions, or to adopt what they consider the best methods for the question at hand, knowing that their work is unlikely to receive a hearing from economists.

(4)   Let us conclude by emphasizing what we are certainly not proposing: we are not arguing against the mainstream approach per se, but against the fact that its dominance is taken for granted in the profession. We are not arguing against mainstream methods, but believe in a pluralism of methods and approaches justified by debate. Pluralism as a default implies that alternative economic work is not simply tolerated, but that the material and social conditions for its flourishing are met, to the same extent as is currently the case for mainstream economics. This is what we mean when we refer to an "opening up" of economics.

References

Baudrillard, Jean. 1994. *Simulacra and Simulation*, 1st ed. Ann Arbor, Michigan: University of Michigan Press.

Black, Fischer. 1972. "Capital Market Equilibrium with Restricted Borrowing." *Journal of Business* 45: 444–455.

Collison, David and George M. Frankfurter. 2000. "Are We Really Maximizing Shareholders' Wealth? Or What Investors Must Know When We Do." *The Journal of Investing* 9(3): 55–63.

de Saussure, Ferdinand. 1959. *Courses in General Linguistics*. New York: McGraw Hill.

Fama, Eugene F. 1965. "The Behavior of Stock Market Prices." *Journal of Business* 38: 34–105.

———. 1970. "Efficient Capital Markets: A Review of Theory and Empirical Work." *Journal of Finance* 25: 383–417.

———. 1998. "Market Efficiency, Long-Term Returns, and Behavioral Finance." *Journal of Financial Economics* 49: 283–306.

Frankfurter, George M. 2001. "Still Autistic Finance." *Alternative Perspectives on Finance and Accounting*, Vol. 1, http://www.departments.bucknell.edu/management/apfa/.

———. 2002. "Method and Methodology." *Homo Oeconomicus* 18: 465–491.

Frankfurter, George M. and Elton G. McGoun. 1999. "Ideology and the Theory of Financial Economics." *Journal of Economic Behavior and Organization* 39: 159–177.

———. 2002. *From Individualism to the Individual: Ideology and Inquiry in Financial Economics*. London: Ashgate Publishing.

———. 2002. "Positive Financial Economics as Catch-22." In *From Individualism to the Individual*, edited by G.M. Frankfurter and E.G. McGoun. Ashgate Publishing.

Friedman, Milton M. 1953. "The Methodology of Positive Economics." In *Essays in Positive Economics*, edited by M.M. Friedman. Chicago: The University of Chicago Press.

Kuhn, Thomas S. 1970. *The Structure of Scientific Revolutions*. Chicago: The University of Chicago Press.

Lawson, Tony. 1997. *Economics and Reality*. London: Routledge.

Lintner, John. 1965. "The Valuation of Risk Assets and the Selection of Risky Investments in Stock Portfolios and Capital Budgets." *Review of Economics and Statistics* 47: 13–37.

Markowitz, Harry M. 1952. "Portfolio Selection." *Journal of Finance* 7: 77–91.

———. 1959. *Portfolio Selection*. New Haven: Yale University Press.

McGoun, Elton G. 1997. "Hyperreal Finance." *Critical Perspectives on Accounting* 8: 97–122.

Mcintosh, Norman B. 2002. "A Linguistic Approach to Understanding Accounting: A 'Wild Card' Possibility." Working Paper, Kingston.

Miller, Merton H. and Franco Modigliani. 1961. "Dividend Policy, Growth and the Valuation of Shares." *Journal of Business* 34: 411–433.

Modigliani, Franco and Merton H. Miller. 1958. "The Cost of Capital, Corporation Finance, and the Theory of Investment." *American Economic Review* 48: 261–297.

Peirce, Charles Sanders. 1991. "Peirce on Signs." In *Peirce on Signs*, edited by J. Hooper. Chapel Hill, NC: The University of North Carolina Press.

Sharpe, William F. 1963. "A Simplified Model of Portfolio Analysis." *Management Science* 9: 277–293.

———. 1964. "Capital Market Prices: A Theory of Market Equilibrium under Conditions of Risk." *Journal of Finance* 14: 425–442.

Strauss, Leo. 1988. *Persecution and the Art of Writing*, 3rd ed. Chicago & London: The University of Chicago Press.

Epilogue

> Postmodernity is the simultaneity of the destruction of earlier values and
> their reconstruction. It is renovation within ruination.
>
> — Jean Baudrillard *Cool Memories*

In a *Harper's* essay, Stanley Fish (2002) succinctly and rather elegantly
demarks the boundaries of postmodernism, quoting Edward Rothstein's
OP-Ed piece from the September 22, 2001 issue of the *New York Times*:

> A full account, or even definition of postmodernism would be out of place
> here, but it may be enough to look at one offered by Rothstein, who begins
> by saying "Postmodernists challenge assertions that truth and ethical judg-
> ment have any objective validity." Well, it depends on what do you mean
> by "objective." If you mean a standard of validity and value that is inde-
> pendent of any historically emergent and therefore revisable system, of
> thought and practice, then it is true that many postmodernists would deny
> that any such standard is or could ever be available. But if by "objective" one
> means a standard of validity and value that is backed up by the tried-and-
> true procedures and protocols of a well-developed practice or discipline —
> history, physics, economics, psychology, etc. — then such standards are all
> around us, and we make use of them all the time without any metaphysi-
> cal anxiety.

Financial economics fancies calling itself modern finance. If one dis-
cards the religious philosophical wrapping of modernism, then the term
modern finance that serves as a synonym to financial economics must
mean the application of scientific methods to the study of a social phenomenon. This phenomenon is the behavior of people, together and individually, with respect to matters that involve anything connected to
money and wealth.

Modern finance has been dominated for the last 40 years by a model,
contrived on the psychology of an imaginary economic being (called the *homo
economicus*), the philosophy of *laissez faire*, and Friedmanian positivism

(Friedman, 1953). It has been the study of a real world that academics often call "out there" with the framing of a non-existent world. So, it developed its "objectivity," a *sine qua non* of the scientific method, and henceforth its "tried-and-true procedures and protocols of a practice or discipline" as per Fish's second criterion of postmodernity, on false pretenses. It also often mistakes its methods for its methodology (sometimes, with a clear purpose, I suspect). Thus, it fails the second understanding of "objectivity," and, consequently, postmodernity. It fails without question Rothstein's interpretation of postmodernity, because modern finance is heavy-handedly ideology-laden.

This ideology is the dogma of free markets, the ultimate benefit of which is market efficiency. Market efficiency is, *de facto*, Pareto optimality, meaning the market knows best, therefore, leave it alone. Modern finance never stops studying market efficiency as its major *raison d'être*. Those that dictate the research program of financial economics, specifically, the Chicago–Rochester School and its many myrmidons, make it sure that very little objection is published to this agenda. Of course, quite often work surfaces that shows lack of market efficiency with undeniable statistical significance. This evidence, if not challenged as inferior work, is termed as an anomaly, in fact reinforcing the myth of market efficiency, because it is quite paradoxically treated as a random occurrence, perfectly consistent with the notion of informationally efficient markets (Fama, 1998).

So, modern finance never became postmodern, and it is, if not a giant ruse, a total scientific failure. In either case, it is the abandonment of one of the intelligencia's sacred duties: making society think over its priorities and where its current course is leading.

Politically, the idea of free markets (a disingenuous euphemism for capitalism, because, according to John K. Galbraith, it creates the impression that the consumer has a voice) started the watershed of lifting regulations, commencing with the thrift institutions' failure in the late 1980s and early 1990s (the greatest reversed Robin Hood act of taking from the poor and giving to the rich in the history of mankind), continued with an unprecedented wave of corporate buyouts and takeovers that made a very few very rich, and segued into Enronism in the early 21st century. Why, Mr. Cheney, while CEO of Halliburton, remarked that Enron should be emulated by all as the model of the new age corporation. And many did, indeed, emulate Enron, whereby institutionalizing corporate larceny. That included Mr. Cheney's own firm, Halliburton, that reported $100 million non-existent revenues under his CEO-ship.

Instead of chasing an ideologically imbued phantom ghost, modern finance should have turned postmodern, concentrating on the causes and effects of cointegration of economics and politics, which is a poisonous symbiosis. This, of course, would have not just stopped the debate over whether markets are efficient or not, or to what degree (if they are), but would have explored the social consequences and loss to society when lawmakers, regulators and the giants of the corporate world are in cahoots to make the process of allocation of wealth as one-sided in favor of capital as much as one can imagine.

For the record, it must be said that modern finance became enamored with agency theory (Jensen and Meckling, 1976) for a while. A substantial component of this theory (more a collection of loose stories than theory) is a scenario Reiter (1994) paints so well. Because of asymmetries of information (an unfortunate monkey wrench in the construct of efficient markets, which before they are efficient must be perfect) and not perfectly enforceable contracts, the dastardly villain (the manager[129]) is just about to tie the damsel in distress (the shareholder) to the railroad tracks. Then comes Dudley "Market" Doright to save the maiden from the rogue executive. Never happens!

What happens is more the story told by the *Los Angeles Times*, quoting a conversation S. David Freeman, the head of the Los Angeles Department of Water and Power, had in late 2000 with Kenneth "Kenny boy" Lay, the then CEO of Enron (very likely committed suicide in 2006). Freeman was debating with Lay the possibility of government intervention of price controls to keep skyrocketing energy prices in California at bay. Lay, of course, argued that government intervention would not work, because it would discourage energy companies from building new power plants.[130] At the end Lay told Freeman, "Well Dave, in the final analysis it doesn't matter what you crazy people in California do, because I got smart guys out there who can always figure out how to make money" (reported in the *New York Times* of June 17, 2002, by *The Associated Press*). Later, it was revealed that the "smart guys" of Enron concocted trading schemes with names such as "Death Star" and "Get Shorty" to distress the already distressed damsel.

---

[129] It is hard to discern just who is the manager, or rather, how low one must go in the corporate ladder as to find someone who cannot qualify as a manager.

[130] Now we know that Enron orchestrated much of the crisis.

One also must not forget that the promoters of agency theory were also very happy to see the LBO craze of the 1980s and the acquisition frenzy of the 1990s, all done with overleveraging. In short, they added a lot of confusion and muck to an otherwise indefensible positive theory.

This is not to say that story-telling was a bad thing. The start of every science is, in fact, story-telling. The metaphor was totally wrong, however. Of course, some managers are villains (as we find in this collection of stories), but not all managers. The market, however, is no Dudley Doright. The market is the damsel in distress, which is losing its efficiency over and over again (a biological impossibility). Given the socio-economic structure of American capitalism, markets cannot be efficient, and thus, one should not waste time and other resources to prove whether they are, or are not.

But I sense, perhaps because of my inherent and foolish optimism, that Enron will open a door for some serious inventory-taking, because in the wake of Enron we are discovering two phenomena with an intensity never experienced before:

(1)   That there are many more Enrons out there, some of which are much, much worse than the original, and
(2)   That politics and economics are inseparably intertwined.

The second phenomenon is especially important for academics to ponder because it may result in a complete change, indeed, a turnaround, of the research program in finance.

Strangely, globalization, which has been one of the trendiest euphemisms for spreading American capitalism all over the globe and succumbing to the rule of the multinational mega-corporation, might be another deterrent of corporate larceny. In an *International Herald Tribune* column of June 8, 2002, William Pfaff argues that the EU might be another challenge facing America. The opening paragraph of Pfaff's is quite explicit:

> Those who believe that the mutation of American capitalism during the past two decades, and the takeover of American politics by corporate money, have done more damage to the United States than the terrorists of Al-Qaeda will ever do, now have encouraging news: A balancing counter-power,[131] skewed as it may be, is at work.

---

[131] I wonder if "a balancing counterpower" is just a slip of the tongue, and what Pfaff really meant to say was the Galbraithian "counterbalancing power."

Pfaff continues with the story of how a new challenge to American business standards is coming from Europe. According to Pfaff, a proposal before EU ministers would require American companies doing business in Europe and listed on European stock exchanges to adopt the International Standards of Accounting (IAS), instead of GAAP which should be adhered to (but are not) in America. The IAS are not just stricter than GAAP, but they are also philosophically different. The IAS require a certification from the accountant that the financial picture that is painted by the accounting statements is, principally, a true picture of the firm's financial health. What is followed in America is a compendium of rules (quite often full of loopholes and subject to interpretation) without any personal guarantee that the accounting statements reflect honestly on the firm's conditions.

This is how it happened that inadequately regulated markets and lax standards ". . . produced the worst abuse: rigged accounts and complaisant auditors' reports; dishonest company statements with dissimulated losses and fictitious profits; looted pension funds; concealed insider loans to managers; and abuse of client and consumer confidence, all in order to inflate stock values and enrich executives." It was Edward Heath, British Conservative Prime Minister (and not a wild-eyed socialist) who, several decades ago already, called the compensation of executives "the unpleasant and unacceptable face of capitalism."

Yet, the panacea offered by the President's much heralded speech on July, 8, 2002 to Wall Street is a lot of soundbites, including one that baffles this writer: a financial SWAT (Special Weapons and Tactics) Team to ferret out corporate criminals and bring them to justice. Are we to expect armed-to-the-teeth Ninjas rappelling down from Apache helicopters on the rooftops of corporate headquarters, spread-eagling green-visored accountants, all the while throwing concussion grenades at frightened secretaries? The suggestion is an absolute nonsense. It is just a lot of macho drivel left over from the war-on-terror rhetoric. What we need is a new philosophy, a set of rules to follow and agencies that will enforce them, instead of grandstanding. What we need is moral leadership by example. And this is something that will not come soon.

Perhaps the title of the concluding section of this book is a misnomer. Perhaps all this is just the beginning; the unfolding of the end, however slowly, of a system that is based on falsehood and casuistry, not unlike the Soviet Union and its satellites that eventually brought about its demise. But I doubt it. The system is so entrenched and so impassive to change due to the moneybag controls of both political parties, that a radical turn in the way and means of the system is next to impossible. In fact, counterbalancing forces are at work, already, to stifle any possible move toward radical and much needed legislation, something akin to the Blue Sky Laws that followed the fraudulent decade of the 1920s. As the *New York Times* reports:

> Two legislative sources said Philip J. Purcell, chairman of Morgan Stanley, had recently made the rounds on Capitol Hill to promote legislation to curb state regulators' powers. One person said Mr. Purcell's idea had gained support among both Republicans and Democrats.

> A Morgan Stanley spokeswoman declined to comment on Mr. Purcell's role in the amendment. But in an interview last Friday, Mr. Purcell said, "I personally believe that legislation could make a positive contribution to restoring investor confidence." He was referring to the Republican legislation on corporate disclosure, supported by Representative Michael G. Oxley of Ohio.

The proposed legislation affirms that "no law, rule, regulation, order, administrative action, judgment, consent order or settlement agreement shall be imposed by any state on people subject to Securities and Exchange Commission rules." And *moto perpetuo*. Or, *déjà vu* all over again. Was this not where we started?

References

Fama, E.F. 1998. "Market Efficiency, Long-Term Returns, and Behavioral Finance." *Journal of Financial Economics* 49: 283–306.

Fish, Stanley. 2002. "Postmodern Warfare." *Harper's* 305: 33–40.

Friedman, M.M. 1953. "The Methodology of Positive Economics." In *Essays in Positive Economics*, edited by M.M. Friedman. Chicago: The University of Chicago Press.

Jensen, M.C. and W.H. Meckling. 1976. "Theory of the Firm: Managerial Behavior, Agency Costs and Ownership Structure." *Journal of Financial Economics* 3: 305–360.

Reiter, S. 1994. "Storytellers, Stories, and 'Free Cash Flow'." *International Review of Financial Analysis* 3: 209–224.

Afterword: Encomium for an Ideologue

While preparing this manuscript for publication, Professor Milton Friedman passed away on November 16, 2006. Without a doubt, the world lost, if not the greatest economist who ever lived on the planet, then the one who made the greatest impact on Western civilization in the post-WWII era.

Nevertheless, the kind of economics that ruled our life during his influence led to a great extent to false, if not mythical, beliefs, and an ideology that created the greatest gap between the poor and the rich, between the "haves" and the "have-nots." His theories and ideology not just ruled the field of economics, but also was the cornerstone of the economic policies of the Cold War and later the Reagan–Bush–Clinton–Bush era, spanning a 50-year horizon.

Perhaps Friedman's passing away will reduce his influence on social policy makers, or will give a better chance for those who question the benefits of his ideas for Western societies. With all my admiration for Friedman's genius in imparting influence, I wish to set the record straight in the following obituary, and hope that his death will serve as a signal for the dominance of a new way of thinking, which much of this manuscript is about and hopes for.

Professor Milton M. Friedman passed away at the age of 94 on November 16, 2006. In a panegyric by Steven Pearlstein (*The Washington Post*, November 17, 2006), Friedman is called "the greatest economist of our times." Whether one agrees with the title or not is a matter of perception. Perhaps not just perception, but also what is important in making history and what is just a symbol.

Although the issue of the title will remain to be solved by future generations with the proper perspective that the passing of time and regimes may so lavishly shower on mankind, one thing I am sure of: Milton Friedman became an icon in his own time. Indeed, Friedman turned out to be the academic white knight of the Cold War, the merciless warrior of the neoclassical school of economics and *laissez faire* (it was once claimed that Friedman was two clicks to the right of Barry Goldwater, if that were possible), and the patriarch of the dynasty that still rules the economics profession, financial or otherwise.

Professor Friedman's influence on economics, especially the financial kind, is still so strong that tossing cabers into the wind could be more productive than challenging the research agenda of the neoclassical school. Even the budding contrarian literature and behavioral finance are framing their models and empirical evidence in the confines of market efficiency, if that were the oracle.

Mr. Pearlstein also writes that because people and circumstances change, two diametrically opposing economic views may well be justified in one era and not in another. This is to make it clear that although at one time John Maynard Keynes might have been the right cure for the world, at another time (meaning the post-WWII era and the Cold War) Friedman was for us what the Catholic Church reserved for Jesus: *ego sum via veritas et vita*.[132]

One, however, cannot disregard the fact that Keynes' (the *fils*) general theory saved the Western world (and ultimately, capitalism) from the jaws of the Great Depression. And that John Kenneth Galbraith (1906–2006), whose writings will become more relevant to life in the 21st century than ever were, too, a contemporary, was regarded with ridicule by the school Friedman created at Chicago.

At the Bretton Woods Conference (July 1–22, 1944) where the monetary future of the post-WWII world had been decided, Keynes was received as the hero of the free world because his theories were adopted by the Allies. In fact, Hitler already practiced Keynesian economics to rebuild Germany's military machine and to pull the Third Reich out from the throes of the Great Depression, before FDR did it in America. It did not take long for the post-war new world order to abandon Keynes and to turn 180° to follow the Friedmanian doctrine.

Because I am a self-proclaimed iconoclast, a fact that might have been lost in the confusion (a lot of this is going around, lately) such persons usually create, let me make one thing perfectly clear. Friedman was first and foremost an ideologue whose dislike of government and absolute espousal of *laissez faire* made another great economist and Nobel Laureate, Franco Modigliani, accuse him of "academic dishonesty."

I also must admit that as early as a Ph.D. student, I became a neo-classical agnostic. In one of my economics classes, my professor accused

---

[132] I am the way, the truth and life.

me of not having Friedman's religion. "No Sir," I replied, "we have the same religion. We just don't believe in the same things."

That Professor Friedman was an ideologue first and economist after is clear when one reads his collection of essays, published under the title *Capitalism and Freedom* (Friedman, 1962, 1982), in which he declares in so many possible ways that capitalism is a necessary condition of freedom, and ultimately, of democracy.

This is so, because, albeit some might argue that socialism and democracy can go hand-in-hand:

> The thesis [of this chapter] is that such a view is a delusion, that there is an intimate connection between economics and politics, that only certain combinations of political and economic arrangements are possible, and that in particular, a society which is socialist cannot also be democratic, in the sense of guaranteeing individual freedom (*ibid.*, p. 8).

Another anthology of Friedman's, titled "The Methodology of Positive Economics" (Friedman, 1953), gave a free hand to economists to concoct models and explanations to economic phenomena based on a dream world, because the assumptions on which economic theories rest are "necessarily wild," (read, unrealistic) and what counts is their predictive ability "for the purpose at hand" which is the formulation of social policy.

The practitioners of positive economics vehemently deny, however, "that there is an intimate connection between economics and politics," and argue that their theories are "value-neutral." There is not a single leading economic model that takes into account the influence of money in politics, and nefarious deeds of firms and managers in order to "maximize shareholders' wealth."

Friedman's relentless pushing of *laissez faire* has been the foundation of the socio-economic policies of Nixon, Reagan, Bush, Sr., and, ultimately, Bush, Jr. Although, truth be told, Jimmy Carter started the epidemic of deregulation which brought about the massive failings of the thrifts in 1989–1991 and the bankruptcies of major airlines as of late. And let us not forget that Bill Clinton made NAFTA possible.

Nevertheless, Friedman was the way, the truth and life in and out of academia. Yet, the political regimes that espoused the Friedmanian doctrine created the biggest government interventionism in the so-called free markets for the sake of destabilizing the ruble, an unheard of military buildup/budget, staggering deficits to cut social spending, totally at variance with the idea of getting the government's dirty hands off the markets, domestic or otherwise.

The very same policies turned the SEC into a paper tiger, manufactured government incompetence to prove the point that government is bad, and left national healthcare, drug and energy policies under the influence of corporate giants. Albeit a bit harsh, the words of Dresden James come to mind: "When a well-packed web of lies has been sold gradually to the masses over generations, the truth will seem utterly preposterous and its speaker a raving lunatic."

What Friedman brought about was Reaganomics in several different monikers[133] that first and foremost resulted in a grossly disproportionate allocation of income, and ultimately wealth, since the Great Depression, certainly since "baby-booming." How many high-paying industrial jobs left this country since 1980 when the Reagan revolution came to pass, destroying, *de facto*, the American labor movement? And how did it happen that after our steel industry collapsed into the dustbin of the rust-belts, the unemployed steelworkers who tried to retrain as computer programmers (at Mr. Reagan's suggestion, if it were possible) are now working for us in Calcutta via satellite? And how did "outsourcing," a sexy-sounding euphemism for importing cheap labor, turn essential for our economy as per Mr. George W. Bush?

What this ideology created was a Wal-Mart economy in which the majority can afford only the bare necessities of livelihood, and the real economic well-being of the masses should be measured by the number of outlets of Dollar General Stores where they live.

The academics who followed the Friedman tune did it because that was the way to fame and fortune. In a market-based economy, science, or rather meta-science which is what economics is, follows the money interests. That is why the corporate sponsors who underwrote the academic chairs were eager to see the *laissez faire* dogma ruling the "predictions" that are instrumental for social policy to keep the government out of their business.

Friedman and the neoclassicals must have been right, were they not? After all, their philosophy is based on Adam Smith, whose work is almost written in stone. And Friedman's *laissez faire* was Adam Smith's idea, was it not?

---

[133] The latest of which is "The Job Growth and Taxpayer Relief Reconciliation Act of 2003."

The funny thing about Friedman and Adam Smith is that neoclassical economics' battle cry was co-opted from the latter's great work, *The Wealth of Nations* (Smith, 1937):

> It is not from the benevolence of the butcher, the brewer, or the baker that we expect our dinner, but from their regard to their own interest (Book I, p. 11).

Smith, a radical individualist, who was a humanist first, a philosopher second and an economist third, also wrote in his great work:

> Whenever the legislature attempts to regulate the differences between masters and workmen, its counselors are always the masters. When regulation, therefore, is in favour of the workmen, it is always just and equitable; but it is sometimes otherwise when in favour of the masters (*ibid.*, pp. 112–113).

I have never heard the neoclassical school quoting this passage from Adam Smith. Moreover, the regimes of Mr. Reagan and those that followed made sure that it was always "otherwise."

One must not forget that Smith's worldview was based on the utopia of perfect competition and a bucolic co-existence between the entrepreneur and craftsmen working in harmony, one for all and all for one. This is certainly not the world we live in.

With all fairness, I must admit that at least to the extent that economics and politics are strongly interconnected, Friedman was right on the button. If I may say so, politics is just the sugar-coating, the correct speech, to swallow a bitter pill, otherwise the majority would not go for in a democracy. That the coating eventually wears off showed up clearly in the 2006 mid-term elections.

The supreme fallacy of the Friedmanian dogma was his belief in capitalism as a necessary condition of freedom, and by transference, that democracy is not possible otherwise. The last six years of erosion of our civil rights with PATRIOT I and II, wiretapping, military tribunals for suspected enemy combatants (Americans and foreigners) and Public Law 109-364 (practically overriding the insurrection and posse comitatus acts), giving the President the power to use the National Guard without the acquiescence of the governor of the state to control civil disobedience, brings us as close to Stalinism as one could ever come in a nightmare.

Perhaps the ideology that Friedman mongered is not the capitalism he had in mind. Can it be that American capitalism and the idea of world domination is Friedman's bastard child? Or is what you have read so far just the incoherent rattling of an iconoclast?

George M. Frankfurter
Lloyd F. Collette Professor, Emeritus
Louisiana State University

References

Friedman, M.M. 1953. "The Methodology of Positive Economics." In *Essays in Positive Economics*, edited by M.M. Friedman. Chicago: The University of Chicago Press.

———. 1962, 1982. *Capitalism and Freedom*. Chicago: The University of Chicago Press.

Smith, A. 1937. *The Wealth of Nations*. New York: Random House.

Author Index

Subject Index